SITING TRANSLATION

SITING TRANSLATION

HISTORY, POST-STRUCTURALISM, AND THE COLONIAL CONTEXT

Tejaswini Niranjana

University of California Press
Berkeley • Los Angeles • Oxford

University of California Press
Berkeley and Los Angeles, California

University of California Press, Ltd.
Oxford, England

© 1992 by
The Regents of the University of California

Library of Congress Cataloging-in-Publication Data

Niranjana, Tejaswini, 1958–
    Siting translation : history, post-structuralism, and the colonial
context / Tejaswini Niranjana.
        p.   cm.
    Includes bibliographical references (p.   ) and index.
    ISBN 0-520-07450-5 (cloth). — ISBN 0-520-07451-3 (paper)
        1. Translating and interpreting.   2. Deconstruction.
    3. Structuralism (Literary analysis).   4. Historicism.
    5. Imperialism.   I. Title.
PN241.N48   1992
428'.02911—dc20   91-21487
                                                                        CIP

Printed in the United States of America

The paper used in this publication meets the minimum requirements
of ANSI/NISO Z39.48-1992 (R 1997) (Permanence of Paper).

To my parents,
Anupama Niranjana
and
K. S. Niranjana

Contents

Acknowledgments

For their generosity and careful criticism, I am indebted to Joseph N. Riddel, Vincent Pecora, and Paul Hernadi, and to R. B. Patankar, who taught me my first course in literary theory. I am especially grateful to those scholars at UCSC who, although I was not one of their students, gave freely of their time and allowed me to participate fully in their class discussions. My thanks, therefore, to Hayden White, Teresa de Lauretis, James Clifford, Gabriel Berns, David Hoy, Marta Morello-Frosch, and Dilip Basu, and to the Group for the Critical Study of Colonial Discourse for providing the context in which my work took shape.

Without the help, encouragement, and affection of David Bass, Sudhir Chella Rajan, Satish Deshpande, Ashok Dhareshwar, Howard Dickler, Ruth Frankenberg, Sasheej Hegde, Mary John, Annette Leddy, Kathryne Lindberg, Lata Mani, Harryette Mullen, Seemanthini Niranjana, Ted Pearson, R. Srivatsan, P. Sudhir, and D. Vasanta, I would not have been able to finish writing and revising this book. To them, then, my less than adequate gratitude.

Susie Tharu's friendship and intellectual example have shown me the importance of continuing to work on the interface of theory and history.

Vivek Dhareshwar provided critical support and sustenance in the darkest hours. Without him, this book would never have been written.

I would like to thank the following for granting fellowships that enabled me to complete this work sooner than I otherwise would have: the Department of English at UCLA, the Phi Beta Kappa Alumni Association, and the American

Association of University Women. Thanks to the anonymous readers of my manuscript for their comments, and to Doris Kretschmer of the University of California Press for being such a wonderful editor.

Different versions of parts of this book have appeared in *Strategies,* the *Journal of Arts and Ideas,* and the *Economic and Political Weekly.* I am grateful to my interlocutors in the many places where these ideas were first presented: the University of California at Irvine; the University of California at Santa Cruz; the University of Delhi; the University of Bombay; the University of Poona; the Indian Institute of Technology, Bombay; the University of California at Los Angeles; and Jadavpur University, Calcutta.

For permission to use copyrighted material, I thank Penguin Books and Karnatak University Press.

T. N.

Abbreviations

ACE	Asad, ed., *Anthropology and the Colonial Encounter*
AR	De Man, *Allegories of Reading*
Babel	Derrida, "Des Tours de Babel"
BI	De Man, *Blindness and Insight*
C	De Man, " 'Conclusions,' Walter Benjamin's 'The Task of the Translator' "
CSS	Spivak, "Can the Subaltern Speak?"
DH	Spivak, "Deconstructing Historiography"
EF	Benjamin, "Eduard Fuchs, Collector and Historian"
HBI	Mill, *A History of British India*
LCP	Foucault, *Language, Counter-Memory, Practice*
LWJ	*The Letters of Sir William Jones*
Memoires	Derrida, *Memoires: For Paul de Man*
OAH	Jones, "On Asiatic History, Civil and Natural"
OG	Derrida, *Of Grammatology*
PA	De Man, "Pascal's Allegory of Persuasion"
PH	Hegel, *The Philosophy of History*
PU	Jameson, *The Political Unconscious*
ResTh	De Man, *The Resistance to Theory*
RhT	De Man, "The Rhetoric of Temporality"
Signature	Derrida, "Signature Event Context"

SP	Derrida, *Speech and Phenomena*
SSH	De Man, "Sign and Symbol in Hegel's Aesthetics"
SW	Bhabha, "Signs Taken for Wonders"
TAD	Jones, "Third Anniversary Discourse"
TAR	Jauss, ed., *Toward an Aesthetic of Reception*
TH	Benjamin, "Theses on the Philosophy of History"
TOL	Jones, *Translations from Oriental Languages*
TpF	Benjamin, "Theologico-Political Fragment"
TT	Benjamin, "The Task of the Translator"
VHL	Ward, *A View of the History, Literature, and Mythology of the Hindoos*

1

Introduction:
History in Translation

The passion for English knowledge has penetrated the most
obscure, and extended to the most remote parts of India.
The steam boats, passing up and down the Ganges, are
boarded by native boys, begging, not for money, but for
books. . . . Some gentlemen coming to Calcutta were as-
tonished at the eagerness with which they were pressed for
books by a troop of boys, who boarded the steamer from
an obscure place, called Comercolly. A Plato was lying on
the table, and one of the party asked a boy whether that
would serve his purpose. "Oh yes," he exclaimed, "give
me any book; all I want is a book." The gentleman at last
hit upon the expedient of cutting up an old *Quarterly Review*, and distributing the articles among them.
　　　　　　　　　　　　—Charles Trevelyan,
　　　　　　　　　　　　　On the Education of the People of India

SITUATING TRANSLATION

In a post-colonial context the problematic of *translation* becomes a significant site for raising questions of representation, power, and historicity. The context is one of contesting
and contested stories attempting to account for, to recount,
the asymmetry and inequality of relations between peoples,
races, languages. Since the practices of subjection/subjectifi-
cation implicit in the colonial enterprise operate not merely
through the coercive machinery of the imperial state but also
through the discourses of philosophy, history, anthropology,
philology, linguistics, and literary interpretation, the colonial
"subject"—constructed through technologies or practices of
power/knowledge[1]—is brought into being within multiple

1. "[Power] produces knowledge . . . [they] directly imply one another,"

1

discourses and on multiple sites. One such site is translation. Translation as a practice shapes, and takes shape within, the asymmetrical relations of power that operate under colonialism. What is at stake here is the representation of the colonized, who need to be produced in such a manner as to justify colonial domination, and to beg for the English book by themselves. In the colonial context, a certain conceptual economy is created by the set of related questions that is the problematic of translation. Conventionally, translation depends on the Western philosophical notions of reality, representation, and knowledge. Reality is seen as something unproblematic, "out there"; knowledge involves a representation of this reality; and representation provides direct, unmediated access to a transparent reality. Classical philosophical discourse, however, does not simply engender a practice of translation that is then employed for the purposes of colonial domination; I contend that, simultaneously, translation in the colonial context produces and supports a conceptual economy that works into the discourse of Western philosophy to function as a philosopheme (a basic unit of philosophical conceptuality). As Jacques Derrida suggests, the concepts of metaphysics are not bound by or produced solely within the "field" of philosophy. Rather, they come out of and circulate through various discourses in several registers, providing a "conceptual network in which philosophy *itself* has been constituted."[2] In forming a certain kind of subject, in presenting particular versions of the colonized, translation brings into being overarching concepts of reality and representation. These concepts, and what they allow us to assume, completely occlude the violence that accompanies the construction of the colonial subject.

---

says Foucault (*Discipline and Punish: The Birth of the Prison*, trans. Alan Sheridan [New York: Random House, Vintage Books, 1979], p. 27). He further suggests that the "individual" or the subject is "fabricated" by technologies of power or practices of subjectification.

2. Derrida, "White Mythology: Metaphor in the Text of Philosophy," in *Margins of Philosophy*, trans. Alan Bass (Chicago: University of Chicago Press, 1982), p. 230.

Translation thus produces strategies of containment. By employing certain modes of representing the other—which it thereby also brings into being—translation reinforces hegemonic versions of the colonized, helping them acquire the status of what Edward Said calls representations, or objects without history.[3] These become *facts* exerting a force on events in the colony: witness Thomas Babington Macaulay's 1835 dismissal of indigenous Indian learning as outdated and irrelevant, which prepared the way for the introduction of English education.

In creating coherent and transparent texts and subjects, translation participates—across a range of discourses—in the *fixing* of colonized cultures, making them seem static and unchanging rather than historically constructed. Translation functions as a transparent presentation of something that already exists, although the "original" is actually brought into being through translation. Paradoxically, translation also provides a place in "history" for the colonized. The Hegelian conception of history that translation helps bring into being endorses a teleological, hierarchical model of civilizations based on the "coming to consciousness" of "Spirit," an event for which the non-Western cultures are unsuited or unprepared. Translation is thus deployed in different kinds of discourses—philosophy, historiography, education, missionary writings, travel-writing—to renew and perpetuate colonial domination.

My concern here is to explore the place of translation in contemporary Euro-American literary theory (using the name of this "discipline" in a broad sense) through a set of interrelated readings. I argue that the deployment of "translation" in the colonial and post-colonial contexts shows us a way of questioning some of the theoretical emphases of post-structuralism.

Chapter 1 outlines the problematic of translation and its relevance to the post-colonial situation. Reading the texts of different kinds of colonial translators, I show how they bring

3. Said, discussion with Eugenio Donato and others ("An Exchange on Deconstruction and History," *Boundary* 2 8, no. 1 [Fall 1979]: 65–74).

into being hegemonic versions of the non-Western other. Because they are underpinned by the powerful metaphysics of translation, these versions are seen even in the post-colonial context as faithful pictures of the decadence or depravity of "us natives." Through English education, which still legitimizes ruling-class power in formerly colonized countries, the dominant representations put into circulation by translation come to be seen as "natural" and "real." In order to challenge these representations, one must also examine the historicist tenets that endorse them. I will, therefore, discuss the pertinence of the critique of historicism to a world undergoing decolonization. Given the enduring nature of Hegelian presentations of the non-West and the model of teleological history that authorizes them, a questioning of the model could underwrite a new practice of translation.

In chapter 2, I examine how "translation" works in the traditional discourse of translation studies and in ethnographic writing. Discussing the last two, which are somewhat marginal to literary theory, may nevertheless help us sharpen our critique of translation. Caught in an idiom of fidelity and betrayal that assumes an unproblematic notion of representation, translation studies fail to ask questions about the historicity of translation; ethnography, on the other hand, has recently begun to question both the innocence of representation and the long-standing asymmetries of translation.

In chapters 3, 4, and 5, my main focus is the work of Paul de Man, Jacques Derrida, and Walter Benjamin (an earlier critic who is becoming increasingly important to post-structuralist thinkers). My analysis shows how translation functions as a "figure" in all three thinkers, becoming synonymous or associated with a major preoccupation in each: allegory or literature in de Man, the problematics of representation and intentionality in Derrida, and the question of materialist historiography in Benjamin. Pointing out the configurations of translation and history in Benjamin's work, I describe the kind of reading provided by de Man and Derrida of Benjamin's important essay "The Task of the Translator." My argument is that Walter Benjamin's early writings on translation are troped in significant ways into his later essays on the writing of history, a troping that goes unrecognized by both de Man and Derrida. (I use *trope* to indicate a metaphorizing that includes a displacement as well as a re-figuring.) The refusal of these major proponents of deconstruction to address the question of history in Benjamin suggests a critical drawback in their theory and perhaps indicates why deconstruction has never addressed the problem of colonialism.

In the final chapter, with the help of a translation from Kannada, a South Indian language, into English, I discuss the "uses" of post-structuralism in post-colonial space. Throughout the book, my discussion functions in all the registers—philosophical, linguistic, and political—in which translation "works" under colonialism. If at any point I seem to dwell on only one of these, it is for a purely strategic purpose.

This work belongs to the larger context of the "crisis" in "English" that is a consequence of the impact of structuralism and post-structuralism on literary studies in a rapidly decolonizing world. The liberal humanist ideology that endorsed and was perpetuated by the civilizing mission of colonialism is still propagated by discourses of "literature" and "criticism" in the tradition of Arnold, Leavis, and Eliot. These disciplines repress what Derrida, in the words of Heidegger, calls the logocentric or ontotheological metaphysics by which they are constituted, which involves all the traditional conceptions of representation, translation, reality, unity, and knowledge.[4]

There have been few systematic attempts to question "English," or literature, or criticism from a post-colonial perspective, let alone such a perspective that also incorporates insights from contemporary theory.[5] In order to help challenge

4. Post-Romantic literary criticism, for example, relies on a concept of the text as a unified, coherent, symbolic whole that can be re-presented or interpreted by the critic. Derrida would argue that the text is "always already" marked by representation; it was not suddenly brought into being through the "originality" of its "author."

5. See, however, Gauri Viswanathan, "The Beginnings of English Literary Study in British India," *Oxford Literary Review* 9, nos. 1–2 (1987): 2–26. Viswanathan's book *Masks of Conquest* (New York: Columbia University Press, 1989) provides a finely detailed discussion of the ideological uses of English

the complicity of these discourses with colonial and neo-colonial domination, I propose to make a modest beginning by examining the "uses" of translation. The rethinking of translation becomes an important task in a context where it has been used since the European Enlightenment to underwrite practices of subjectification, especially for colonized peoples. Such a rethinking—a task of great urgency for a post-colonial theory attempting to make sense of "subjects" already living "in translation," imaged and re-imaged by colonial ways of seeing—seeks to reclaim the notion of translation by deconstructing it and reinscribing its potential as a strategy of resistance.

Given the dispersed nature of its existence, we shall have to approach an understanding of the "post-colonial" through a variety of nodes: the intersection of the present with a history of domination,[6] the formation of colonial "subjects," the workings of hegemony in civil society,[7] and the task, already under way, of affirmative deconstruction.[8]

In beginning to describe the post-colonial, we might reiterate some of the brute facts of colonialism. Starting with the

---

literature in colonial India. I should also mention here Ngũgĩ wa Thiong'o's famous challenge to Eng. Lit. (Ngũgĩ et al., "On the Abolition of the English Department," reprinted in Ngũgĩ, *Homecoming* [1972; reprint, Westport, Conn.: Lawrence Hill, 1983]); Chinua Achebe's essays in *Morning Yet on Creation Day* (London: Heinemann, 1975); and Chinweizu, Onwuchekwa Jemie, and Ihechukwu Madubuike, *Toward the Decolonization of African Literature*, vol. 1 (1980; reprint, Washington, D.C.: Howard University Press, 1983).

6. *History*, like *translation*, is a term under constant interrogation in my text. I shall suggest later some of its relevant uses in the post-colonial situation.

7. *Hegemony* and *civil society* are terms used by Antonio Gramsci. Definitions will be provided later in the discussion. Gramsci's famous work is the series of fragments collected in *Quaderni del carcere*, available in English as *Selections from the Prison Notebooks*, trans. Quintin Hoare and Geoffrey Nowell Smith (New York: International Publishers, 1971). Autobiographical circumstances determine my examples of "practices of subjectification," most of which are from colonial and post-colonial India.

8. See chapter 6 for an example of translation as affirmative deconstruction.

period around the end of the seventeenth century and continuing beyond World War II, Britain and France, and to a lesser extent Spain, Portugal, Germany, Russia, Italy, and Holland, dominated—ruled, occupied, exploited—nearly the entire world. By 1918, European powers had colonized 85 percent of the earth's surface.[9] Not until after World War I (referred to by some non-Western writers as the European Civil War) was the process of decolonization initiated. Of course, we cannot speak here of a swift or complete transition to a postcolonial society, for to do so would be to reduce the ruptured complexities of colonial history to insignificance. The term *decolonization* can refer only crudely to what has, in the language of national liberation struggles, been called the "transfer of power," usually from the reigning colonial power to an indigenous elite.

Although one cannot see as negligible the importance of the transfer, it would be naive to believe it marks the "end" of domination, for the strength of colonial discourse lies in its enormous flexibility. By colonial discourse I mean the body of knowledge, modes of representation, strategies of power, law, discipline, and so on, that are employed in the construction and domination of "colonial subjects." *Discourse* is used here in a sense not incompatible with Michel Foucault's notion; as the rest of this chapter will show, however, my use of the term is not exclusively dependent on the Foucauldian framework. Colonial relations of power have often been reproduced in conditions that can only be called neocolonial, and ex-colonials sometimes hunger for the "English book" as avidly as their ancestors.[10]

9. For a graphic description of the ambitions of imperial powers, see Edward Said's classic, *Orientalism* (London: Routledge & Kegan Paul, 1978).

10. Although many critics of imperialism describe contemporary Third World societies as "neocolonial," I shall use the term *post-colonial* in order not to minimize the forces working against colonial and neocolonial domination in these societies. I have in mind especially the Indian context, from which I draw most of my examples. Also, it is more likely that economists rather than cultural theorists would use *neocolonial*. This is not to posit two separate realms

The post-colonial (subject, nation, context) is therefore still scored through by an absentee colonialism. In economic and political terms, the former colony continues to be dependent on the ex-rulers or the "West." In the cultural sphere (using *cultural* to encompass not only art and literature but other practices of subjectification as well), in spite of widely employed nationalist rhetoric, decolonization is slowest in making an impact. The persistent force of colonial discourse is one we may understand better, and thereby learn to subvert, I argue, by considering translation.

By now it should be apparent that I use the word *translation* not just to indicate an interlingual process but to name an entire problematic. It is a set of questions, perhaps a "field," charged with the force of all the terms used, even by the traditional discourse on translation, to name the problem, to translate translation. *Translatio* (Latin) and *metapherein* (Greek) at once suggest movement, disruption, displacement. So does *Übersetzung* (German). The French *traducteur* exists between *interprète* and *truchement*, an indication that we might fashion a translative practice *between* interpretation and reading, carrying a disruptive force much greater than the other two. The thrust of displacement is seen also in other Latin terms such as *transponere, transferre, reddere, vertere*. In my writing, *translation* refers to (a) the problematic of translation that authorizes and is authorized by certain classical notions of representation and reality; and (b) the problematic opened up by the post-structuralist critique of the earlier one, and that makes translation always the "more," or the *supplement*, in Derrida's sense.[11] The double meaning of *supplement*—as providing both

---

of analysis, but merely to suggest that a term appropriate at one level may not be as accurate at another.

11. In *Positions* (trans. Alan Bass [Chicago: University of Chicago Press, 1981]), Derrida defines *supplement* as an "undecidable," something that cannot any longer "be included within philosophical (binary) opposition," but that resists and disorganizes philosophical binaries *"without ever constituting a third term . . . ; the supplement is neither a plus nor a minus, neither an outside nor the complement of an inside, neither accident nor essence"* (p. 43).

what is missing as well as something "extra"—is glossed by Derrida thus: "The *overabundance* of the signifier, its *supplementary* character, is . . . the result of a finitude, that is to say, the result of a lack which must be *supplemented*."[12] Where necessary, however, I shall specify narrower uses of *translation*.

My study of translation does not make any claim to solve the dilemmas of translators. It does not propose yet another way of theorizing translation to enable a more foolproof "method" of "narrowing the gap" between cultures; it seeks rather to think through this gap, this difference, to explore the positioning of the obsessions and desires of translation, and thus to describe the economies within which the sign of translation circulates. My concern is to probe the absence, lack, or repression of an awareness of asymmetry and historicity in several kinds of writing on translation. Although Euro-American literary modernists such as Ezra Pound, Gertrude Stein, and Samuel Beckett persistently foregrounded the question of translation, I have not discussed their work, since it has, in any case, been extensively dealt with by mainstream literary critics, and since the focus of my interrogation is not poetics but the discourses of what is today called "theory."

The post-colonial distrust of the liberal-humanist rhetoric of progress and of universalizing master narratives has obvious affinities with post-structuralism.[13] Derrida's critique of representation, for example, allows us to question the notion of re-presentation and therefore the very notion of an origin or an original that needs to be re-presented. Derrida would argue that the "origin" is itself dispersed, its "identity" undecidable. A representation thus does not re-present an "original"; rather, it re-presents that which is always already represented. The notion can be employed to undo hegemonic

12. Derrida, "Structure, Sign, and Play in the Discourse of the Human Sciences," in *Writing and Difference*, trans. Alan Bass (Chicago: University of Chicago Press, 1978), p. 290.
13. In fact, I use even the terms *post-colonial* and *Third World* with some hesitation, since they too can be made to serve a totalizing narrative that disregards heterogeneity.

"representations" of "the Hindus," like, for example, those put forward by G. W. F. Hegel and James Mill.[14]

Another aspect of post-structuralism that is significant for a rethinking of translation is its critique of historicism, which shows the genetic (searching for an origin) and teleological (positing a certain end) nature of traditional historiography. As I have already suggested, of immediate relevance to our concern with colonial practices of subjectification is the fact that "historicism" really presents as *natural* that which is *historical* (and therefore neither inevitable nor unchangeable). A critique of historicism might show us a way of deconstructing the "pusillanimous" and "deceitful" Hindus of Mill and Hegel. My concern here is not, of course, with the alleged misrepresentation of the "Hindus." Rather, I am trying to question the withholding of reciprocity and the essentializing of "difference" (what Johannes Fabian calls a denial of coevalness) that permits a stereotypical construction of the other. As Homi Bhabha puts it: "The stereotype is not a simplification because it is a false representation of a given reality. It is a simplification because it is an arrested, fixated form of representation that, in denying the play of difference (that the negation through the Other permits), constitutes a problem for the *representation* of the subject in significations of psychic and social relations."[15]

The "native boys" about whom Charles Trevelyan, an ardent supporter of English education for Indians, wrote in 1838, are "interpellated" or constituted as subjects by the discourses of colonialism. Trevelyan shows, with some pride, how young Indians, without any external compulsion, beg for "English."[16]

---

14. Hegel, *The Philosophy of History* (1837), trans. J. Sibree (New York: P. F. Collier, n.d.), pp. 203–35; cited henceforth as *PH*. Mill, *A History of British India* (1817; New Delhi: Associated Publishing House, 1972); cited henceforth as *HBI*.

15. Bhabha, "The Other Question," *Screen* 24, no. 6 (November–December 1983): 27.

16. Under colonial rule, "the individual *is interpellated as a (free) subject in order that he shall submit freely to the commandments of the Subject, i.e. in order that he shall (freely) accept his subjection, i.e. in order that he shall make the*

"Free acceptance" of subjection is ensured, in part, by the production of hegemonic texts about the civilization of the colonized by philosophers like Hegel, historians like Mill, Orientalists like Sir William Jones.[17] The "scholarly" discourses, of which literary translation is conceptually emblematic, help maintain the dominance of the colonial rule that endorses them through the interpellation of its "subjects." The colonial subject is constituted through a process of "othering" that involves a teleological notion of history, which views the knowledge and ways of life in the colony as distorted or immature versions of what can be found in "normal" or Western society.[18] Hence the knowledge of the Western orientalist appropriates "the power to represent the Oriental, to translate and explain his (and her) thoughts and acts not only to Europeans and Americans but also to the Orientals themselves."[19]

TRANSLATION AS INTERPELLATION

That translation became part of the colonial discourse of Orientalism is obvious from late-eighteenth-century British efforts to obtain information about the people ruled by the merchants of the East India Company. A. Maconochie, a scholar connected with the University of Edinburgh, urged the Brit-

---

gestures and actions of his subjection 'all by himself' " (Louis Althusser, "Ideology and Ideological State Apparatuses," in *Lenin and Philosophy, and Other Essays*, trans. Ben Brewster [New York: Monthly Review Press, 1971], p. 182; emphasis in original). *Interpellation* is a term used by Althusser to describe the "constitution" of subjects in language by ideology.

17. I do not mean to lump together Hegel's idealism, Mill's utilitarianism, and Jones's humanism-romanticism. Their texts are, however, based on remarkably similar premises about India and the Hindus. For a discussion of how these premises led eventually to the introduction of English education in India, see my "Translation, Colonialism and the Rise of English," *Economic and Political Weekly* 25, no. 15 (1990): 773–79. I am grateful to Rajeswari Sunder Rajan for her perceptive criticism of my attempt to relate translation to the beginnings of "English" in India.

18. Ronald Inden, "Orientalist Constructions of India," *Modern Asian Studies* 20, no. 3 (1986): 401–46.

19. Ibid., p. 408.

ish sovereign (in 1783 and again in 1788) to take steps "as may be necessary for discovering, collecting and translating whatever is extant of the ancient works of the Hindoos."[20] Although Maconochie hoped that by these translations European astronomy, "antiquities," and other sciences would be advanced, it became clear in the projects of William Jones—who arrived in India in 1783 to take his place on the bench of the Supreme Court in Calcutta—that translation would serve "to domesticate the Orient and thereby turn it into a province of European learning."[21]

As translator and scholar, Jones was responsible for the most influential introduction of a textualized India to Europe. Within three months of his arrival, the Asiatic Society held its first meeting with Jones as president and Warren Hastings, the governor-general, as patron. It was primarily through the efforts of the members of the Asiatic Society, themselves administrators and officials of the East India Company's Indian Government, that translation would help "gather in" and "rope off" the Orient.[22]

In a letter, Jones, whose Persian translations and grammar of Persian had already made him famous as an Orientalist before he came to India, declared that his ambition was "to know *India* better than any other European ever knew it."[23] His translations are said to have been read by almost everyone in the West who was literate in the nineteenth century.[24] His works were carefully studied by the writers of the age, especially the Germans—Goethe, Herder, and others. When Jones's new writings reached Europe, the shorter pieces were eagerly picked up and reprinted immediately by different pe-

20. Quoted in Dharampal, *The Beautiful Tree: Indigenous Indian Education in the Eighteenth Century* (New Delhi: Biblia Impex, 1983), p. 9.

21. Said, *Orientalism*, p. 78.

22. Ibid.

23. Letter to Lord Althorp, 2d Earl Spencer, August 17, 1787, in *The Letters of Sir William Jones*, ed. Garland Cannon (London: Oxford University Press, 1970), 2:751; emphasis in original. Hereafter abbreviated as *LWJ*.

24. A. J. Arberry, *Oriental Essays: Portraits of Seven Scholars* (London: George Allen & Unwin, 1960), p. 82.

riodicals. His translation of Kālidāsa's *Śākuntala* went through successive reprints; Georg Forster's famous German translation of the translation came out in 1791, after which the play was translated into other European languages as well. As a twentieth-century scholar puts it, "It is not an exaggeration to say that he altered our [i.e., Europe's] whole conception of the Eastern world. If we were compiling a thesis on the influence of Jones we could collect most of our material from footnotes, ranging from Gibbon to Tennyson."[25] Evidence for Jones's lasting impact on generations of scholars writing about India can be found even in the preface of the 1984 Indian edition of his discourses and essays, where the editor, Moni Bagchee, indicates that Indians should "try to preserve accurately and interpret the national heritage by treading the path chalked out by Sir William Jones."[26]

My main concern in examining the texts of Jones is not necessarily to compare his translation of *Śākuntala* or Manu's *Dharmaśāstra* with the so-called originals. Rather, what I propose to do is to examine the "outwork" of Jones's translations—the prefaces, the annual discourses to the Asiatic Society, his charges to the Grand Jury at Calcutta, his letters, and his "Oriental" poems—to show how he contributes to a historicist, teleological model of civilization that, coupled with a notion of translation presupposing transparency of representation, helps construct a powerful version of the "Hindu" that later writers of different philosophical and political persuasions incorporated into their texts in an almost seamless fashion.

The most significant nodes of Jones's work are (a) the need for translation by the European, since the natives are unreliable interpreters of their own laws and culture; (b) the desire to be a lawgiver, to give the Indians their "own" laws; and (c) the desire to "purify" Indian culture and speak on its behalf. The interconnections between these obsessions are ex-

25. R. M. Hewitt, quoted by ibid., p. 76.
26. Bagchee, foreword to Jones's *Discourses and Essays* (New Delhi: People's Publishing House, 1984), p. xvi.

tremely complicated. They can be seen, however, as feeding into a larger discourse of improvement and education that interpellates the colonial subject.

In Jones's construction of the "Hindus," they appear as a submissive, indolent nation unable to appreciate the fruits of freedom, desirous of being ruled by an absolute power, and sunk deeply in the mythology of an ancient religion. In a letter, he points out that the Hindus are "incapable of civil liberty," for "few of them have an idea of it, and those, who have, do not wish it" (*LWJ*, p. 712). Jones, a good eighteenth-century liberal, deplores the "evil" but recognizes the "necessity" of the Hindus' being "ruled by an absolute power." His "pain" is "much alleviated" by the fact that the natives are much "happier" under the British than under their former rulers. In another letter, Jones bids the Americans, whom he admired, not to be "like the deluded, besotted Indians, among whom I live, who would receive Liberty as a curse instead of a blessing, if it were possible to give it them, and would reject, as a vase of poison, that, which, if they could taste and digest it, would be the water of life" (p. 847).

Jones's disgust is continually mitigated by the necessity of British rule and the "impossibility" of giving liberty to the Indians. He brings up repeatedly the idea of "Orientals" being accustomed to a despotic rule. In his tenth annual discourse to the Asiatic Society, he says that a reader of "history" "could not but remark the constant effect of despotism in benumbing and debasing all those faculties which distinguish men from the herd that grazes; and to that cause he would impute the decided inferiority of most Asiatic nations, ancient and modern."[27] The idea of the "submissive" Indians, their inability to be free, and the native laws that *do not permit* the question of liberty to be raised are thus brought together in the concept of Asian despotism. Such a despotic rule, continued by the British, can only fill the coffers of the East India Company: "In these Indian territories, which providence has thrown into

27. "On Asiatic History, Civil and Natural," in *Discourses and Essays*, p. 99. Cited hereafter as OAH.

the arms of Britain for their protection and welfare, the religion, manners, and laws of the natives preclude even the idea of political freedom; but . . . our country derives essential benefit from the diligence of a placid and submissive people" (OAH, pp. 99–100).

The glorious past of India, according to Jones, is shrouded in superstition, "marked and bedecked in the fantastic robes of mythology and metaphor" (OAH, p. 100), but the now "degenerate" and "abased" Hindus were once "eminent in various knowledge."[28] This notion of an Indian Golden Age seems to contradict Jones's insistence on the unchanging nature of Hindu society: "By *Indian* I mean that whole extent of the country in which the primitive religion and languages of the *hindus* prevail at this day with more or less of their ancient purity" (TAD, p. 6). He appears to avoid the contradiction, however, by distinguishing, although tenuously, the "religion and languages," which have not changed, from "arts," "government," and "knowledge," which have become debased (pp. 7–8). Jones's distinction seems to sustain the paradoxical movement of colonial discourse in simultaneously "historicizing" (things have *become* debased) as well as "naturalizing" (things have remained unchanged) the degradation of the natives. We shall see the same movement in the historian James Mill, although he dismisses Jones's notion of a previous Golden Age and posits instead an unchanging state of barbarism.

The presentation of the Indians as "naturally" effeminate as well as deceitful often goes hand in hand in Jones's work. In an essay on Oriental poetry, he describes the Persians as characterized by "that *softness,* and *love of pleasure,* that *indolence,* and *effeminacy,* which have made them an easy prey to all the western and northern swarms."[29] Persian poetry is said

28. "Third Anniversary Discourse," in *Discourses and Essays,* pp. 7–8. Abbreviated in my text as TAD.

29. Jones, *Translations from Oriental Languages* (Delhi: Pravesh Publications, n.d.), 1:348. Cited henceforth as *TOL.* The feminization of the "native" is a fascinating trope in colonial discourse but will not be discussed further at this time.

to greatly influence the Indians, who are "soft and voluptuous, but artful and insincere."[30] Jones's obsession with the insincerity and unreliability of the natives is a trope that appears in his work—usually in relation to translation—as early as the 1777 *Grammar of the Persian Language,* a copy of which was sent by Samuel Johnson to Warren Hastings. In his preface to the *Grammar,* Jones stresses the need for East India Company officials to learn the languages of Asia. Speaking of the increasing interest in Persian (used as a court language in India), he puts it down to the frustration of the British administrators at receiving letters they could not read: "It was found highly dangerous," says Jones, "to employ the natives as interpreters, upon whose fidelity they could not depend."[31]

As a Supreme Court judge in India, Jones took on, as one of his most important projects, the task of translating the ancient text of Hindu law, Manu's *Dharmaśāstra.* In fact, he began to learn Sanskrit primarily so that he could verify the interpretations of Hindu law given by his pandits. In a letter, he wrote of the difficulty of checking and controlling native interpreters of several codes, saying: "Pure Integrity is hardly to be found among the Pandits [Hindu learned men] and Maulavis [Muslim learned men], few of whom give opinions without a culpable bias" (*LWJ,* p. 720). Before embarking on his study of Sanskrit, Jones wrote to Charles Wilkins, who had already translated a third of the *Dharmaśāstra:* "It is of the utmost importance, that the stream of Hindu law should be pure; for we are entirely at the devotion of the native lawyers, through our ignorance of Shanscrit [*sic*]" (p. 666). Interestingly enough, the famous Orientalist attempt to reveal the former greatness of India often manifests itself as the British or European task of translating and thereby *purifying* the debased native texts. This Romantic Orientalist project slides

---

30. *TOL,* 2:358.
31. Jones, preface to *A Grammar of the Persian Language* (1771; 8th ed., London: W. Nicol, 1823), p. vii. The recurring emphasis on *infidelity* suggests the existence of a long, if repressed, tradition of resistance on the part of the colonized. I hope to explore this notion elsewhere.

almost imperceptibly into the Utilitarian Victorian enterprise of "improving" the natives through English education.[32]

Even before coming to India, Jones had formulated a solution for the problem of the translation of Indian law. Writing to Lord Cornwallis in 1788, he mentions once again the deceiving native lawyers and the unreliability of their opinions. "The obvious remedy for this evil," he writes, "had occurred to me before I left England" (*LWJ*, p. 795). This obvious remedy is, of course, the substitution of British translators for Indian ones. Jones, like his patron Warren Hastings, was a staunch advocate of the idea that Indians should be ruled by their own laws. However, since the "deluded," "besotted" Indians thought of liberty as a curse rather than a blessing, since they certainly could not rule themselves or administer their own laws, these laws had first to be taken away from them and "translated" before they could benefit from them. Another manifestation of the natives' insincerity was what Jones called "the frequency of perjury."[33] The "oath of a low native" had hardly any value at all, for everyone committed perjury "with as little remorse as if it were a proof of ingenuity, or even a merit."[34] Jones hoped to make this perjury "inexpiable" by settling once and for all—in another act of translation—the method of taking "evidence" from Indians (p. 682), making them punishable by their own (translated) laws.

32. For a discussion of the shared assumptions of "Orientalists" and "Anglicists" with regard to the practice of *sati*, or widow-burning, see Lata Mani, "Contentious Traditions: The Debate on SATI in Colonial India," *Cultural Critique* (Fall 1987): 119–56. Viswanathan, "Beginnings of English Literary Study," suggests that the move to anglicize education for Indians actually draws on the "discoveries" of Orientalism. See also Eric Stokes, *The English Utilitarians and India* (1959; reprint, Delhi: Oxford University Press, 1989) for a finely differentiated comparison of James Mill's attitudes with Thomas Macaulay's. Stokes argues that Mill was no Anglicist, since he did not think English education fulfilled the criterion of "utility," and since he did not in any case believe in the efficacy of formal education. However, I am concerned here with the larger utilitarian discourse on education that informed the changes in British educational policy in India.

33. Jones, "Charge to the Grand Jury, June 10, 1787," in *Works*, vol. 7 (1799; reprint, Delhi: Agam Prakashan, 1979).

34. Ibid., 7:286.

It is clear that Jones saw the compilation and translation of Manu as "the fruit of [his] Indian Studies," for he hoped it would become "the standard of justice to eight millions of innocent and useful men" in a kingdom that Fortune threw into Britain's lap while she was asleep (*LWJ*, p. 813). The discourse of law functions here in such a way as to make invisible the extensive violence of the colonial encounter. The translated laws would discipline and regulate the lives of "many millions of *Hindu* subjects, whose well-directed industry would add largely to the wealth of *Britain*" (p. 927). For, according to the translator, "those laws are actually revered, as the word of the Most High, by nations of great importance to the political and commercial interests of *Europe*."[35] Jones's translation went through four editions and several reprints, the last published in Madras in 1880. Although in the later years of Company rule and under the direct rule of the British Crown Indian law was ostensibly formulated according to Western models, the presence to this day of separate civil codes for different religions suggests that the laws actually derive from Orientalist constructions and translations of "Hindu" and "Muslim" scriptures.

Apart from the fact that giving the Indians their own laws would lead in Jones's logic to greater efficiency and therefore to greater profit for England, there is perhaps also another reason for employing Indian law. As Jones had pointed out in his tenth anniversary discourse, the "laws of the natives preclude even the idea of political freedom" (OAH, p. 100). This idea, seen as a reliable (because Western) interpretation of the "original" text, begins to circulate among various styles of discourse, having been set in motion by a concept of translation endorsing, as well as endorsed by, the "transparency" of representation. This kind of deployment of translation, I argue, colludes with or enables the construction of a teleological and hierarchical model of cultures that places Europe at the pinnacle of civilization, and thus also provides a position for the colonized.

35. Jones, preface to *Institutes of Hindu Law*, in *Works*, 7:89.

As I suggested earlier, William Jones's desire to purify Hindu law, art, and philosophy is another version of the British discourse of improvement. Jones, who wished to recover for Indians the glories of their own civilization, describes his task in "A Hymn to Surya" (1786), one of his series of "Indian" hymns, immensely popular in Europe, structured by the figures of the lost Golden Age, the debased and ignorant present, and the translator from a remote land:

> And, if they [the gods] ask, "What mortal pours the strain?"
> . . . .
> Say: from the bosom of yon silver isle,
> "Where skies more softly smile,
> "He came; and, lisping our celestial tongue,
> "Though not from *Brahma* sprung,
> "Draws Orient knowledge from its fountains pure,
> "Through caves obstructed long, and paths too long obscure."[36]

In some poems, like "A Hymn to Ganga" (1785–86), Jones shifts the first-person pronoun away from himself to create a subject-position for the colonized, making the "Hindu" speak in favor of the British, who "preserve *our* laws, and bid *our* terror cease" (*TOL*, 2:333; emphasis mine). Here the discourse of law seems to foreground violence, but only to place it in a *pre*-colonial time, or, in other words, to suggest that the coming of the British led to the *proper* implementation of the Indians' *own* laws and the end of "despotic" violence and "terror."

Two main kinds of translators of Indian literature existed in the late eighteenth and early nineteenth centuries: administrators like William Jones and Christian missionaries like the Serampore Baptists William Carey and William Ward. The latter were among the first to translate Indian religious texts into European languages. Often these were works they had themselves textualized, by preparing "standard versions" based on classical Western notions of unity and coherence. On the evidence of these authoritative translations, missionaries berated Hindus for not being true practitioners of Indian re-

---

36. *TOL*, 2:286; punctuation original.

ligion.[37] Their only salvation, the missionaries would then claim, lay in *conversion* to the more evolved religion of the West. The missionaries' theology arises from a historicist model that sets up a series of oppositions between traditional and modern, undeveloped and developed. This kind of attempt to impose linear historical narratives on different civilizations obviously legitimizes and extends colonial domination.

William Ward's preface to his three-volume *A View of the History, Literature, and Mythology of the Hindoos*[38] is instructive for the virulence with which it attacks the depravity and immorality of the natives. Their religion, manners, customs, and institutions are shown to be characterized, like those of other pagans, by "impurity" and "cruelty," which appear in their most "disgusting" and "horrible" manifestations among the "Hindoos" (*VHL*, p. xxxvii). The author claims, in his obsessive references to "native" sexuality, to have witnessed innumerable scenes of "impurity," for the Hindu institutions are "hotbeds of impurity," and the very services in the temples present "temptations to impurity" (pp. xxxvi–vii). Unlike William Jones, however, Ward does not see the present state of the Hindus as a falling away from a former Golden Age. Instead, like James Mill, who quotes him approvingly and often, Ward sees the Hindus as corrupt by nature, lacking the means of education and improvement. He suggests that the "mental and moral improvement" of the Hindus is the "high destiny" of the British nation. Once she was made "enlightened and civilized," India, even if she became independent, would "contribute more to the real prosperity of Britain" by "consuming her manufactures to a vast extent." Ward remarks on the "extraordinary fact" that the British goods

---

37. For a discussion of the textualization of Indian religion in the context of widow-burning, see Lata Mani, "The Production of an Official Discourse on SATI in Early Nineteenth-Century Bengal," in *Europe and Its Others*, ed. Francis Barker et al. (Colchester: University of Essex Press, 1985), 1:107–27.

38. Ward, *A View of the History, Literature, and Mythology of the Hindoos: Including a Minute Description of their Manners and Customs, and Translations from their Principal Works*, 2d ed. (London: Kingsbury, Parbury & Allen, 1822). Cited henceforth as *VHL*.

purchased annually by India "are not sufficient to freight a single vessel from our ports":

> But let Hindoost'han receive that higher civilization she needs, that cultivation of which she is so capable; let European literature be transfused into all her languages, and then the ocean, from the ports of Britain to India, will be covered with our merchant vessels; and from the centre of India moral culture and science will be extended all over Asia, to the Burman empire and Siam, to China, with all her millions, to Persia, and even to Arabia. (*VHL*, p. liii)

The entire "Eastern hemisphere" would then become Christian. In the age of the expansion of capitalism, interpretation and translation help create a market for European merchandise. As the missionary texts help us understand, translation comes into being overdetermined by religious, racial, sexual, and economic discourses. It is overdetermined not only because multiple forces act on it, but because it gives rise to multiple practices. The strategies of containment initiated by translation are therefore deployed across a range of discourses, allowing us to name translation as a significant technology of colonial domination.

The righteous disgust of Ward's writing is echoed uncannily by the "secular" historiography of James Mill, who constructs a version of "Hindoo nature" from the translations of Ward, Jones, Charles Wilkins, Nathaniel Halhed, Henry Colebrooke, and others. Mill's *History of British India*, published in three volumes in 1817, until quite recently served as a model for histories of India.[39] The Indian people, both Hindus and Muslims, were for Mill characterized by their insincerity, mendacity, perfidy, and venality. "The Hindu, like the eunuch," he said, "excels in the qualities of a slave." Like the Chinese, the Hindus were "dissembling, treacherous, mendacious, to an excess which surpasses even the usual measure of uncultivated society." They were also cowardly, un-

39. Mill's writings are still used in Indian history classes, often with the barest mention of his racism, and with sad approval of the wisdom of his characterizations.

feeling, conceited, and physically unclean (*HBI*, p. 486).[40] In defining the Indian, Mill sought to give by contrast a proper picture of the "superior" European civilization. As Edward Said has pointed out, "the Orient has helped to define Europe (or the West) as its contrasting image, idea, personality, experience."[41]

Mill declares that to "ascertain the true state of the Hindus in the scale of civilization" is of the greatest practical importance for the British. The Hindus need to be understood before they can be properly ruled, and to consider them as highly civilized would be a grave mistake (*HBI*, p. 456). In order to prove his thesis, Mill sets out to discredit the Orientalists who spoke of a Golden Age, often by a skillful citation of their own works. Mill's strategy is, first, to demolish the idea that India ever had a history, and then, to suggest that the state of the Hindus bears comparison with primitive societies, including that belonging to Britain's own past, that show evidence of the childhood of humankind. The maturity-immaturity, adulthood-childhood opposition feeds right into the discourse of improvement and education perpetuated by the colonial context.

Framing Mill's *History* is his comment that "rude nations seem to derive a peculiar gratification from pretensions to a remote antiquity. As a boastful and turgid vanity distinguishes remarkably the oriental nations they have in most instances carried their claims extravagantly high" (*HBI*, p. 24). Throughout the book, Mill again and again uses the adjectives *wild*, *barbaric*, *savage*, and *rude* in connection with the "Hindus," thus forming by sheer force of repetition a counterdiscourse to the Orientalist hypothesis of an ancient civilization.

The same descriptions provided by the Orientalists as evidence of the high civilization of the Hindus are declared by

40. The German Indologist Max Müller declared that Mill's *History* "was responsible for some of the greatest misfortunes that had happened to India" (J. P. Guha's prefatory note to the 1972 reprint of *HBI*, p. xii).
41. Said, *Orientalism*, pp. 1–2.

Mill to be "fallacious proof." The "feminine softness" and gentleness of the Hindus, for example, was taken to be the mark of a civilized community. Mill, on the other hand, suggests that the *beginnings* of civilization are compatible with "great violence" as well as "great gentleness" of manners. As in the "savages" of North America and the islanders of the South Seas, mildness and the "rudest condition of human life" often go together (*HBI*, pp. 287–88). As for the austerities prescribed by Hinduism, they tend to coexist with the encouragement of the "loosest morality" in the religion of a rude people (p. 205). Where an Orientalist might remark on the rough tools but neat and capable execution of tasks by the Hindu, Mill comments that "a dexterity in the use of its own imperfect tools is a common attribute of a rude society" (p. 335). Should anyone suggest that the Hindus possess beautiful poetry, Mill comes back with the remark that poetry points to the first stage of human literature, where the literature of the Hindus seems to have remained (p. 365).

Drawing on what he calls his knowledge of human nature, which appears in a variety of guises but displays an "astonishing uniformity" with regard to the different stages of society (*HBI*, p. 107), Mill further consolidates his teleological model of world history. The trial by ordeal prescribed by Hindu law, for example, was common "in the institutions of our barbaric ancestors" (p. 108). Mill seems to pick up the theories of, say, William Jones, about the Indo-Aryan origins of European civilization and employ them in a way that actually clarifies their ideological underpinnings for us. Both the Orientalist and the Utilitarian discourses end up producing the same historicist model and constructing the colonial subject in a very similar fashion. Mill actually draws directly on Jones's view of Hindu law when he says that the account of creation in Manu is "all vagueness and darkness, incoherence, inconsistency and confusion" (p. 163) and the religious ideas of the Hindus are also "loose, vague, wavering, obscure, and inconsistent." The "wild mythology" and "chain of unmeaning panegyric which distinguishes the religion of ignorant men" (p. 182) is characteristic of the rude mind's propensity to create that which is extravagant, "fantastic and senseless" (p. 163). Compare this with Jones's description in the preface to his translation of Manu of the system created by "description and priestcraft," "filled with strange conceits in metaphysicks and natural philosophy, with idle superstitions . . . it abounds with minute and childish formalities, with ceremonies generally absurd and often ridiculous" (p. 88).

Nearly half of the twenty-eight footnotes in chapter 1 of Mill's *History* mention William Jones, while the footnotes of chapter 2 are divided primarily between Halhed's translation of the *Code of Gentoo Laws*[42] and Jones's translation of Manu's *Institutes*. Quoting judiciously from these two texts (as well as from Colebrooke's *Digest of Hindu Law on Contracts and Successions*),[43] Mill manages to establish that the Hindu laws are both absurd and unjust. He quotes from Halhed's preface to the *Code of Gentoo Laws* to the effect that Hindu morals are as gross as Hindu laws, the latter grossness being a result of the former (*HBI*, p. 125 n. 90). From Charles Wilkins's translation of the *Hitopadeśa* (a collection of fables),[44] Mill obtains a picture of the "abject," "grovelling" Hindus, whose self-abasement provides him with proof of the despotic Hindu state; and from William Ward, of course, Mill procures "superabundant evidence of the immoral influence of the Hindu religion" and the "deep depravity" produced by it.

Translations of inscriptions on monuments are used selectively by Mill (*HBI*, p. 469; p. 504 n. 30). Claims of nobility or antiquity are immediately dismissed as wild fabrications, while anything that shows the depravity of the Hindus is considered legitimate evidence. Mill trashes the Purāṇas (mythological tales) as false history, but is willing to accept evidence from the play *Śākuntala* regarding the political

42. Nathaniel Halhed, *Code of Gentoo Laws, or, Ordinations of the Pundits, from a Persian Language translation made from the original writings in the Shanscrit Language* (London: n.p., 1777).
43. Henry Colebrooke and Jagannatha Tarakapanchanana, *Digest of Hindu Law*, 3d ed. (Madras: Higginbotham, 1864).
44. See the collated version by Henry Colebrooke, *Hitōpadeśa* (Serampore: Mission Press, 1804).

arrangements and laws of the age (pp. 133, 473). History is dismissed as fiction, but fiction—translated—is admissible as history. Mill embeds in his text several quotations from Captain Wilford's writings (Wilford is also one of Hegel's authorities) in *Asiatic Researches*, saying: "The Hindu system of geography, chronology, and history, are all equally monstrous and absurd" (p. 40). The whole stock of Hindu historical knowledge could thus be contained in a few quarto pages of print (p. 423). The language is remarkably similar to that Macaulay was to use barely a decade later to denounce Indian education. As the historian Ranajit Guha has pointed out, Mill begins his *History* with a chapter on the ancient history of the Hindus, and then interrupts the text with nearly five hundred pages (or nine chapters) on the "nature" of the Hindus (that is, their religion, customs, manners, etc.).[45] These nine chapters, predominantly in the present tense, perform the function of dehistoricizing the situation of the Hindus, thereby establishing their eternal and unchanging nature, as well as fixing their place in a hierarchy of civilizations.

Not only do secular historiography and philosophy of history participate in colonial discourse, Western metaphysics itself (and the "historicism" that is emblematic of it) seems to emerge in a certain age *from* colonial translation. The concept of representation put into circulation by eighteenth- and nineteenth-century translators of non-Western texts grounds, for example, the Hegelian theory of world history.

Whether we acknowledge it or not, whether we know it or not, says Paul de Man, we are all "orthodox Hegelians."[46] De Man's concern is to perform a critique of the kind of traditional historicism that is suggested by Hegel's teleological scheme of the coming to consciousness of Spirit. In India, says Hegel, "Absolute Being is presented . . . as in the ecstatic state of a dreaming condition"; and since "the generic

---

45. Ranajit Guha, "Remarks on Power and Culture in Colonial India" (MS), p. 59.
46. De Man, "Sign and Symbol in Hegel's Aesthetics," *Critical Inquiry* 8, no. 4 (Summer 1982): 761–75. For discussing this and other related points in chapter 1 with me, I am grateful to Sanjay Palshikar.

principle of Hindoo Nature" is this "character of Spirit in a state of Dream," the Indian has not attained to "self" or to "consciousness."[47] Because "History" for Hegel refers to the "development of Spirit," and because Indians are not "individuals" capable of action, the "diffusion of Indian culture" is "pre-historical," "a dumb, deedless expansion" (*PH*, p. 206); hence "it is the necessary fate of Asiatic Empires to be subjected to Europeans" (p. 207).

While Hegel is willing to grant that Indian literature depicts its people as mild, tender, and sentimental, he emphasizes that these qualities often go hand in hand with absolute lack of "freedom of soul" and "consciousness of individual right" (*PH*, p. 225). The idea of the "pusillanimous," "effeminate" Hindus with their despotic Asian rulers, and their inevitable conquest by the West, is part of a Hegelian philosophy of history that not only interpellates colonial subjects but is *authorized* by colonial translations. Hegel's condemnation of the Hindu as cunning and deceitful, habituated to "cheating, stealing, robbing, murdering," echoes the writings of James Mill, and the translations of Colebrooke, Wilkins, and other Orientalists.

Mill's model of history participates, as I have pointed out, in the British discourse of improvement that found such enthusiastic adherents in Macaulay and Trevelyan. The ideologists of "utility" and "efficiency" used the opposition between traditional and modern, created in part by Orientalist projects of translation, to make feasible the dismissal of indigenous education and the introduction of Western education.

As examiner or chief executive officer of the East India Company in London from 1830 on, James Mill influenced a number of modifications in Company policy. His son J. S. Mill wrote in his *Autobiography* that his father's despatches to India, "following his History, did more than had ever been done before to promote the improvement of India, and teach

47. *PH*, pp. 204–25.

Indian officials to understand their business."[48] When William Bentinck became governor-general in 1828, he acknowledged his indebtedness to and discipleship of James Mill. Although Mill was skeptical about the efficacy of formal education,[49] in his passion for "useful knowledge" he supported Bentinck's attempts to introduce educational reforms. For Bentinck, "the British language" was "the key to all improvements" and "general education" would lead to "the regeneration of India."[50]

The radical or utilitarian discourse was supplemented by the Evangelicals, whose horror of Jacobin atheism spurred them to propagate missionary activity in all parts of the rapidly consolidating British empire. Evangelicals such as William Wilberforce and Charles Grant (members of the Clapham Sect) and their supporters held positions of great power in government, as well as in the East India Company. However, Wilberforce's 1793 motion to allow Christian missionaries into India was defeated in Parliament because of British fears that proselytizing would enrage the natives. It was only with the Charter Act of 1813 that the Evangelicals won a major victory: although the act renewed the Company's charter for operations, it also broke the Company's monopoly by allowing free trade and cleared the way for missionary work in India. Given the Evangelicals' belief in the transformation of human character through education, and their conviction that conversion to Christianity required some amount of learning, their victory with the 1813 Act included the provision of an annual sum of £10,000 for the promotion of education for the natives.[51]

As early as 1797, however, Charles Grant, a director of the Company and its chairman for many years, presented to the

48. J. S. Mill, *Autobiography*, cited in Stokes, *English Utilitarians and India*, p. 49.

49. See Stokes, *English Utilitarians and India*, p. 57.

50. Bentinck, quoted in Percival Spear, *A History of India* (Harmondsworth: Penguin Books, 1970), 2:126.

51. Stokes, *English Utilitarians and India*, p. 30.

Court of Directors a privately printed treatise in which he advocated English education in India.[52] Entitled *Observations on the State of Society among the Asiatic Subjects of Great Britain, Particularly with Respect to Morals; and on the Means of Improving It*, Grant's treatise argued that the "lamentably degenerate and base Hindus," "governed by malevolent and licentious passions" and possessed of only a "feeble sense of moral obligation," were "sunk in misery" owing to their religion. Supporting his allegations with copious quotations from Orientalist and missionary translations of Indian texts, Grant contended that only education in English would free the minds of the Hindus from their priests' tyranny and allow them to develop individual consciences.[53] Anticipating his opponents' argument that English education would teach the Indians to desire English liberty, Grant asserted that "the original design" with which the British had come to India—that is, "the extension of our commerce"—would best be served by the spread of education. In phrases we hear echoed by William Ward and later by Macaulay, Grant points out that British goods cannot be sold in India because the taste of the people has not been "formed to the use of them"; besides, they have not the means to buy them. English education would awaken invention among the Indians; they would initiate "improvements" at home as well as "acquire a relish" for the ingenious manufactures of Europe. For Grant, as for Macaulay after him, this was "the noblest species of conquest": "Wherever, we may venture to say, our principles and language are introduced, our commerce will follow."[54] In a phase described by Ramakrishna Mukherjee as the period of transition from mercantile capitalism to the hegemony of the British industrial bourgeoisie, Grant's arguments seemed espe-

52. Grant's treatise was reprinted as a Parliamentary Paper in 1813 and again in 1832.
53. For a discussion of the Clapham's Sect's "interests," see Stokes, *English Utilitarians and India*, pp. 30–33.
54. Grant, quoted in Ramakrishna Mukherjee, *The Rise and Fall of the East India Company* (1955; rev. ed., Bombay: Popular Prakashan, 1973), p. 421.

cially appropriate.[55] British commerce would benefit substantially from the coinciding of "duty" and "self-interest."[56]

For years a controversy raged between "Orientalists" and "Anglicists" as to whether the money set aside for education by the act of 1813 was to be used for indigenous education or Western education.[57] Finally, the compulsions of the changing nature of Company rule enabled, during Bentinck's tenure, the Resolution of March 7, 1835, which declared that the funds provided should "be henceforth employed in imparting to the Native population knowledge of English literature and science through the medium of the English language."[58] Schools and colleges were set up by the British; Persian gave way to English as the official language of the colonial state and the medium of the higher courts of law. Bentinck's "westernization" of the administrative system went hand in hand, therefore, with a reversal of Cornwallis's exclusionary

55. Ibid., passim.

56. See Stokes, *English Utilitarians and India*, p. 33.

57. For an extensive discussion of this debate, see B. K. Boman-Behram, *Educational Controversies of India: The Cultural Conquest of India under British Imperialism* (Bombay: Taraporevala Sons, 1942). Dharampal suggests that the uprooting of indigenous education could have been prompted by the British fear that the cultural and religious content of Indian education would provide grounds for resistance to colonial hegemony (Dharampal, *Beautiful Tree*, p. 75). Charles Trevelyan wrote in 1838 that it was unreasonable to expect the British to sponsor indigenous education: "Our bitterest enemies could not desire more than that we should propagate systems of learning which excite the strongest feelings of human nature against ourselves" (Trevelyan, *On the Education of the People of India* [London: Longman, Orme, Brown, Green & Longmans, 1838], p. 189).

58. *History of India*, 2:127. Eric Stokes argues that as early as 1813 the East India Company could not justify its trade monopoly. Indian "piece-goods" no longer had a market in Europe, and with the Company becoming a "purely military and administrative power," it absorbed all available revenue surpluses (Stokes, *English Utilitarians and India*, pp. 37–38). What British rule could now do in India was not to extract tribute but to create a new market for British goods. Besides, after the defeat of the Marathas in 1818, the last resistance to the British crumbled, and the main task became one of effectively administering the large territories acquired by the Company (ibid., p. xv). English education would produce not only large numbers of native bureaucrats but also begin to create the taste for European commodities.

policies and induction of more and more Indians into the hierarchy, a move enabled by English education. Given this rather obvious "use" of English, the Committee on Public Instruction, of which Macaulay was president, emphasized higher education in English and disregarded large-scale primary schooling.

Macaulay did not think it necessary for the entire Indian populace to learn English: the function of anglicized education was "to form a class who may be interpreters between us (the British) and the millions whom we govern; a class of persons, Indian in blood and colour, but English in taste, in opinions, in morals, and in intellect."[59] A lawgiver like William Jones, Macaulay, who also formulated the Indian Penal Code, spoke of the time when India might become independent, when the British would leave behind an empire that would never decay, because it would be "the imperishable empire of our arts and our morals, our literature and our laws."[60]

Macaulay's brother-in-law, Charles Trevelyan, wrote about how the influence of the indigenous elite would secure the "permanence" of the change wrought by Western education: "Our subjects have set out on a new career of improvement: they are about to have a new character imprinted on them."[61] The agent of this change would be "English literature," which would lead to Indians speaking of great Englishmen with the same enthusiasm as their rulers: "Educated in the same way, interested in the same objects, engaged in the same pursuits with ourselves, they become more English than Hindus" and look upon the British as their "natural protectors and benefactors," for "the summit of their [the Indians'] ambition is, to resemble us."[62]

<hr>

59. Macaulay, "Indian Education" (Minute of the 2nd of February, 1835), in *Prose and Poetry,* ed. G. M. Young (Cambridge, Mass.: Harvard University Press, 1967), p. 729.
60. Macaulay, "Speech of 10 July 1833," in *Prose and Poetry,* p. 717.
61. Trevelyan, *Education of the People of India,* p. 181.
62. Ibid., pp. 189–92.

In his 1835 minute on Indian education, Macaulay, who was an avid reader of Mill's *History*, claimed he had not found a single Orientalist "who could deny that a single shelf of a good European library was worth the whole native literature of India and Arabia,"[63] and Trevelyan agreed that the latter was "worse than useless."[64] The British propagation of English education resulted ultimately in people being compelled and encouraged "to collaborate in the destruction of their instruments of expression."[65]

As Gauri Viswanathan has pointed out, the introduction of English education can be seen as "an embattled response to historical and political pressures: to tensions between the English Parliament and the East India Company, between Parliament and the missionaries, between the East India Company and the native elite classes."[66] Extending her argument, I would like to suggest that the specific resolution of these tensions through the introduction of English education was enabled discursively by the colonial practice of translation. European translations of Indian texts prepared for a Western audience provided the "educated" Indian with a whole range of Orientalist images. Even when the anglicized Indian spoke a language other than English, "he" would have preferred, because of the symbolic power conveyed by English, to gain access to his own past through the translations and histories circulating through colonial discourse. English education also familiarized the Indian with ways of seeing, techniques of translation, or modes of representation that came to be accepted as "natural."

The philosopheme of translation grounds a multiplicity of discourses, which feed into, as well as emerge out of, the

---

63. Macaulay, "Minute," in *Prose and Poetry*, p. 722.

64. Trevelyan, *Education of the People of India*, p. 182.

65. Pierre Bourdieu, *Ce que parler veut dire: L'Economie des échanges linguistiques* (Paris: Fayard, 1981), cited by John Thompson in *Studies in the Theory of Ideology* (Berkeley and Los Angeles: University of California Press, 1984), p. 45.

66. Viswanathan, "Beginnings of English Literary Study," p. 24.

colonial context. And just as translation is overdetermined, so is the "subject" under colonialism, overdetermined in the sense that it is produced by multiple discourses on multiple sites, and gives rise to a multiplicity of practices. The demand for English education on the part of the colonized is clearly not a simple recognition of "backwardness" or mere political expedience, but a complex need arising from the braiding of a host of historical factors, a need produced and sustained by colonial translation.

The construction of the colonial subject presupposes what Pierre Bourdieu has called "symbolic domination." Symbolic domination, and its violence, effectively reproduce the social order through a combination of recognition and misrecognition *(reconnaissance* and *méconnaissance)*—recognition that the dominant language is legitimate (one thinks again of the use of English in India) and "a misrecognition of the fact that this language . . . is imposed *as* dominant. The exercise of symbolic violence is so invisible to social actors precisely because it presupposes the complicity of those who suffer most from its effects."[67] Bourdieu's analysis suggests that the colonized—or even the post-colonial—recolonizes him/herself again and again through her/his participation in "the discursive practices of everyday life," which, rather than any powerful system imposed from above, maintain the asymmetrical relations characteristic of colonialism.

The notion of autocolonization implicit in the story about the "native boys" begging for English books could be explored in greater depth through Antonio Gramsci's concept of hegemony. Gramsci makes a distinction between the state apparatus and "civil society": the first includes the entire coercive mechanism of the state, including army, police, and legislature, while the second includes the school, the family, the church, and the media. The dominant group exercises *domination* through the state apparatus, with the use of force or coercion, and ensures its *hegemony* through the production

---

67. Thompson, *Studies in the Theory of Ideology,* p. 58.

of ideology in civil society, where it secures its power through consent.[68]

Colonial society presents a good example of the workings of a hegemonic culture.[69] The discourses of education, theology, historiography, philosophy, and literary translation inform the hegemonic apparatuses that belong to the ideological structure of colonial rule. We may turn again to Gramsci's work for a conception of ideology that breaks away from the traditional notion of "false consciousness."[70] Ideology, which for Gramsci is inscribed in practices (for example, colonial practices of subjectification), produces "subjects" and has therefore a certain materiality.[71] Influential translations (from Sanskrit and Persian into English in the eighteenth century, for example) interpellated colonial subjects, legitimizing or authorizing certain versions of the Oriental, versions that then came to acquire the status of "truths" even in the countries in which the "original" works were produced. The introduction of Western education was facilitated by what Trevelyan calls "seminaries," missionary-run schools sponsored by the government. European missions, which played an important role in easing colonies into the global economy, often ran the

68. For an illuminating discussion of Gramsci's ideas, see Chantal Mouffe, "Hegemony and Ideology in Gramsci," in *Gramsci and Marxist Theory*, ed. Mouffe (London: Routledge & Kegan Paul, 1979).

69. But see Ranajit Guha's argument in "Dominance without Hegemony and Its Historiography," in *Subaltern Studies VI: Writings on South Asian History and Society*, ed. Guha (Delhi: Oxford University Press, 1989). Guha suggests that *domination* more appropriately describes colonial society than *hegemony*, because *hegemony* implies the consent of all classes, whereas colonial rule had the "sanction" only of the elites. It seems to me that Guha does not sufficiently account for what even Macaulay saw as the filtration effect—that is, the gradual pervading by different forms of colonial rule of all sections of the colonized. This notion, I should admit, however, may not apply to all colonized societies; colonialism may be hegemonic, for example, in Barbados, but not in Jamaica; in Martinique, but not in Guadeloupe, and so on.

70. Ideology as false consciousness, a classical Marxist notion, suggests a distorted representation of "reality." Gramsci's conception, which stresses the "material nature" of ideology, is more useful in examining the persistence of colonial discourse.

71. Mouffe, "Hegemony and Ideology," p. 199. Althusser draws on Gramsci's notion of ideology in formulating the theory of interpellation.

entire education system in other colonial societies, such as the Belgian Congo, for example. The *systemic* collaboration of anthropologists, missionaries, and colonial administrators in the non-European world, in being independent of the willing participation of "individuals," is characteristic of the workings of hegemonic colonial discourse.[72] Missionaries, therefore, functioned as colonial agents in the formation of practices of subjectification, not only in their roles as priests and teachers but also in the capacity of linguists, grammarians, and translators.[73]

The desire of colonial discourse to translate in order to contain (and to contain and control in order to translate, since symbolic domination is as crucial as physical domination) is evidenced in colonial-missionary efforts to compile grammars of "unknown" languages. European missionaries were the first to prepare Western-style dictionaries for most of the Indian languages, participating thereby in the enormous project of collection and codification on which colonial power was based. Administrators and Asiatic Society members like Jones and Halhed published grammars as their first major works of scholarship: Jones's Persian grammar came out in 1777, and Halhed's Bengali grammar, the first one to use Bengali script, in 1778. Halhed complained in the preface to his work about the "unsettled" orthography of Bengali, and the difficulty of applying European principles of grammar to a language that seemed to have lost "its general underlying principles."[74] The establishment of the College of Fort William in Calcutta, closely associated with the Asiatic Society and devoted to the "Oriental" education of East India Company employees, provided a major impetus to translators and grammarians. As

72. I discuss the relationship between anthropologists and colonial rule at greater length in chapter 2. For a discussion of "systemic" collaboration, see Johannes Fabian, *Language and Colonial Power* (Cambridge: Cambridge University Press, 1986).

73. For a comprehensive description of the convergence of missionary and imperial efforts in Bengal, the first center of British government in India, see David Kopf, *British Orientalism and the Bengal Renaissance* (Berkeley and Los Angeles: University of California Press, 1969).

74. Halhed, *A Grammar of the Bengali Language* (Hooghly: n.p., 1778), cited in Kopf, *British Orientalism and the Bengal Renaissance*, p. 57.

David Kopf puts it, "By 1805 the college had become a veritable laboratory where Europeans and Asians worked out new transliteration schemes, regularized spoken languages into precise grammatical forms, and compiled dictionaries in languages relatively unknown in Europe."[75] When a fire in 1812 destroyed the printing shop of the Serampore missionaries, one of whom—William Carey—taught in the college, among the manuscripts destroyed was that of a polyglot dictionary "containing words of every known oriental tongue."[76]

The drive to study, to codify, and to "know" the Orient employs the classical notions of representation and reality criticized by post-structuralists like Derrida and de Man. Their work offers a related critique of traditional historicism that is of great relevance in a post-colonial context. The critique of historicism may help us formulate a complex notion of *historicity*, which would include the "effective history" of the text; this phrase encompasses questions such as: Who uses/interprets the text? How is it used, and for what?[77] Both the critique of representation and the critique of historicism empower the post-colonial theorist to undertake an analysis of what Homi Bhabha (following Foucault) has called technologies of colonial power.[78] These critiques also enable the reinscription of the problematic of translation: the deconstruction of colonial texts and their "white mythology" helps us to see how translation brings into being notions of representation and reality that endorse the founding concepts of Western philosophy as well as the discourse of literary criticism.

THE QUESTION OF "HISTORY"

In a recent essay on Fredric Jameson's *The Political Unconscious*, Samuel Weber charges Jameson with using the gesture

---

75. Kopf, *British Orientalism and the Bengal Renaissance*, p. 67.

76. Ibid., p. 78.

77. See the next section of this chapter for my discussion of the notion of historicity/history.

78. Bhabha, "Signs Taken for Wonders: Questions of Ambivalence and Authority under a Tree outside Delhi, May 1817," *Critical Inquiry* 12, no. 1 (Autumn 1985): 144–65; cited henceforth as SW.

of "capitalizing History" to address the "challenge of 'post-structuralist' thought."[79] Weber's is one of the latest salvoes in the prolonged skirmishing between the defenders of "post-structuralism" and those (on the right as well as the left) who accuse it of denying "history." The early attacks on deconstruction by M. H. Abrams and others now read like the despairing cries of traditional literary historians intent on preserving their notions of tradition, continuity, and historical context against the onslaught of a violent, disruptive Nietzscheanism.[80] Jameson, however, has consistently attempted to come to terms with structuralist and post-structuralist thought, and his imperative to historicize derives from the "priority" he gives to "a Marxian interpretive framework."[81]

As the post-structuralists (I have in mind Derrida and the American deconstructionists in particular) perceive it, the demand that they address "history" comes increasingly from the "left," especially from those who have "taken on" (the phrase is Geoff Bennington's) deconstruction in more senses than one.[82] With all the quibbling about "history," it is curious that both the post-structuralists and those who maintain an antagonistic, but admiring, stance toward them should have such a monolithic view of what *history* means. If the former polemicize against history as "phallogocentrism," the latter argue that is an "untranscendable horizon." Neither specify whether the "history" in question refers to a mode of writing history (a certain conception of the past) or to the "past" itself.

My central concern here is not to elaborate on the battle for "history" now being staged in Euro-American theory but to

79. Samuel Weber, "Capitalizing History: *The Political Unconscious*," in *Institution and Interpretation* (Minneapolis: University of Minnesota Press, 1987), pp. 40–58.

80. See, e.g., Abrams, "The Deconstructive Angel," *Critical Inquiry* 3, no. 3 (Spring 1977): 425–38.

81. Jameson, *The Political Unconscious* (Ithaca, N.Y.: Cornell University Press, 1981), p. 10; cited henceforth as *PU.*

82. See the recent anthology *Post-Structuralism and the Question of History*, ed. Derek Attridge, Geoff Bennington, and Robert Young (New York: Cambridge University Press, 1987).

ask a series of questions from a strategically "partial" perspective—that of an emergent post-colonial practice willing to profit from the insights of post-structuralism, while at the same time demanding ways of writing history in order to make sense of how subjectification operates.

Since one of the classic moves of colonial discourse (as, for example, in Orientalism) is to present the colonial subject as unchanging and immutable, historicity—which includes the idea of change—is a notion that needs to be taken seriously. For my purposes, I take *historicity* to mean—although not unproblematically—effective history (Nietzsche's *wirkliche Historie* or Gadamer's *Wirkungsgeschichte*), or that part of the past that is still operative in the present.[83] The notion of effective history helps us read against the grain Jones's late-eighteenth-century translations of ancient Sanskrit texts; it also suggests the kinds of questions one might work with in re-translating those texts two hundred years later. The term *historicity* thus incorporates questions about how the translation/re-translation worked/works, why the text was/is translated, and who did/does the translating.

I use the word *historicity* to avoid invoking History with a capital H, my concern being with "local" practices (or micropractices as Foucault calls them) of translation that require no overarching theory to contain them. As Foucault declares, "effective history affirms knowledge as perspective"; it may be seen as a radical kind of "presentism," which we may be able to work from.[84] I indicated earlier that post-colonials have good reason to be suspicious of teleological historicism, which Derrida has rightly characterized as a manifestation of Western metaphysics.[85] But since the facts of "history" are ines-

83. Nietzsche, *The Use and Abuse of History*, trans. Adrian Collins (Indianapolis: Bobbs-Merrill, 1957), 2d ed.; Hans-Georg Gadamer, *Truth and Method*, trans. Garrett Barden and John Cumming (1975; reprint, New York: Crossroad, 1985).

84. Foucault, "Nietzsche, Genealogy, History," in *Language, Counter-Memory, Practice*, ed. Donald Bouchard (Ithaca, N.Y.: Cornell University Press, 1977), p. 156.

85. Derrida uses this term to refer to the edifice of Western philosophy, a system of thought built on a first principle or foundation that remains un-

capable for the post-colonial, since attention to history is in a sense *demanded* by the post-colonial situation, post-colonial theory has to formulate a narrativizing strategy in addition to a deconstructive one. The use of historicity / effective history may help us sidestep the metaphysics of linearity.

We may also find useful Louis Althusser's critique of historicism, which leads him, in Jameson's words, to formulate the notion that "history is a process without a *telos* or a subject," "a repudiation of . . . master narratives and their twin categories of narrative closure *(telos)* and of character (subject of history)" *(PU,* p. 29). The latter assumption may be seen as an attack on the individualist idea of the subject, which Althusser's own notion of subject deconstructs. Jameson further suggests that history for Althusser is an "absent cause," that it is like Jacques Lacan's "Real," "inaccessible to us except in textual form" *(PU,* p. 82). The notion that history can be "apprehended only through its effects" (p. 102) is directly relevant to a theorist seeking, like Foucault's genealogist, to understand the "play of dominations" and "systems of subjection" *(LCP,* p. 148). The genealogist, says Foucault, "needs history to dispel the chimeras of the origin" *(LCP,* p. 144). A theory emerging from the post-colonial context needs to ally itself with the critique of origin and *telos* as it tries to practice a way of writing history that is anti-essentialist. In this project, another source of support is the work of Walter Benjamin, who sees the historian (or we may even say the translator) seizing the past image that comes into a constellation with the present. The discontinuity of the past we construct may provoke us to discuss the "why" of a translation and how it manifests effective history.[86] Perhaps post-colonial theory can show that we need to *translate* (that is, disturb or displace)

---

questioned. He sees his task as one of "deconstructing" this body of assumptions that underwrites the whole of Western culture.

86. For an extended discussion of Benjamin's notions of translation and history, see chapters 4 and 5.

history rather than to interpret it (hermeneutically) or "read" it (in a textualizing move).

The most profound insight Derrida's work has afforded to post-colonials is the notion that *origin* is always already heterogeneous, that it is not some pure, unified source of meaning or history. It would be a mistake for historiographers (literary or otherwise) to challenge colonial representations as "false" or "inadequate"; the striving for adequacy based on such a challenge would trap post-colonial writing in a metaphysics of presence, in what Derrida has called "the generative question" of the age, the question of the value of representation.[87]

In "Speech and Phenomena," his essay on Husserl, Derrida says:

> When in fact I *effectively* use words . . . I must from the outset operate (within) a structure of repetition whose basic element can only be representative. A sign is never an event, if by event we mean an irreplaceable and irreversible empirical particular. A sign which would take place but "once" would not be a sign. . . . Since this representative structure is signification itself, I cannot enter into an "effective" discourse without being from the start involved in unlimited representation.[88]

What Derrida is claiming is that there is no primordial "presence" that is then re-presented. The "re-" does not *befall* the original. It is the concept of representation that suppresses the difference that is already there in the so-called origin and grounds the whole of Western metaphysics. This is a meta-

87. Derrida, "Sending: On Representation," trans. Peter and Mary Ann Caws, *Social Research* 49, no. 2 (Summer 1982): 294–326. Another problem with seeing colonial representations as "false" is that the colonial "reality" can be said to be *produced* by the colonizer. The representation of a "cheating Hindoo," for example, implies the production of a reality in which "cheating" can be a form of resistance to colonial domination. Instead of challenging the colonial representation as false, perhaps we should look at its *effects*, arguing that different representations can produce other, more enabling or empowering effects.

88. Derrida, *Speech and Phenomena*, trans. David B. Allison (Evanston, Ill.: Northwestern University Press, 1973), p. 50. Cited henceforth as *SP*.

physics of presence, of the "absolute proximity of self-identity" (*SP*, p. 99) and of presence to oneself. Perhaps the predominant characteristic of the metaphysics of presence is the privileging of voice and speech over "writing" *(écriture)* that Derrida calls phonocentrism or logocentrism, wherein writing, as a derived form, the copy of a copy, comes to signify a distant, lost, or broken origin, a notion Derrida contests by revealing that any notion of the simple, the center, or the primordial is always already characterized by an irreducible or untranscendable heterogeneity.

In a series of detailed readings of Husserl, Heidegger, Saussure, Lévi-Strauss, and Rousseau, Derrida demonstrates how representation—and writing—already belong to the sign and to signification: "In this play of representation, the point of origin becomes ungraspable. . . . There is no longer a simple origin."[89] It is interesting to speculate what impact this notion of a dispersed origin might have on deep-rooted European histories of the cradle of civilization (Asia or Africa) and on post-colonial peoples' images of themselves.

To deconstruct logocentric metaphysics, Derrida proposes we use the notion of writing as he has reinscribed it. Derrida's "writing" is another name for difference at the origin; it signifies "the most formidable difference. It threatened the desire for living speech from the closest proximity, it *breached* living speech from within and from the very beginning" (*OG*, p. 56). The sign of origin, for Derrida, is a writing of a writing that can only state that the origin is originary translation. Metaphysics tries to reappropriate presence, says Derrida, through notions of adequacy of representation, of totalization, of history. Cartesian-Hegelian history, like the structure of the sign, "is conceivable only *on the basis* of the presence that it defers and *in view* of the deferred presence one intends to reappropriate" (*SP*, p. 138). Here Derrida points to historicism's concern with *origin* and *telos* and its desire to construct a totalizing narrative. "History," in the texts of post-structur-

---

89. Derrida, *Of Grammatology*, trans. Gayatri C. Spivak (Baltimore: Johns Hopkins University Press, 1974), p. 36. Cited henceforth as *OG*.

alism, is a repressive force that obliterates difference and belongs in a chain that includes meaning, truth, presence, and logos. We shall see later how Walter Benjamin, in a similar critique of monolithic histories, instead uses materialist historiography as a means of destabilization.

Derrida's critique of representation is important for postcolonial theory because it suggests a critique of the traditional notion of translation as well. In fact, the two problematics have always been intertwined in Derrida's work. He has indicated more than once that translation perhaps escapes "the orbit of representation" and is therefore an "exemplary question."[90] If representation stands for the reappropriation of presence, translation emerges as the sign for what Derrida would call "dissemination."[91] We must, however, carefully interrogate the conventional concept of translation that belongs to the order of representation, adequacy, and truth.

While post-colonial theory would willingly dispense with the historical narratives that have underwritten the imperialistic enterprise, that come into being with the denial of historicity to conquered peoples, and that suppress history in order to appear as history, it is aware that the situation of the post-colonial "subject," who lives always already "in translation," requires for its articulation some notion of what history is. The translations by Calcutta's Fort William College scholars from Indian languages into English, in constructing the colonial subject, provided representations of the "Asiatik" to generations of Europeans.

The point is not just to criticize these characterizations as "inadequate" or "untrue"; one should attempt to show the complicity of the representations with colonial rule and their part in maintaining the asymmetries of imperialism. The post-colonial desire for "history" is a desire to understand the traces of the "past" in a situation where at least one fact is singularly irreducible: colonialism and what came after. Historiography

90. Derrida, "Sending: On Representation," p. 298.
91. Derrida, *Dissemination*, trans. Barbara Johnson (Chicago: University of Chicago Press, 1981).

in such a situation must provide ways of recovering occluded images from the past to deconstruct colonial and neocolonial histories. In India, for example, the Subaltern Studies group, which has initiated such a project of rewriting history, is grappling with the conceptual problems of essentialism and representation.

In an essay on the Subaltern Studies historians, Gayatri Spivak argues that their practice is akin to "deconstruction," since they put forward a "theory of change as the site of displacement of function between sign-systems" and this is "a theory of reading in the strongest possible general sense."[92] Spivak's essay is a persuasive, if somewhat anxious, attempt to account for the similarities (and a few of the differences) between these post-colonial historiographers and the projects of post-structuralism. She provides a useful parallel when she suggests that the Subaltern Studies historians focus on the "site of displacement of the function of signs," which is "the name of reading as active transaction between past and future," and that this "transactional reading"—perhaps we can also call it translation—may indicate the possibility of action (DH, p. 332).

Since it is part of my argument that the problematics of translation and the writing of history are inextricably bound together, I shall briefly go over Spivak's main points regarding the Subaltern historians. Their strategic use of post-structuralist ideas (whether self-declared or emerging from Spivak's reading of their work) may help us see more clearly how the notions of history and translation I wish to reinscribe are not only enabled by the post-colonial critique of historiography but might also further strengthen that critique.

The significant post-structuralist "themes" Spivak refers to are the critique of origins, writing and the attack on phonocentrism, the critique of bourgeois liberal humanism, the notion of the "enabling" discursive failure, and the notion of

92. Spivak, "Subaltern Studies: Deconstructing Historiography," in *Subaltern Studies IV: Writings on South Asian History and Society* (Delhi: Oxford University Press, 1985). Cited henceforth as DH.

"affirmative deconstruction." The Subaltern historians are concerned with revealing the discursivity of a history (colonial or neocolonial) that has come into being through a suppression of historicity. They use the term *subaltern* "as a name for the general attribute of subordination in South Asian society whether this is expressed in terms of class, caste, age, gender and office or in any other way."[93] Through elaborate construction of the figure of the insurgent subaltern and a series of sustained miscognitions, elite historiography presents a history that purports to be "disinterested" and "true." The post-colonial historian tries to show how this discursive field is constituted, and how, as Spivak puts it, the "Muse of History" and counterinsurgency are "complicit" (DH, p. 334). History and translation function, perhaps, under the same order of representation, truth, and presence, creating coherent and transparent texts through the repression of difference, and participating thereby in the process of colonial domination.

The problem of subaltern consciousness, according to Spivak, "operates as a metaphysical methodological presupposition" in the group's work, but "there is always a counterpointing suggestion" that "subaltern consciousness is subject to the cathexis of the elite, that it is never fully recoverable, that it is always askew from its received signifiers, indeed that it is effaced even as it is disclosed, that it is irreducibly discursive" (DH, p. 339). As I tried to suggest in the first section of this chapter, translations into English by colonialists in India in the eighteenth and nineteenth centuries offered authoritative versions of the Eastern self not only to the "West" but to their (thereby interpellated) subjects. The introduction of English education after 1835 and the decline of indigenous learning ensured that post-colonials would seek their unrecoverable past in the translations and histories constituting colonial discourse. The subaltern, too, exists only "in translation," always already cathected by colonial domination.

93. Ranajit Guha, preface to *Subaltern Studies I: Writings on South Asian History and Society* (Delhi: Oxford University Press, 1982), p. vii.

In a move that some may see as imperialistic in its own way, Spivak appropriates the Subaltern historians' critique of origins: "What had seemed the historical predicament of the colonial subaltern can be made to become the allegory of the predicament of *all* thought, *all* deliberative consciousness, though the elite profess otherwise" (DH, p. 340, emphasis in original). What she refers to is the creation of the subaltern as a "subject-effect," its operation *as subject* in an enormous "discontinuous network" or "text." In order to function as subject, it is assigned a "sovereign and determining" role; what is really an effect is presented as a cause—a metalepsis is posited. Spivak indicates that elements in the work of Subaltern Studies "warrant a reading of the project to retrieve the subaltern consciousness as the attempt to undo a massive historiographical metalepsis and 'situate' the effect of the subject as subaltern" (DH, pp. 341–42).

The notion of consciousness, then, is used strategically, deliberately, unnostalgically, in the service of "a scrupulously visible political interest" (DH, p. 342), to refer to an "emergent collective consciousness" rather than that of the liberal humanist subject. The strategic use of essentialist concepts marks what Spivak, and Derrida, would call "affirmative deconstruction." A comment of Derrida's from *Of Grammatology* offers an important clue to the way in which post-colonial theory will have to situate itself:

> The movements of deconstruction do not destroy structures from the outside. They are not possible and effective, nor can they take accurate aim, except by inhabiting those structures. Inhabiting them *in a certain way,* because one always inhabits, and all the more when one does not suspect it. Operating necessarily from the inside, borrowing all the strategic and economic resources of subversion from the old structure, borrowing them structurally, that is to say without being able to isolate their elements and atoms, the enterprise of deconstruction always in a certain way falls prey to its own work.
>
> (*OG*, p. 24)

How can theory, or translation, avoid being trapped in the order of representation when it uses the very concepts it criticizes? Derrida would say that it should aim to be the kind of writing that "both marks and goes back over its mark with an undecidable stroke," for this "double mark escapes the pertinence or authority of truth," reinscribing it without overturning it. This displacement is not an *event;* it has not "taken place." It is what "writes / is written."[94] The double inscription Derrida mentions has a parallel in Walter Benjamin's strategy of citation or quotation. For Benjamin, the historical materialist (the critical historiographer) quotes without quotation marks in a method akin to montage. It is one way of revealing the constellation a past age forms with the present without submitting to a simple historical continuum, to an order of origin and *telos.*

Derrida's double writing can help us challenge the practices of "subjectification" and domination evident in colonial histories and translations. The challenge will not, however, be made in the name of recovering a lost essence or an undamaged self. Instead, the question of the *hybrid* will inform our reading. As Bhabha puts it:

> Hybridity is the sign of the productivity of colonial power, its shifting forces and fixities; it is the name for the strategic reversal of the process of domination through disavowal (that is, the production of discriminatory identities that secure the "pure" and original identity of authority). Hybridity is the revaluation of the assumption of colonial identity through the repetition of discriminatory identity effects. It displays the necessary deformation and displacement of all sites of discrimination and domination.   (SW, p. 154)

Colonial discourse, although it creates identities for those it transfixes by its gaze of power, is profoundly ambivalent at the source of its authority. Hybridity leads to proliferating differences that escape the "surveillance" of the discriminatory eye. "Faced with the hybridity of its objects," says Bhabha, "the *presence* of power is revealed as something other than what its rules of recognition assert" (SW, p. 154). When we begin to understand how colonial power ends up *producing*

94. Derrida, *Dissemination,* p. 193.

hybridization, "the discursive conditions of dominance" can be turned into "the grounds of intervention" (p. 154). The hybrid (subject or context), therefore, involves translation, deformation, displacement. As Bhabha is careful to point out, colonial hybridity is not a problem of cultural identity that can be resolved by a relativistic approach; it is, rather, "a *problematic* of colonial representation and individuation that reverses the effects of the colonialist disavowal, so that other 'denied' knowledges enter upon the dominant discourse and estrange the basis of its authority" (p. 156).[95]

Clearly, the notion of hybridity, which is of great importance for a Subaltern critique of historiography as well as for a critique of traditional notions of translation, is both "ambiguous and historically complex."[96] To restrict "hybridity," or what I call "living in translation," to a post-colonial elite is to deny the pervasiveness, however heterogeneous, of the transformations wrought across class boundaries by colonial and neocolonial domination. This is not to present a meta-narrative of global homogenization, but to emphasize the need to reinvent oppositional cultures in nonessentializing ways. Hybridity can be seen, therefore, as the sign of a post-colonial theory that subverts essentialist models of reading while it points toward a new practice of translation.

95. For a forceful description of the hybrid, see Aijaz Ahmad, "Jameson's Rhetoric of Otherness and the 'National Allegory,' " *Social Text* 15 (Fall 1986): 3–25.

96. James Clifford, *The Predicament of Culture* (Cambridge, Mass.: Harvard University Press, 1988), p. 16.

2

Representing Texts and Cultures: Translation Studies and Ethnography

> It was found highly dangerous to employ the natives as interpreters, upon whose fidelity they could not depend.
> —William Jones,
> *A Grammar of the Persian Language*

Translation—in the narrowest sense of the word, that is, to turn something from one language into another, or interlingual translation—has traditionally been viewed by literary critics in the West (at least since the Renaissance) as the noble task of bridging the gap between peoples, as the quintessential humanistic enterprise.[1] Social anthropologists and ethnographers, since the beginnings of their discipline in the nineteenth century, have also seen their task as epitomizing humanism in its desire to provide their (Western) audience with a body of knowledge about "unknown" peoples; it is a task that anthropologists themselves would define as intercultural translation, or the translating of one culture into terms intelligible to another.[2]

What has only recently begun to be discussed, however, is the question of the historical complicity in the growth and expansion of European colonialism in the nineteenth and twentieth centuries of those interested in translating non-

1. We must not forget here that the conception of the humanistic enterprise is enabled by the repression of heterogeneity *within* the "West." Imperialism allows the West to conceive of the other as *outside* it, to constitute itself as a unified subject.

2. "The problem of describing to others how members of a remote tribe think . . . begins to appear largely as one of translation" (Godfrey Lienhardt, "Modes of Thought," in *The Institutions of Primitive Society* [Oxford: Basil Blackwell, 1961], p. 96).

Western texts (for example, missionaries engaged in spreading Christianity) and those involved in the study of "man." Is there something in the very nature of the problems posed—and the kinds of solutions adopted—in translation studies[3] and ethnography that lends itself, borrows from, authorizes the discourse of colonization that underwrites the project of imperialism?

In this chapter, I shall discuss the debates in these two very different discourses concerned with translation.[4] *Translation studies* is a rubric for traditional theories of translation and their contemporary formulations; *ethnography* refers to the writings of cultural/social anthropologists, who, until recently, in a more or less unproblematic fashion, saw the object of their study as "man" and their mission as one of translation. The discussion of ethnography will be the most suggestive for our purpose, since it has been able to generate an internal critique of the asymmetries implicit in its enterprise. Translation studies, on the other hand, seems to be by and large unaware that an attempt should be made to account for the relationship between "unequal" languages.

I suggest we need to draw attention to those questions constituting "translation studies" as a field, questions that are normally left unconsidered because to do so would be to interrogate the very project of translation as a "humanistic" enterprise. The self-conception of translation studies is deeply imbued with what Derrida has called a "metaphysics of presence." Its notions of text, author, and meaning are based on an unproblematic, naively representational theory of lan-

---

3. I use the name proposed by André Lefevere in 1978 in an appendix to the published proceedings of the 1976 Louvain Colloquium on literature and translation.

4. It should be clear by now that I use the term *translation* "under erasure." In the translator's preface to Derrida's *Of Grammatology*, Gayatri Spivak glosses *under erasure* thus: "to write a word, cross it out, and then print both word and deletion. . . . In examining familiar things we come to such unfamiliar conclusions that our very language is twisted and bent even as it guides us. Writing 'under erasure' is the mark of this contortion" (*OG*, p. xiv). In what follows, I shall constantly have occasion to question the ways in which *translation* has been used.

guage. I shall shortly discuss the implications of these blind-
nesses and explore their connection with the refusal to consider questions of power and historicity.

TRANSLATION STUDIES AND HUMANISM

After the preliminary outlining of the importance of the translation problematic for a post-colonial context, we can now begin to unravel the discourses of (on) translation. Our task will
be to study the uses of the *site* and *sign* of translation, and to
see what questions are posed through translation, as well as
which are displaced, excluded, or repressed.

Although the same concepts of adequacy and fidelity pre-
side over both translation studies and literary criticism in the
traditional sense, the former does not bear the same relationship to the practice of translation as the latter does to "literature." Writers on translation have always been concerned with
how to translate, and their evaluations and assessments belong properly to the question of "method." Nearly all specu-
lation on translation exists in the form of translators' *prefaces*
to specific texts, and the tone they adopt ranges from the
apologetic to the aggressively prescriptive. This positioning
of translators in what Derrida would call the "exergue," or
"outwork," of their offerings may suggest that they are aware
of their marginality. But it is they who have drawn the margins, demarcated the text. The work from which they seem
to exclude themselves is constituted by the traces of *their* historicity, and the gesture of exclusion they perform makes
possible the presentation of the text as a unified and transparent whole.

Western writings on translation go back at least to the beginning of Judeo-Christian time. There never seems, however, to have been much of an attempt to formulate a discipline or an institutional apparatus to regulate translators. Only
in the present century—coinciding with, but largely un-
marked by, the rise of post-structuralism in literary studies—
have there been efforts to give an institutional character to
translation through the publication of journals devoted to

translation and the formation of professional organizations.[5]
The liberal-humanist conceptual framework of the new field
of *translation studies*, however, differs very little from the ideas
that have informed debates on translation over the centuries.
We may be justified, therefore, in considering the debates as
leading to the "founding" of the discipline, and the discipline
as crystallizing and perpetuating the debates.

What I propose to do is to pick out some of the obsessions
of writings on translation and indicate to what conceptions of
text, author, and meaning they appear to be bound. Occasional books and collections of essays on translation have appeared over the past twenty-five years or so, but the terms of
the debate have not changed significantly since the earliest
discussions of Bible translation.[6] "Over some two thousand
years of argument and precept, the beliefs and disagreements
voiced about the nature of translation have been almost the
same," George Steiner observes. "Identical theses, familiar
moves and refutations in debate recur, nearly without exception, from Cicero and Quintilian to the present day."[7] The
most important obsession is, of course, manifested in the opposition between the faithful and the unfaithful, freedom and
slavery, loyalty and betrayal. It points to a notion of "text"
and "interpretation" that comes out of the classical concept
of the mimetic relationship between "reality" and "knowledge."

A rapid survey of translation studies would show that for
the past few centuries thinking on translation has remained
within an empiricist-idealist conceptual framework that,
structured by what Gramsci would call "common sense," in
turn upholds the premises of humanism. I suggested in the

5. The American Literary Translators' Association, for example, was
founded in 1978. Journals focusing on translation include *Babel, Translation
Review,* and the now defunct *Delos.*

6. An exception is the anthology *Difference in Translation,* ed. Joseph Graham (Ithaca, N.Y.: Cornell University Press, 1985), the essays in which attempt to take post-structuralism into account. I shall have occasion to refer
to this volume again.

7. George Steiner, *After Babel* (New York: Oxford University Press, 1975),
p. 239.

previous chapter that translation/ethnography's humanistic enterprise was based on a naively representational theory of language and that there could be a connection between the conception of this enterprise and the "civilizing" ideology of liberal humanism. As Catherine Belsey points out,

> Common sense proposes a *humanism* based on an *empiricist-idealist* interpretation of the world. In other words, common sense urges that "man" is the origin and source of meaning, of action, and of history *(humanism)*. Our concepts and our knowledge are held to be the product of experience *(empiricism)*, and this experience is preceded and interpreted by the mind, reason or thought, the property of a transcendent human nature whose essence is the attribute of each individual *(idealism)*.[8]

"British" empiricism and "German" idealism come together in humanistic interpretation, the framework of which underwrites the classics of Orientalism at the same time as it is underwritten *by* them. The premises of humanism, explicitly problematized by post-structuralism, give rise to notions of reading and translation based on what Belsey calls the theory of expressive realism, which suggests "that literature reflects the *reality* of experience as it is perceived by one (especially gifted) individual, who *expresses* it in a discourse which enables other individuals to recognize it as true."[9] Again, here is a notion of representation based on classical conceptions of author, meaning, and art as mimesis. It is a notion we find widely adopted, implicitly or explicitly, in the debates on translation.

George Chapman, the "first self-conscious poetic translator in English,"[10] who in 1608 published *Homer Prince of Poets (Iliad, I–XII)*, prefaced his translation with a poem "To the Reader," filled with insights into the translative act. Chapman's thoughts on translation were also contained in his prose

8. Catherine Belsey, *Critical Practice* (London: Methuen, 1980), p. 7.
9. Ibid.
10. T. R. Steiner, *English Translation Theory, 1650–1800* (Assen/Amsterdam: Van Gorcum, 1975), p. 11.

preface to the complete *Iliad* (1611) and the commentaries he wrote for ten of the books. He greatly influenced Sir John Denham, Abraham Cowley, and others who formulated neoclassical principles of translation in England. He is supposed to have taken the middle path between *sensum-sensu* and *verbum-verbo*, between "overfree" and "overliteral," a path seen as governed by decorum. T. R. Steiner suggests that

> Chapman's particular achievement [was] that he turned from the words themselves . . . to the entire *artistic world* of the original author, to the whole work filled with the *soul* of a native and *natural expression*. . . . what Chapman ultimately envisioned was *spiritual commerce* between the translator and original author, an *empathic art*. . . . the translator attempts to *inhabit the consciousness* capable of this particular work.[11]

Steiner's selection and "translation" of Chapman's comments on translation weaves together a vocabulary of expressive realism (or empiricist-idealism) with a phenomenological concern for "inhabiting" the original's "consciousness," and for the empathy achieved by the translator with the "artistic world" of the original work. This concern, akin to phenomenological criticism's nostalgia for full presence,[12] evades the insistence of what Derrida calls inscription: "Diaphanousness is the supreme value; as is univocity."[13] Derrida's remark about phenomenology can be legitimately extended here to the obsessions of translation studies. Seventeenth- and eighteenth-century translation theory, according to Steiner, insisted on the true translator's identification with the original author, on his imaginative taking on of the author's consciousness: "By secret sympathy combin'd, / The faithful glass reflects its kindred mind."[14]

11. Ibid., pp. 10–11; emphasis added.
12. The term *phenomenological criticism* refers to the work of Jean Starobinski, Georges Poulet, and Jean-Pierre Richard, among others.
13. Derrida, "Force and Signification," in *Writing and Difference*, trans. Alan Bass (Chicago: University of Chicago Press, 1978), p. 27.
14. Thomas Francklin, "Translation: A Poem" (1753), quoted in Steiner, *English Translation Theory*, p. 114.

Perhaps because the language of faithfulness and identification is threatened by what, to my mind, is a significant indication of Chapman's translative practice, Steiner quotes and then passes in silence over a passage from Chapman's poem "The Tears of Peace" where the ghost of Homer addresses his translator:

> . . . thou didst inherit
> My true sense, for the time then, in my spirit;
> And I, invisibly, went prompting thee
> To those fair greens where *thou didst English me*.[15]

In this phrase we see a foreshadowing of the nature of the translative acts performed more than a hundred years later by Charles Wilkins, William Jones, and others associated with the East India Company. It is a theme even in the writings of Luther, who saw it as his duty to translate the holy books into German, to Germanize them. In his 1530 *Sendbrief* on translation (the word for circular letter evokes Derrida's meditation on *Sendung*, representation, and translation),[16] Luther used *uebersetzen* (to translate) synonymously with *verdeutschen* (to Germanize).[17]

Long before Chapman, the Frenchman Etienne Dolet had published in 1540 an essay on the principles of translation, *La Manière de bien traduire d'une langue en aultre*. Dolet spoke of being faithful to the "intention" of the work, while his contemporary Joachim du Bellay focused on the "spirit." Neither these writers nor the early seventeenth-century theorists of translation who came after them break out of the central obsession with fidelity. Writers following the interpretative tradition of Horace and Cicero argued for complete equivalence between a translation and the original work, while others wanted "artistic *altitudo*" in translation.[18] The issues do not

---

15. Chapman, quoted in Steiner, *English Translation Theory*, p. 10.

16. Derrida, "Sending: On Representation," trans. Peter and Mary Ann Caws, *Social Research* 49, no. 2 (Summer 1982): 294–326.

17. Luther, *Sendbrief vom Dolmetschen* (1530), cited in André Lefevere, *Translating Literature: The German Tradition from Luther to Rosenzweig* (Assen/Amsterdam: Van Gorcum, 1977), p. 7.

18. Steiner, *English Translation Theory*, p. 13.

change: should a translator be literal or licentious, faithful or unfaithful?

Midcentury saw the publication of Cowley's *Pindarique Odes* (1656), in a preface to which he expounded his theory of "imitation"—later to become an important neoclassical genre. Cowley declared that he wished to be faithful not to the letter of the original but to its *"way* and *manner* of speaking,"[19] while his contemporary Denham condemned the "servile path" and the vulgarity of being *fidus interpres* in translation. Cowley and Denham's concept of translation, like the Ciceronian, is based on the notion that languages have clearly defined boundaries or identities, that works in these languages have authors who control their meaning, and that translation deals with these works, whose boundaries are controlled and regulated. The term *translation* in this context obviously shores up the entire tissue of basic presuppositions about "work," "author," and "meaning" that, in spite of repeated changes in models of interpretation, has existed virtually unquestioned until recently.

These presuppositions persist in the neoclassical principles of translation that are likely to have most directly influenced early Orientalists like Wilkins and Jones. John Dryden, exemplary neoclassicist, discussed three kinds of translation: metaphrase (line by line, word for word), paraphrase (translating with "latitude"), and imitation, claiming that his own practice steered between the first two.[20] In a preface to his translation of the *Iliad*, William Cowper indicated that "fidelity is indeed the very essence of translation."[21] Samuel Johnson, to whose exclusive circle of friends Jones belonged, declared in 1759: "[He] will deserve the highest praise . . . who can convey the same thoughts with the same graces, and who, when he translates, changes nothing but the language."[22] In

19. Ibid., p. 66.

20. Dryden, "Preface to *Ovid's Epistles*" (1680), cited in Steiner, *English Translation Theory*, p. 68.

21. Cowper, "Preface to *The Iliad of Homer* (1791), quoted in Steiner, *English Translation Theory*, p. 135.

22. Johnson quoted in Steiner, *English Translation Theory*, pp. 120–21.

Germany, which was to become another haven for Orientalists, Johnson's contemporary Johann Jacob Breitinger suggested that languages were "so many collections of totally equivalent words and locutions which are interchangeable, and which fully correspond to each other in meaning."[23] Clearly, translation here is based on a kind of mimesis that effaces the materiality of language, which then becomes a mere transmitter of an essential meaning.

As Barbara Johnson points out, translation "has always been the translation of *meaning*."[24] The idea that signified and signifier can be separated informs the classical conception of philosophy as well as translation. Derrida has long contended that translatability as transfer of meaning is the very *thesis* of philosophy. The notion of the transcendental signified that for him is a founding concept of Western metaphysics "[takes] shape within the horizon of an absolutely pure, transparent, and unequivocal translatability."[25] The concept of translation that grounds Western metaphysics is the same one that presides over the beginnings of the discourse of Orientalism. Neither is prepared to acknowledge, in its humanism and universalism, the heterogeneity that contaminates "pure meaning" from the start, occluding also the project of translation.

Traditional theories of translation appear persuasive because of the role they assign to meaning, which is what good translations are assumed to preserve. It has been suggested, "after Derrida," that "epistemological considerations" underlie the role meaning plays.[26] If, as Walter Benjamin points out in "The Task of the Translator," the language of truth is concealed in translations, its elucidation may be all that philoso-

23. Breitinger, *Critische Dichtkunst* (1740; reprinted, Stuttgart: Metzler, 1966), quoted in Lefevere, *Translating Literature*, p. 24.

24. Johnson, "Taking Fidelity Philosophically," in *Difference in Translation*, ed. Graham, p. 145.

25. Derrida, *Positions*, trans. Alan Bass (Chicago: University of Chicago Press, 1981), p. 20.

26. Robert J. Matthews, "What Did Archimedes Mean by 'χευσός'?" in *Difference in Translation*, p. 162.

phy can hope to undertake. Given that meaning is not "present," epistemology "must now be practiced in the limit, if it is to be practiced at all."[27] As my reading of Benjamin in chapter 4 indicates, he fashioned out of his theory of translation a theory of writing history, where the deferred epistemological desire of translation was troped into the need for political intervention.

In his famous essay "On Linguistic Aspects of Translation," Roman Jakobson declares that "the meaning of any linguistic sign is its translation into some further, alternative sign."[28] He was perhaps the only writer on translation at the time who realized the implications of a post-Saussurean linguistics, and pointed in the direction of a post-structuralist conception of perpetually deferred meaning, denying the existence of a transcendental signified to which the linguistic sign refers.

The significance of Jakobson's remark has by and large gone unnoticed in subsequent writing in translation studies, however, perhaps because his classification of kinds of translation into intralingual, intersemiotic, and interlingual (or "translation proper") is what Derrida calls a "reassuring tripartition" that presupposes our ability "to determine rigorously the unity and identity of a language, the decidable form of its limits."[29] A recent book tracing the development of the field does suggest that it is "pointless . . . to argue for a definitive translation, since translation is intimately tied up with the context in which it is made."[30] This insight is never pushed far enough by any writer, however, with the result that once again we circle back to the opposition between betrayer and true interpreter, imitator and literalist, and to the timeworn

27. Ibid., p. 161.
28. Roman Jakobson, "On Linguistic Aspects of Translation," in *On Translation*, ed. Reuben Brower (Cambridge, Mass.: Harvard University Press, 1959), pp. 232–33.
29. Derrida, "Des Tours de Babel," in *Difference in Translation*, ed. Graham, p. 173.
30. Susan Bassnett-McGuire, *Translation Studies* (London: Methuen, 1980), p. 9.

suggestion that the translator steer a path between the two extremes, through a combination perhaps of individual intuition, talent, skill, and good fortune. It should be all too obvious that the conceptions of text (unified, "whole," a totality), of author and translator (unified subjects, individuals who are the source of meaning), of language (admittedly somewhat opaque, but ultimately capable of yielding an "immediacy" of experience) prevalent in translation studies effectively keep writers from problematizing the ancient debates structuring their field.

In essays included in a 1961 collection still quoted widely in translation studies, William Arrowsmith speaks of the extremes of "intolerable literalism" and "spurious freedom" and Jean Paris of "extreme freedom" and "extreme slavery."[31] The language of fidelity is accompanied, not surprisingly, by the idea of "equivalence"; Anton Popovič proposes four types of equivalence: linguistic (word for word), paradigmatic (at the level of grammar), stylistic (where meaning must remain identical) and textual (at the level of shape and form).[32]

The problem of fidelity, spirit, and truth is the subject of an entire chapter in a recent book on translation.[33] The chapter concludes with the remark that "great books have been translated countless times," affording different insights each time; however, "such translations float on a sludge of failures where the flow of energy between time, language and reader has been distorted by alien values and made to yield a false message."[34] The vocabulary of truth and falsehood, adequacy and inadequacy, shows that current theory of translation still operates under the aegis of the transcendental signified. Even if prepared to admit that definitive translations

31. Arrowsmith, "The Lively Conventions of Translation," in *The Craft and Context of Translation*, ed. William Arrowsmith and Roger Shattuck (Austin: University of Texas Press, 1961), p. 124. Paris, "Translation and Creation," in ibid., p. 60.

32. Popovič, *Dictionary for the Analysis of Literary Translation* (Edmonton: Department of Comparative Literature, University of Alberta, 1976).

33. Louis Kelly, *The True Interpreter* (New York: St. Martin's Press, 1979).

34. Ibid., p. 218.

do not exist, the theorist returns repeatedly to the theme of fidelity.

The notion of fidelity to the "original" holds back translation theory from thinking the *force* of a translation. The intimate links between, for example, translations from non-Western languages into English and the colonial hegemony they helped create are seldom examined. Although Louis Kelly remarks that "the Americans developed translation theory in the context of anthropological research and Christian missionary activity; the English to fit the needs of colonial administration,"[35] he does not necessarily use the observation to initiate a critique of either colonialism or translation theory. European missionaries in Africa and Asia were among the first to stress the importance of translation and prepare bilingual dictionaries of a host of Asian and African languages for the use not only of their own workers but also for merchants and administrators.[36]

In spite of a recognition on the part of some writers of the colonial beginnings of modern translation studies,[37] there has not as yet been any serious attempt to explore the relationship between the kind of debates generated by translation studies (and the assumptions underlying them) and the complicity with the liberal humanist rhetoric of colonialism. There is clearly a similarity between James Mill's remark that India must discard her Indianness in order to become civilized,[38] and the *Rubaiyat* translator Edward Fitzgerald's comment in 1851: "It is an amusement to me to take what liberties I like

35. Ibid., p. 225.
36. For a fascinating discussion of how this led to "pidginization" of the languages concerned, see Johannes Fabian, *Language and Colonial Power* (Cambridge: Cambridge University Press, 1986).
37. Bassnett-McGuire suggests in *Translation Studies* that the authoritarian relationship between the translator and an "inferior" source culture was compatible with the rise of imperialism in the nineteenth century. Again, she does not follow through on the implications of her remarks.
38. Macaulay in a similar vein suggested that Indians become "anglicized" in order to acquire civilization. See the "Minute on Indian Education," in Macaulay, *Prose and Poetry*, selected by G. M. Young (Cambridge, Mass.: Harvard University Press, 1967).

with these Persians, who . . . are not Poets enough to frighten one from such excursions, and who really do want *a little Art to shape them.*"[39] In both kinds of statements, we see the surfacing of the rigid dichotomies between modern and primitive, West and non-West, civilized and barbaric, culture and nature. As I suggested in chapter 1, one of the ways in which colonial discourse functions is by setting up and "naturalizing" or dehistoricizing this series of oppositions. This has the effect also of naturalizing the historical asymmetry between languages, to the point where theorists of translation can speak blithely of "general principles" that "can be determined and categorized, and, ultimately, utilized in the cycle of text-theory-text *regardless of the languages involved.*"[40] Statements like this one seem oblivious to the relations of power implicit in translation.

A similar blindness can be observed in hermeneutic theorists of translation like Louis Kelly or George Steiner who claim that the translation situation is one of "dialogue," of achieving "a balance between I and thou."[41] Steiner suggests that the faithful translator "creates a condition of significant exchange. The arrows of meaning, of cultural, psychological benefaction, move both ways. There is, ideally, exchange without loss."[42] I need not reiterate the idea of the futility of such remarks in the colonial context, where the "exchange" is far from equal and the "benefaction" highly dubious, where the asymmetry between languages is perpetuated by imperial rule.

Translation studies seems to ignore not just the power relations informing translation but also the historicity or effective history of translated texts. Gideon Toury, the well-known theorist of descriptive translation studies, indicates that "from

39. Fitzgerald, letter to Cowell, March 20, 1851, quoted in Bassnett-McGuire, *Translation Studies*, p. 3; emphasis added. Fitzgerald is said to have been initiated into the study of Persian by William Jones's dictionary of Persian.
40. Bassnett-McGuire, *Translation Studies*, p. 11; emphasis added.
41. Kelly, *True Interpreter*, p. 214.
42. Steiner, *After Babel*, p. 302.

the standpoint of the source text and source system, translations have hardly any significance at all. . . . Not only have they left the source system behind, but they are in no position to affect its linguistic and textual rules and norms, its textual history, or the source text as such."[43] The intertextuality of translations, the canonical nature of certain translations and their participation in colonial practices of subjectification, the largely unilinear borrowing from European languages in the colonial period—these are some of the issues that drop out of Toury's "description" which for him is part of "a *systematic scientific branch*" of "an empirical science" (that is, translation studies). Translations form an intertextual web: Orientalist translations from the Sanskrit—Charles Wilkins's *Bhagavad-Gītā*, William Jones's *Śākuntala*, Jones and Wilkins's *Manu's Institutes*, H. H. Wilson's Kālidāsa—form a canon, interpellate a colonial subject, construct a Hindu character, a Hindu psyche, a Hindu way of life. The "empirical science" of translation comes into being through the repression of the asymmetrical relations of power that inform the relations between languages.

A search for references to "politics" by writers on translation would yield a poor haul. One of the earliest direct references in this century is in Werner Winter's essay "Translation as Political Action."[44] The entire essay is devoted to a discussion of Soviet translation activities after Stalin. It is marked by a pronounced hysteria regarding Soviet "indoctrination efforts" and the sinister attempts to earn the goodwill of African and Asian countries by translating their literature into Russian. Marcia Nita Doron and Marilyn Gaddis Rose's recent essay "The Economics and Politics of Translation" refers to the poverty of translators and provides a simplistic analysis of the politics of the translation-publishing marketplace.[45] It

43. Toury, "A Rationale for Descriptive Translation Studies," in *The Manipulation of Literature*, ed. Theo Hermans (London: Croom Helm, 1985), p. 19.
44. Winter, in *Craft and Context of Translation*, ed. Arrowsmith and Shattuck, p. 172.
45. Doron and Rose, "The Economics and Politics of Translation," in

would be too much to expect translation studies, given their inherent limitations, to initiate or sustain a serious discussion of the political nature of translation, political in the sense that it is enmeshed in effective history and relations of power.

Translation theory's obsession with the humanistic nature of translation seems to blind writers to their own insights into the complicitous relationship of translation and the imperialistic vision. George Steiner, for example, mentions in *After Babel* that Ezra Pound and Arthur Waley "invented" China in their translations. European translations from the Chinese follow such similar conventions that they resemble one another much more than they do the Chinese texts. Steiner criticizes the "simplified history" and "stylized, codified markers" that aid the Western translator in "getting behind" the remote non-Western language.[46] Failing to pursue these insights, however, he remains finally committed to an idealistic vision of "exchange without loss," of a humanist enterprise summed up for him in Samuel Daniel's poem about the "happie Pen / Whom neither Ocean, Desarts, Rockes nor Sands, / Can keep from th' intertraffique of the minde."[47]

In his book on Renaissance French translation theory, Glyn Norton speaks approvingly of the "principal transcendent impulse of humanism, the credo of *translatio studiorum* or the narrowing of gaps between cultures remote in time and space."[48] Norton claims that

> translation, in humanist thought, was simply the sign of a wider transcendent impulse under which empires and learning (*imperia* and *studia*), entire segments of human consciousness, came forward to merge with the articulated experience of the pres-

---

Translation Spectrum, ed. M. G. Rose (Albany: State University of New York Press, 1981).

46. Steiner, *After Babel*, pp. 359–61. The connection between "translation" as Pound saw it and the development of "modernism" will not be discussed here, but see Pound, *Selected Essays, 1909–1965*, ed. William Cookson (New York: New Directions, 1973).

47. Quoted in Steiner, *After Babel*, p. 248.

48. Norton, *The Ideology and Language of Translation in Renaissance France and their Humanist Antecedents* (Geneva: Librairie Droz, 1984), p. 18.

ent. . . . Every translation was bound, by fate, to be a new performance, an undulating instant in the cultural and linguistic tide that was the unity of human consciousness.[49]

Although Norton points out in passing that meanings and cultures are unstable as well as "contaminated," his book lauds, on the whole, those theorists of translation who stress "the unity of human consciousness." This universalism prevents him from addressing the issue of what happens when *imperia* and *studia* merge. As William Jones, who untiringly emphasized the importance of Oriental studies and translations to the efficient administration of the British colonies, pointed out in the preface to his grammar of Persian, the languages of Asia needed to be studied closely, for then "the manners and sentiments of the Eastern nations will be perfectly known, and the limits of our knowledge will be no less extended than the bounds of our empire."[50]

Before we move on to the discussion of ethnography and its preoccupation with translation, it might be useful—given the intimate links between translation studies, the activities of missionaries, the work of anthropologists, and the role of colonial administrators—to look briefly at how "much of the Western theory and practice of translation stems immediately from the need to disseminate the Gospels, to speak holy writ in other tongues."[51] Although the reference here is to the early activities of the Christians and Bible translation into European languages, the comment is pertinent to our times, given the prevalence of examples from Bible translation in twentieth-century works of translation theory.

"Principles of Translation as Exemplified by Bible Translation" by Eugene A. Nida is the very first essay in the classic 1959 anthology *On Translation*. The prominent position of the essay is worth noting. Nida points out that the Scriptures are available at least in part in 1,109 languages, most of the trans-

49. Ibid., pp. 335–36.
50. Jones, *A Grammar of the Persian Language* (1771; 8th ed., London: W. Nicol, 1823), p. vii.
51. Steiner, *After Babel*, p. 245.

lations having been made in the nineteenth century and the first half of the twentieth.[52] Since he does not mention, of course, that the period was also one in which European colonialism grew and flourished, he has to explain the phenomenon of large-scale translation by putting it down to the Bible's "wide appeal." In his frequently quoted *The Art of Translation*, T. H. Savory devotes an entire chapter to the translating of the Bible into English, omitting completely all reference to the proselytizing function of scriptural translation in the past two hundred years.[53]

Translation itself is seen "as a function of religion" in a twentieth-century classic of translation theory, Hilaire Belloc's *On Translation*, for it "has been an essential to the maintenance of religion among men." The author believes that religion—and in the context this can only mean Christianity—is "universal" and "its application to various societies demands the rendering of its fundamental doctrines into the idiom of each in such fashion that all the renderings shall make for unity of thought."[54]

Again the movement toward totalization, again the desire for univocity and diaphanousness, this time marked deeply by the effort to erase difference, by the colonial violence of the Gospel "applied" to "various societies." *Traducir* in Spanish means to translate as well as to convert.[55] To recognize the striving for self-presence and self-identity of the concepts of text and meaning that underpin classical translation theory is to understand, to some extent, the widespread impact translations have had. The refusal of translation studies to question these concepts is a refusal to examine the political consequences of translation rigorously.

52. Nida, "Principles of Translation as Exemplified by Bible Translation," in *On Translation*, ed. Reuben Brower (Cambridge, Mass.: Harvard University Press, 1959), pp. 11–14.

53. Savory, *The Art of Translation* (Boston: The Writer, 1968).

54. Belloc, *On Translation* (London: Oxford University Press, 1931), p. 6.

55. I borrow this comment from Vicente Rafael, "Gods and Grammar: The Politics of Translation in the Spanish Colonization of the Tagalogs of the Philippines," in *Notebooks in Cultural Analysis*, ed. Norman F. Cantor and Nathalia King (Durham, N.C.: Duke University Press, 1986).

TRANSLATION IN ETHNOGRAPHY

In the now famous "Structure, Sign, and Play in the Discourse of the Human Sciences," which introduced his thought to Anglo-American theory, and forever transformed the nature of its debates, Jacques Derrida speaks of ethnology[56] as occupying a privileged place among the "human sciences":

> One can assume that ethnology could have been born as a science only at the moment when a decentering had come about: at the moment when European culture—and, in consequence, the history of metaphysics and of its concepts—had been *dislocated*, driven from its locus, and forced to stop considering itself as the culture of reference. This moment is not first and foremost a moment of philosophical or scientific discourse. It is also a moment which is political, economic, technical, and so forth. One can say with total security that there is nothing fortuitous about the fact that the critique of ethnocentrism—the very condition of ethnology—should be systematically and historically contemporaneous with the destruction of the history of metaphysics. . . . [Ethnology] is primarily a European science employing traditional concepts, however much it may struggle against them. Consequently, whether he wants to or not—and this does not depend on a decision on his part—*the ethnologist accepts into his discourse the premises of ethnocentrism at the very moment when he denounces them* [emphasis mine]. This necessity is irreducible.[57]

Derrida accurately indicates the questioning of European ethnocentrism as the necessary condition for the "birth" or self-conscious formulation of ethnology in the 1920s.[58] This very

56. Following the common practice in recent critiques of anthropology, I use the terms *ethnology, ethnography,* and *anthropology* (social and cultural) synonymously.

57. Derrida, "Structure, Sign, and Play in the Discourse of the Human Sciences," in *Writing and Difference,* trans. Alan Bass (Chicago: University of Chicago Press, 1978), p. 282.

58. Stephan Feuchtwang, "The Discipline and Its Sponsors: Colonial Formation of British Social Anthropology," in *Anthropology and the Colonial Encounter,* ed. Talal Asad (New York: Humanities Press, 1973), pp. 71–100, suggests that in Britain social anthropology as a discipline was formulated in the mid 1920s and fully formed by the late 1940s. This seems to be applicable to European anthropology in general. Asad's anthology, on which I have drawn extensively, is henceforth cited as *ACE.*

critique of ethnocentrism is seen by him as "contemporaneous" with the critique of Western "metaphysics," one way
of deconstructing which he demonstrates, for example, in *Of
Grammatology*, whose exemplary figures include the anthropologist Claude Lévi-Strauss.[59] In introducing a discussion of
Lévi-Strauss's work, Derrida wants to pose "the problem of
the status of a discourse which borrows from a heritage the
resources necessary for the deconstruction of that heritage itself."[60] Just as philosophy finds it extremely difficult to take
a step "outside" its boundaries, ethnology too is confined by
the concepts it inherits.

The discursive legacy of anthropology ties it firmly to a
concept of representation that, for Derrida, presumes the existence of a "reality" or an originary presence that it "befalls"
and re-presents. The striving for meaning or truth and the
concept of the *epistēmē* (the discursive structures that organize
cognition in a given age) belong to a metaphysics that is logocentric and nostalgic. The birth of anthropology has for its
precondition the shaking or "soliciting" of the foundations of
metaphysics. But does not anthropology, by the very nature
of its conception, remain within the orbit of logocentrism?
Does it not depend for its "knowledge" on notions of translation, representation, and reality that in turn show its complicity with the vocabulary of liberal humanism or empiricist-
idealism? And do not these notions and this vocabulary
ultimately serve the idiom of domination that is colonial
discourse?

Even Lévi-Strauss, who rigorously thinks through the relationship of anthropology to the history of metaphysics, remains unaware, says Derrida, of the ethnocentrism of phonetic, alphabetic *writing*.[61] His employment of this notion of

59. Derrida, *Of Grammatology*, trans. Gayatri C. Spivak (Baltimore: Johns
Hopkins University Press, 1976).

60. Derrida, "Structure, Sign, and Play," p. 282.

61. In the "Exergue" to the first edition of *Of Grammatology*, Derrida points
out that logocentrism is "the metaphysics of phonetic writing (for example,
of the alphabet)" which he sees as "nothing but the most original and powerful ethnocentrism" (*OG*, p. 3).

writing is what enables his structural anthropology to translate other cultures. Lévi-Strauss is caught, finally, in the *epistēmē* "within which are produced, without ever posing the
radical question of writing, all the Western methods of analysis, explication, reading, or interpretation."[62]

It is commonly assumed, and not least by anthropologists
themselves, that anthropology studies "societies without
writing." This idea depends on what Derrida calls a vulgar or
ethnocentric misconception: that writing refers only to phonetic and linear notation, whereas any society capable of producing proper names, of "bringing classificatory difference
into play," can be said to practice writing. Lévi-Strauss's refusal to see that the Nambikwara of Brazil already possess
writing in the general sense leads him to imagine that it is he
(that is, the West) who subjects them to "A Writing Lesson,"
disrupting a primal innocence by this violent pedagogy.[63] Lévi-
Strauss's analysis scorns, "[by] one and the same gesture, (alphabetic) writing, servile instrument of a speech dreaming of
its plenitude and its self-presence," at the same time as it refuses to "nonalphabetic signs" the "dignity of writing."[64] This
is a gesture, suggests Derrida, learned by Lévi-Strauss from
Rousseau and Saussure.

The Nambikwara, claimed Lévi-Strauss, could not write.
When he gave them paper and pencil, they drew wavy lines,
an act the anthropologist interpreted as their imitation of his
actions without knowing what they meant. "They called the
act of writing iekariukedjutu, namely: 'drawing lines.' "[65] In
the face of this linguistic evidence—that is, the existence of a
word for the act of writing—Lévi-Strauss persists in repeating

---

62. *OG*, p. 46.
63. While granting the validity of Derrida's critique, we should remain
wary of deconstructive analyses that may appear to erase the *violence* of colonial encounters, a violence Lévi-Strauss admittedly does not forget.
64. *OG*, p. 110.
65. *OG*, p. 123. This comment, made in Lévi-Strauss's dissertation on the
Nambikwara, is omitted from his book *Tristes Tropiques*, which describes the
same incident.

that the Nambikwara did not know how to write. As Derrida comments:

> Is not ethnocentrism always betrayed by the haste with which it is satisfied by certain translations or certain domestic equivalents? To say that a people do not know how to write because one can translate the word which they use to designate the act of inscribing as "drawing lines," is that not as if one should refuse them "speech" by translating the equivalent word by "to cry," "to sing," "to sigh?" Indeed "to stammer". . . . And ought one to conclude that the Chinese are a people without writing because the word *wen* designates many things besides writing in the narrow sense?[66]

The ethnocentrism of Lévi-Strauss's translation appears in the guise of an anti-ethnocentrism concerned about colonial violence. This is not to fault his individual good intentions, or those of other anthropologists or missionaries. What I am concerned about is the larger discursive formation of imperialism in which liberal anti-ethnocentrism participates.[67]

The moment of dislocation of European culture is also the moment when anthropology as a science is born. Bronislaw Malinowski, commonly regarded as one of the "founding fathers" of the discipline, was himself a "dis-located" European who celebrated professional, scientific ethnography as being free of the ethnocentrism of earlier discursive genres like travel-writing and accounts by missionaries or colonial officials.[68] But, as Malinowski's writings show, and as Derrida himself points out, the ethnographer accepts the premises of ethnocentrism "at the very moment when he denounces them."[69] The consequences of this acceptance for the growth of the discipline are far more drastic than Derrida's

66. *OG*, p. 123.

67. See Lévi-Strauss's defense of ethnocentrism in his recent *The View from Afar*, trans. J. Neugroschel and P. Hoss (New York: Basic Books, 1985).

68. See Mary Louise Pratt, "Fieldwork in Common Places," in *Writing Culture: The Poetics and Politics of Ethnography*, ed. James Clifford and George E. Marcus (Berkeley and Los Angeles: University of California Press, 1986), pp. 27–50.

69. Derrida, "Structure, Sign, and Play," p. 282.

discussion of Lévi-Strauss indicates, drastic, that is, in terms of the discourse's deliberate as well as unwitting complicities in the power relations of colonial administration in Africa and Australasia, whose inhabitants have usually been ethnography's objects of study.

Implicitly or explicitly, ethnography always conceived of its project as one of *translation*. In his inaugural lecture at the Collège de France, Lévi-Strauss emphasized the idea of translation and its links with signification: "When we consider some system of belief . . . the question which we ask ourselves is indeed, 'what does all this mean or *signify?*,' and to answer it, we force ourselves to *translate* into our language rules originally stated in a different code."[70]

What is this model of translation based on? According to George Steiner, whose own model derives its inspiration from Lévi-Strauss, structural anthropology "regards social structures as attempts at dynamic equilibrium achieved through an exchange of words, women, and material goods. All capture calls for subsequent compensation. . . . Within the class of semantic exchanges, translation is . . . the most graphic, the most radically equitable."[71] Translation for Steiner is, therefore, an "act of double-entry" where "the books must balance." The "exchange without loss" posited by Steiner's (and also Lévi-Strauss's) structural model seems to lapse into the classic ahistoricism that Derrida warns against in *Of Grammatology* and "Structure, Sign, and Play," for it does not account for the inequality of languages perpetuated by the colonial encounter. Lévi-Strauss's notion of translation is obviously linked to the "new humanism" he advocates in *The Scope of Anthropology*. Derrida's perceptive naming of Rousseau as a precursor of Lévi-Strauss helps us link the translation model of anthropology with the projects of the eighteenth-century Orientalists in India, themselves heirs of the

70. Lévi-Strauss, *The Scope of Anthropology*, trans. Sherry Ortner Paul and Robert A. Paul (London: Jonathan Cape, 1967), p. 80; emphasis original. The lecture was delivered in 1960.

71. Steiner, *After Babel*, p. 302.

philosophes, taking their inspiration from the universalist premises of Voltaire's and Rousseau's humanism.

That the task of anthropology is one of *translation* is proposed explicitly by Godfrey Lienhardt:

> When we live with savages and speak their languages, learning to represent their experience to ourselves in their way, we come as near to thinking like them as we can without ceasing to be ourselves.
>
> Eventually, we try to represent their conceptions systematically in the logical constructs we have been brought up to use. . . .
>
> The problem of describing to others how members of a remote tribe think . . . begins to appear largely as one of *translation*, of making the coherence primitive thought has in the language it really lives in, as clear as possible in our own.[72]

In understanding or translating the "coherence" of primitive thought, says Lienhardt, "We mediate between their habits of thought, which we have acquired with them, and those of our own society; in doing so, it is not finally some mysterious 'primitive philosophy' that we are exploring but the further potentialities of our own thought and language."[73]

Lienhardt's cultural relativism contains an implicit critique of some anthropologists' dismissal of the "primitive mentality" and "pre-logical thought."[74] In stressing the unity of human consciousness, however, he makes a now familiar move: the language that "primitive thought . . . really lives in" has to be translated, transformed, clarified, in "our own" (here, English). The "primitive" becomes the anthropologist's civilizational other. Because it does not depend on logic or consistency, the primitive society's science is "defective compared with ours."[75] The unity of human consciousness does not preclude—in fact, it helps construct—an inner hierarchy: primitive thought needs to be translated into modern, for it

72. Lienhardt, "Modes of Thought," pp. 96–97; emphasis added.
73. Ibid.
74. Notably Lucien Levy-Bruhl, cited in Lévi-Strauss, *Scope of Anthropology*, p. 41.
75. Lienhardt, "Modes of Thought," p. 100.

is that which is not yet modern. The hierarchy also indicates to us the operation of a teleological model of history.

Present-day critics of ethnography, while commending Lienhardt's notion that the anthropologist needs to explore her/his "own thought and language," suggest at the same time that this is something which the ethnographer is often not equipped, or is unwilling, to do.[76] Although the institutionalization of fieldwork as the supreme method of a professionalized ethnography ensured that anthropologists spent some time with the people they eventually wrote about, the transformation of ethnology into a scientific discipline also endowed the fieldworker with the professional "tools" that would enable her/him to construct entire cosmologies on the basis of a one- or two-year acquaintance with a tribe and its language. It was often emphasized that the anthropologist need not be absolutely fluent in the language. One could always depend on native interpreters. The idea of translation in such a context is a metonymy for the desire to achieve transparent knowledge and provide for a Western audience immediacy of access to "primitive thought." The desire to translate is a desire to *construct* the primitive world, to *represent* it and to *speak on its behalf*.[77] What the discourse of ethnography traditionally represses, however, is any awareness of the asymmetrical relations between colonizer and colonized that *enabled* the growth of the discipline and provided the context for translation.

The "difficulties" of translation are emphasized by writers from E. E. Evans-Pritchard to Edmund Leach, who see it as the central problem for ethnographers. Leach indicates that the social anthropologist "devotes his efforts to trying to understand, not just the spoken language of the people with whom he interacts, but their whole way of life. That, in itself, is a problem of translation, of finding categories in his own ways of thought which can be fitted to *the complex of observed*

76. Talal Asad, "The Concept of Cultural Translation in British Social Anthropology," in *Writing Culture*, ed. Clifford and Marcus, pp. 141–64.
77. The parallels with "Orientalism" should be obvious.

facts that he records."[78] There is no suggestion here of the contemporary crisis in representation.[79] The language of "observing" and "recording" presupposes a conception of reality as something "out there" that is re-presented by the anthropologist. An awareness of the constructed, or always already represented, nature of "reality" makes us cautious about accepting the translations underwritten by these theorists.

The "knowledge" produced by anthropology has only recently been questioned, in particular by those who have for a long time been the objects of its gaze. The transparency of the knowledge and its univocity serve to mask the inequalities between cultures and languages that the knowledge has actually helped create. The notions of reality and representation that are the premises of the translation project allow not only anthropologists but also historians and translators to assume the totalizing, teleological concept of a universal history. If ethnographers possess the discursive legacy of Rousseau, historians (and Orientalists) inherit the hegemonic writings of Montesquieu, Hegel, and Marx. Derrida's reading of Lévi-Strauss shows the latter's indebtedness to Rousseau's notion of the primitive as the past of humankind, and of a primal state of innocence befallen by civilization, or writing. Ideas like "the feudal system" or "the hunting stage," often left unthought in anthropology and historiography, presuppose a Eurocentric view of history. And those who study the non-Western societies that possess writing (in the narrow sense) speak, in accents derived from Hegel and Marx, of the "Asiatic mode of production" and "Oriental despotism" as "natural" to certain civilizations. The naturalizing, dehistoricizing move is, of course, accompanied by a situating of the "primitive" or the "Oriental" in a teleological scheme that shows them to be imperfect realizations of the Spirit or of Being. Faced with

78. Leach, *Social Anthropology* (London: Oxford University Press, 1982), p. 53; emphasis added.

79. For a discussion of how the crisis in representation has been tackled by what the authors call "interpretive anthropology," see George E. Marcus and Michael M. J. Fischer, *Anthropology as Cultural Critique* (Chicago: University of Chicago Press, 1986).

these powerful discourses of domination that employ classical notions of knowledge, reality, and representation, any attempt to come up with a new conception of translation will first have to take into account what the discourses suppress: the asymmetrical relations between languages.

A post-colonial practice of translation must necessarily be aware of how the problematic has been addressed in a discourse (that of ethnography) to which it is so central—a discourse, moreover, with historical ties to the relations of power that constituted colonialism. It is to a quick examination of these ties that we shall now turn, drawing upon the first critiques of ethnography.

In 1968 the American anthropologist Kathleen Gough described ethnography as "the child of Western imperialism."[80] Ethnographers in general, however, showed "a strange reluctance to consider seriously the power structure within which their discipline has taken shape."[81] Social anthropology before World War II was made possible by the unequal relationship between colonial powers and colonized cultures, and its analyses were assimilated without difficulty into the discourse of colonialism. Professional anthropology did not deal in stereotypical ethnocentric notions of primitive peoples. Like Indology or other Orientalist discourses, anthropology provided a vast quantity of detailed, meticulously collected information about the social-cultural institutions of its subjects. Both colonial administrators and missionaries began to see the usefulness of such information in furthering their aims. In *Other Cultures*, John Beattie asks what social anthropology, whose "stock in trade" includes "objectivity and disinterestedness," can do for administrators, traders, and missionaries. He suggests that new "facts" important for these three significant branches of the colonial enterprise can be discovered with the help of the anthropologist's framework of "theoretical and

80. Gough, "New Proposals for Anthropologists," *Current Anthropology*, 9 (1968): 403.
81. Asad, introduction to *ACE*, p. 15.

comparative knowledge."[82] Beattie's book, which is still used as an undergraduate textbook in many parts of the world, appears to be quite unaware of the relations of power in which his "disinterested" science is enmeshed.

The close connections between *imperia* and *studia* can be seen in the resolution passed at a meeting in 1920 attended by government officials and university and British Museum representatives asking for the establishment of an imperial School of Applied Anthropology:

> In the highest interests of Empire, it is necessary so to extend and complete the organisation of the teaching of Anthropology at the Universities of Great Britain [so that those intending to spend their lives in outposts of Empire] will acquire . . . a sound and accurate knowledge of the habits, customs, social and religious ideas and ideals of the Eastern and non-European races subject to his Majesty the King-Emperor.[83]

It was not the first time the British had thought of strengthening the alliance between scholarship and administration. In 1800 Lord Wellesley, the governor-general of India, established in Calcutta the College of Fort William to train young Englishmen for the civil service. The proposal to found the college had been put forward by Wellesley's predecessor, Warren Hastings, who was also responsible, with William Jones, for bringing into being the Royal Asiatic Society, the first Orientalist institution of its kind. Hastings, who was proficient in the languages of South Asia, believed that administrative efficiency depended on knowledge of the subjects' culture. He paid enormous sums for the translation of Hindu and Muslim law into English for the use of East India Company officials, and sponsored the translation of Company regulations into Indian languages.[84]

---

82. Beattie, *Other Cultures: Aims, Methods and Achievements in Social Anthropology* (New York: Free Press of Glencoe, 1964). Evans-Pritchard, Beattie's teacher and a major twentieth-century anthropologist, read and approved the manuscript of the book.

83. *Man* 21 (1921): 151, quoted in Helen Lackner, "Colonial Administration and Social Anthropology: Eastern Nigeria, 1920–1940," in *ACE*, p. 139.

84. For a detailed discussion of Hastings's cultural policies, see David

Once the Fort William College was set up, employees of the Company were met at the docks and taken to live in the college for three years while they learnt Persian (the court language of the Moghuls), Urdu, Hindustani, and other Indian languages. The Asiatic Society, which was to be closely associated with the college, had, under the leadership of William Jones, already been engaged for more than a decade in the task of collecting, codifying, and translating manuscripts, and writing new "histories" of the Asian subcontinent. Jones and Hastings both belonged to an eighteenth-century elite influenced by the ideas of Voltaire and the *philosophes*, and their cultural relativism has much in common with the attitudes of a post-Enlightenment Lévi-Strauss or a Lienhardt.[85] Although an aggressive imperialism became ascendant in the 1820s, and the College of Fort William was eventually dissolved, policies of cultural "understanding" were implemented again after the 1857 "Mutiny" and the takeover of India by the British Crown. In both periods, the translation of Indian culture was used to further the British technique of "indirect rule."

Anthropology, too, was of immediate relevance in the years when the doctrine of "indirect rule" was explicitly formulated, "a strategy which allowed Britain to control her colonies *cheaply*, by co-opting precolonial ruling classes into the new colonial hierarchy."[86] This doctrine was set out in *The Dual Mandate in British Tropical Africa* (1922), whose author, Lord Lugard, became the first chairman of the executive council of the International Institute of African Languages and Cultures in London. The repressive measures advocated by Lu-

---

Kopf, *British Orientalism and the Bengal Renaissance* (Berkeley and Los Angeles: University of California Press, 1969), part 1.

85. Lévi-Strauss's Rousseauistic nostalgia is paralleled by William Jones's "discovery" of the Golden Age of India, although Jones's triumphant joy manifests itself as guilt in Lévi-Strauss.

86. Omafume F. Onoge, "The Counterrevolutionary Tradition in African Studies: The Case of Applied Anthropology," in *The Politics of Anthropology*, ed. Gerrit Huizer and Bruce Mannheim (The Hague: Mouton, 1979), p. 47.

gard were fully endorsed by Malinowski, who "believed that an important task of anthropology was to provide scientific recipes for facilitating colonial control."[87]

Malinowski suggested that anthropology should study "culture contact" and the "changing native" in the colonial situation. But he allied the emerging discipline with the colonial administration, so that it could facilitate greater European control, based not only on the "unquestionable military superiority" of the Europeans, with which "the natives have to be impressed, even cowed," but also on scientific policies to stabilize and maintain the colonial system. What was the political significance of Malinowski's cultural functionalism? The most momentous seems to be the dismissal of precolonial history as mythology and the repression of historicity into "moments of equilibrium."[88] This thrust of anthropology, argue its critics, comes out of a colonial setup and continues to survive in neocolonial societies.

Refusing the name of "history" to the precolonial past implies that the anthropologist bestows on it the name of "nature." Even an ethnologist like Lévi-Strauss who professes to be anti-colonial and anti-ethnocentric repeats the dehistoricizing gesture, inherited from Rousseau, that marks non-Western peoples as "natural." Both the functionalist (Malinowski) and the neo-Romantic (Lévi-Strauss) propose a teleology that includes "the dream of a full and immediate presence" and "the suppression of contradiction and difference."[89] Frantz Fanon and others have written about the revolutionary potential of a *historical sense* in the hands of the colonized.[90] This sense is crucial also for a practice of translation in the colonial/post-colonial setting. By reading against the grain of colonial his-

87. Ibid. Remarkably similar rationales are offered by present-day Indian anthropologists who see the tribal Indian as the uncivilized other.

88. Feuchtwang, "Discipline and Its Sponsors," p. 73.

89. However, the functionalist teleology would suggest a movement toward "modernity" and the neo-Romantic one a movement toward "decadence." Lévi-Strauss's gesture is analyzed by Derrida in OG. The phrases quoted here are from OG, p. 115.

90. The point is made forcefully in Onoge, "Counterrevolutionary Tradition in African Studies."

toriography, the translator/historian discovers areas of contradiction and silent resistance that, being made legible, can be deployed against hegemonic images of the colonized. The dismissal of the precolonial past as "savagery" in the case of Africa or "Oriental despotism" in the case of India was accompanied by the substitution of European history for local history in the curriculum of the colonized. This kind of substitution was strengthened, for example, by the introduction of English as the language of higher education in the colonies, a move that usually made European texts the only ones available to the "educated" colonial subject.

The dismissal of precolonial history was accompanied by the production of static images of the subjects of anthropology. These privileged "representations" acquired the status of facts when they began to be employed by policymakers. The value of the functionalist approach, which sought a "totalization without contradictions," is described by Malinowski as that of teaching "the relative importance of various customs, how they dovetail into each other, how they have to be handled by missionaries, colonial authorities, and those who economically have to exploit savage trade and savage labor."[91] Malinowski's "totalization" suggests a seamless knowledge, a "reality" rendered transparent. In its bringing together of knowledge and power, his project of translation resembles that of the early Orientalists, who, like William Jones, were not only translators but lawmakers and administrators.

With the onset of World War II, the translation enterprises of British anthropology became professionalized with the help of state sponsorship. There was the sudden need to ensure that colonial subjects cooperated with the war effort; and with the increasing strength of nationalist struggles, colonial governments prepared to abandon direct rule and fashion the conditions for absentee colonialism.[92] More than ever before, administrators and anthropologists collaborated in devising

---

91. Cited in Marvin Harris, *The Rise of Anthropological Theory* (New York: Crowell, 1968), p. 558.
92. Feuchtwang, "Discipline and Its Sponsors," p. 86.

colonial policy. Malinowski wrote of the administrator's "professional and implicit duty to look after the interests of the natives, who do not and cannot share in deciding about their own destinies."[93] This functionalist paternalism is matched by Lévi-Strauss's concern for "newly created states" that are "insufficiently trained in the use of the written word" and are therefore "vulnerable" to propaganda.[94]

On the basis of a 1929 article by Malinowski, the International Institute of African Languages and Cultures, headed by Lord Lugard, proposed a plan to study the processes of change scientifically. Financial assistance was to be provided to missionaries and colonial administrators to take courses in anthropology, many under Malinowski at the London School of Economics. Research fellowships were given to social scientists studying language change and "culture contact."

Social anthropology claimed its main concern was primitive society in transformation. But its elaborate translations of non-Western "tribals" set them in a synchronic present time, essentializing their habits and customs, repressing the context of colonial power that was rapidly changing tribal society. It has been suggested that since colonial governments (and later, international foundations funded by multinational corporations) were the main sponsors of anthropological research, ethnographers tended to maintain a discreet silence as to the havoc wreaked by colonialism on their subjects.[95]

Studies of social change committed to policies for achieving equilibrium often translated native resistance as "maladjustment" (as in S. F. Nadel's famous studies of the Sudan). The refusal to pay taxes or to obey a chief supported by the colonial government was seen by anthropologists as an in-

93. Malinowski, "The Rationalisation of Anthropology and Administration," *Afrika* 3, no. 4 (1930): 432–34, quoted in Feuchtwang, "Discipline and Its Sponsors," p. 91.

94. Lévi-Strauss, *Tristes Tropiques*, trans. John Weightman and Doreen Weightman (1973; reprint, New York: Washington Square Press, 1977), p. 338. Spivak's translation of *OG* (which cites the same passage from Lévi-Strauss) substitutes "not yet ready to be edified" for "insufficiently trained in the use of the written word."

95. See Feuchtwang, "Discipline and Its Sponsors."

ability to adjust to change that must be corrected by ther-
apy.[96] Ethnographic and Orientalist images of African and Is-
lamic political traditions helped legitimize colonialism by their
"refusal to discuss *how* Europe had imposed its power and its
own conception of a just political order."[97]

Lord Lugard and Sir Malcolm Hailey, the architects of absentee colonialism and indirect rule, drew on their experience
of administering the Indian Empire to formulate policy for
Africa, and anthropologists with their translations assisted the
administrators on both continents. In fact, as the nationalist
struggle in India reached its peak in the 1940s, British anthropologists shifted their interest from the Asian subcontinent to
British Africa. Clearly, the ethnographers could not afford to
analyze colonialism or the premises of their own discourse,
for "they reproduced the colonial divide in an inverted form
as a colonial 'us' interpreting or representing a colonized
'them'."[98] Granting "agency" or the capacity for resistance to
"primitives" or "Orientals" would breach the coherence of
ethnography's or Orientalism's knowledge of an unchanging
society that was the "reality" these discourses proclaimed.[99]

The simultaneous recognition and repression of the reasons for change in societies dominated by colonial rule is paralleled by the naturalizing, dehistoricizing moves made by
anthropologists. The timeless ethnological present that is the
recurrent theme of anthropology in this century is the creation of a hidden evolutionism manifested in the series of oppositions between nature and culture, primitivism and modernism that permeate ethnographic discourse. This series of
oppositions is also perpetuated in strategies of translation from
non-Western languages into European ones.

96. James Faris, "Pax Britannica and the Sudan: S. F. Nadel," in *ACE*, p.
165.
97. Talal Asad, "Two European Images of Non-European Rule," in *ACE*,
p. 118.
98. Feuchtwang, "Discipline and Its Sponsors," p. 98.
99. See Ronald Inden's insightful discussion of the denial of agency by
Orientalism, in "Orientalist Constructions of India," *Modern Asian Studies* 20,
no. 3 (July 1986): 401–46.

The attempt to turn "history" into "nature" is linked to anthropology's use of the notion of time. The process of secularizing, generalizing, and universalizing Judeo-Christian time is seen by Johannes Fabian as contemporaneous with the rise of colonialism. Anthropology's use of "temporal devices" in the construction of its relationship with its "Other" suggests, according to Fabian, an "affirmation of difference as *distance*."[100] The "primitive" or the "traditional" become, in the discourse of ethnology, not objects of study but temporal categories of Western thought. This leads to a *denial of coevalness*, a use of time to distance the observed from the observer; the denial functions schizophrenically to create a different time for anthropological writing than that of fieldwork (which implies some kind of living together in the same time for ethnographer and subjects). The denial of coevalness removes the other from "the dialogic situation" and contributes to an intellectual justification of colonialism.

The rise of anthropology in the colonial era helped establish fieldwork as an important methodology, for imperial rule and its "products" helped make the "primitive" world safe for ethnographers.[101] The privileging of fieldwork suggests the significance given to techniques of observation and the recording of "facts." This epistemological model, based on classical concepts of reality and representation, seems to align fieldwork with the systematic effort to establish an unequal relationship between the "West" and its "Other." Fabian suggests that while the maintenance and renewal of this relationship requires a "coeval recognition of the Other as object of power/knowledge" the justification and rationalization of the relationship "needs schemes of allochronic distancing"

100. Johannes Fabian, *Time and the Other* (New York: Columbia University Press, 1983), p. 16.

101. Among these products were the steam engine, the telegraph, improved rifles, and quinine (followed by the discovery of penicillin). For a useful discussion of the relationship between colonialism and technological advances, see Daniel R. Headrick, *The Tools of Empire: Technology and European Imperialism in the Nineteenth Century* (New York: Oxford University Press, 1981).

or the denial of coevalness.[102] The project of translation, whether literary or ethnographic, is caught up in this double movement.

The critique of anthropology's project of translation, sometimes manifested as the attempt to write a different kind of ethnography, has been mainly the critique of the complicity of the discipline in sustaining Euro-American colonial and neocolonial relations with the non-Western world. The anthropologist's search for immediacy of experience, and the transparency of her/his "written-up" findings (Clifford Geertz calls the lucid studies of Evans-Pritchard "African transparencies")[103] is belied by the dependence on native interpreters and the denial of "coevalness." The transparencies are of timeless, synchronically presented, self-contained societies, where the violent changes inflicted by colonial rule are either ignored by the ethnographer or assimilated as a movement toward equilibrium. The naturalizing, dehistoricizing tendencies characteristic of colonial discourse are seen not only in ethnographies but also in other kinds of translations; persistent tropes in one type of translation may alert us to similar figures—with similar complicities—in another.

Whereas some writers have offered critiques of the conditions and the context of ethnographic translation, others have drawn attention to the *tropes* of translation that structure ethnographies.[104] Compared to the earlier critics of ethnography, these theorists are post-Saussurean (even post-structuralist) in their orientation. They see how it is not sufficient to criticize the conditions of the formation of anthropology as a discipline; they recognize the importance of putting in question the status of the ethnographic text by problematizing classical notions of text, author, and meaning. Such a problematization, they seem to suggest, will help us understand

---

102. Fabian, *Time and the Other*, p. 149.
103. Geertz, "Slide Show: Evans-Pritchard's African Transparencies," *Raritan Review* 3, no. 2 (Fall 1983): 62–80.
104. See *Writing Culture*, ed. Clifford and Marcus, which not only offers critiques of classical and modern ethnographies but also proposes and assesses new ways of writing anthropology and translating culture.

the enduring force of colonial discourse and open up ways of undermining it. They accept the disruption of the Enlightenment ideology that claims "transparency of representation" and "immediacy of experience."[105] A traditional theory of meaning supports the notion that the sign unproblematically represents reality, makes it "present." But to see the sign as reflection or representation is to deny what Roland Barthes has called the productive character of language, and what Derrida would call "writing." Drawing inspiration from post-structuralist literary theory, the new ethnographers emphasize that writing is "central to what anthropologists do" and that language is not a transparent medium, for ethnographers invent rather than represent cultures.[106] Some of these writers suggest that works of cultural translation use literary procedures, and that literary processes influence not only the writing but also the reading of ethnographies.[107] Revealing the constructed nature of cultural translations shows how translation is always *producing* rather than merely reflecting or imitating an "original."

Classical ethnography, however, bases itself on concepts of representation and reality that efface the heterogeneity of the original. One strategy of effacement is the textual inscription of ethnographic authority that compels readers to accept the anthropologist's translation. The presentation of "authority" is linked to the tropes ethnographers use, often borrowed from earlier genres like travel-writing and the memoirs of missionaries and colonial officials. Mary Louise Pratt gives the example of the utopian figure of first contact, or the "arrival scene," which remains remarkably unchanged from Louis de Bougainville (1767) to Raymond Firth (1936). The figure of

105. James Clifford, introduction, ibid., p. 2.
106. Ibid.
107. See, especially, Mary Louise Pratt, "Fieldwork in Common Places," in ibid., and "Scratches on the Face of the Country; or, What Mr. Barrow Saw in the Land of the Bushmen," *Critical Inquiry* 12, no. 1 (Autumn 1985): 119–43. And see, too, Vincent Crapanzano, "Hermes' Dilemma: The Masking of Subversion in Ethnographic Description," in *Writing Culture*, ed. Clifford and Marcus, pp. 51–76.

the intrepid Victorian colonial explorer seen in Richard Burton (1868) surfaces in classic ethnographies like Evans-Pritchard's (1940). Another discursive convention is the complete effacement of the speaking or experiencing subject from the scientific texts of anthropology and its displacement into the genre of personal narrative. Pratt shows how, in spite of this displacement, ethnographic authority is "anchored in subjective experience," since fieldwork is a methodological norm.[108]

Constituting the authority of the ethnographer is seen as a crucial moment that employs a variety of discursive conventions. In classical ethnographic writing, the individual anthropologist makes "an unquestioned claim to appear as the purveyor of truth in the text," reducing to a coherent little world an "overdetermined, cross cultural encounter shot through with power relations."[109] The privileging of "observation" stressed immediacy of experience at the cost of the materiality of text, language, and culture. It was assumed "that the experience of the researcher can serve as a unifying source of authority in the field."[110] The dialogic aspects of fieldwork, the relations of power determining the nature of the anthropologist's interaction with his/her subjects, disappear from the text into which field notes are translated.

The translation of field notes into ethnography is marked, of course, by what Fabian has called allochronic distancing, or the denial of coevalness. "Writing-up" as an established practice uses metaphoric or stylistic conventions that may assimilate too easily, "exclude, or diminish in significance" many facets of the "unequal cultures" translated by ethnographers.[111] Recognizing the tropes of translation can help show us how to problematize ethnographic representations of the non-Western "Other."

108. Pratt, "Fieldwork in Common Places," p. 32.
109. James Clifford, "On Ethnographic Authority," *Representations* 1, no. 2 (1983): 120.
110. Ibid., p. 128.
111. Talal Asad and John Dixon, "Translating Europe's Others," in *Europe and Its Others*, ed. Francis Barker et al. (Colchester: University of Essex Press, 1985), 1:176.

The recognition may also show how contemporary anthropology often *reproduces* its discursive legacy even while repudiating it. The "remorse" that informs anthropology today inspires a critique of ethnocentrism, but the critique "has most often the sole function of constituting the other as a model of original and natural goodness,"[112] thus removing the "subject" of ethnography from "history" and placing her/him in "nature." The gesture that claims to grant difference actually denies it. In the work of Lévi-Strauss, for example, ethnocentrism will seem to have been avoided "at the very moment when it will have already profoundly operated."[113] Self-conscious contemporary ethnographers like Clifford Geertz establish authority by "a collusive relationship" between anthropologist and readers, created through the use of puns and allusions intelligible only to a Western audience. The hierarchical relationship between the two worlds places the ethnographer and his readers at the top.[114] Even a writer like Emmanuel Le Roy Ladurie, who employs polyphony in his texts, is shown as setting up ethnographic authority through this device; the relationship between the historian or ethnographer and his subjects remains "insensitive to power relations and cultural differences."[115]

The personal authority of the ethnographer is less important, according to Talal Asad, than his/her "social authority." An ethnographer's translation of a culture occupies a privileged position as a "scientific text," and is not only more powerful than folk memory, but also constructs folk memory. As Asad points out, "The anthropologist's monograph may return, retranslated, into a 'weaker' Third World language." The social authority of the anthropologist tends to reduce and simplify "the implicit meanings of subordinate societies," for the process of cultural translation is inescapably caught

---

112. *OG*, p. 114.
113. *OG*, p. 121.
114. Crapanzano, "Hermes' Dilemma," p. 69.
115. Renato Rosaldo, "From the Door of His Tent: The Fieldworker and the Inquisitor," in *Writing Culture*, ed. Clifford and Marcus, p. 82.

up in relations of power—"professional, national, international."[116]

Cultural translation for Asad implies translation not merely
into English but into the established discursive game of academia. By the same token, interlingual translation—for example, translation from Sanskrit into English—also implies
translation into an entire discourse on the Orient, with its
own sets of conventions. Ethnographic conventions of cultural translation, says Asad, are not all that flexible, and iso-
lated individual experiments in ethnographic representation
may not make any lasting impact on them. An unskilled
Western translator "may simplify in the direction of his own
'strong' language."[117] Remarking on Lienhardt's notion that
the translator must explore the potential of his/her own thought
and language, Asad stresses that the ethnographer/translator
cannot decide this by an individual effort, since it is governed
by relations of power that are institutional. Although Asad's
notion of translation draws attention to the asymmetries between languages, he seems to assume that the only translators are Euro-American ones re-presenting a non-Western
other. What happens in a post-colonial situation where bilingual translators challenge earlier Western versions through
retranslation? Can one not include under the practice of
translation the rewriting of history in the post-colonial period
by reading against the grain of hegemonic representations?
Asad's conception of cultural translation leaves too little room
for the use of translation as an act of resistance.

The "identity" of the translator is left unproblematized even
in attempts to theorize a post-modern ethnography. Stephen
Tyler, who seems to imagine that substituting the term *evo-
cation* for *representation* will alter the discursive legacy to which
he remains bound, sees a post-modern ethnography as shaping "a cooperatively evolved text consisting of fragments of
discourse intended to evoke in the minds of both reader and

116. Asad, "Concept of Cultural Translation in British Social Anthropology," p. 163.
    117. Ibid., p. 158.

writer an emergent fantasy of a possible world of common-
sense reality, and thus to provoke an aesthetic integration that
will have a therapeutic effect." What Tyler is suggesting is
that ethnography will function as "poetry," which will "sa-
cralize" the participant through an encounter with "occult
practices." Although Tyler argues that the post-modern ethnography should be a "cooperatively evolved text," the co-
operation for him seems always to be between "the ethnographer and his native partners."[118] Even if the new
ethnography denies the totalizing impulse toward unity characteristic of colonial anthropology, Tyler's envisioning of *who*
will write the ethnography places the new discipline firmly
within a neocolonial framework. He, like Asad, does not indicate the possibility of a situation where the "natives" do
their own translating. Though he declares that anthropology
must make "its own contextual grounding part of the question," his conception of a post-modern ethnography does not
permit us to raise the question of domination or relations of
power. Tyler's concern with dialogism, like that of the hermeneutic theorists of translation, does not sufficiently take
into account the hegemonic strength and persistence of the
discursive legacy of colonialism.

The new critique of anthropology accepts that neither culture nor text is unified. Both are enmeshed in relations of power
and both have more than one subject. To see the split nature
of subject/author is to take into account the role of language
in constructing both "subject" and "reality" and to challenge
the notion of language as transparent. One of the accomplish-
ments of the critique of anthropology is the scrupulous attention it pays to power relations and historicity in discussing
the colonial construction of the discipline. The critics are aware
of the hegemonic strength of classic ethnographic texts and
the need to problematize the conditions of their creation. They
help us see that the discipline's refusal of history and historicity and its willful blindness to the workings of power go

118. Tyler, "Post-Modern Ethnography: From Document of the Occult to
Occult Document," in *Writing Culture*, ed. Clifford and Marcus, pp. 125, 127.

hand in hand with its self-declared enterprise of translation. The critique of anthropology acknowledges the importance of rehistoricizing non-Western cultures and of developing a post-colonial perspective on the ethnographic project of translation. There is a tendency in the new ethnography, however, that leads to a continual troping of "politics" into "poetics."[119] Does this, perhaps, point to a concern with figure and "rhetoric" that marks the lapse into the "classic ahistoricism" of which Derrida says Lévi-Strauss is guilty?

In "Structure, Sign, and Play," Derrida's critique of ethnology leads him to a notion of "interpretation" that has cast off the concern with origins and presence and tries to move beyond "humanism." But, as we have seen, recent Western critiques of ethnography, in spite of their professed anti-ethnocentrism, seem to be performed by "those who . . . turn their eyes away when faced by the as yet unnamable which is proclaiming itself and which can do so, as is necessary whenever a birth is in the offing, only under the species of the nonspecies, in the formless, mute, infant, and terrifying form of monstrosity."[120] Derrida's perceptive comment may help us call the unnamable by one of its names—an emergent post-colonial practice of translation, wary of the rhetoric of humanism, informed by a critique of telos and origin, alert to relations of power and historicity.

119. See my discussion of Paul de Man and Walter Benjamin in chapter 4.
120. Derrida, "Structure, Sign, and Play," p. 293.

3

Allegory and the Critique of Historicism: Reading Paul de Man

> Some have asked why Paul de Man always speaks of reading rather than of writing. Well, perhaps because the allegory of reading is writing—or the inverse. But perhaps also because every reading finds itself caught, engaged precisely by the promise of saying the truth, by a promise which will have taken place with the very first word, within a scene of signature which is a scene of writing.
> —Jacques Derrida,
> *Memoires: For Paul de Man*

Speaking at the memorial service for Paul de Man in January 1984, some of the most significant American literary theorists paid tribute to a colleague they unanimously acclaimed as one of the most important thinkers in the discipline. Adding his voice to theirs was Jacques Derrida, who along with de Man had brought "deconstruction" to the North American academy.[1] Derrida hailed de Man's contribution as "undoubtedly one of the most influential of our time," since he had "transformed the field of literary theory," merging the languages of literature and philosophy with the resources of a polyglot.[2] Even one of de Man's detractors acknowledges that "the dominant literary-critical movement of the American 1970's

---

1. I use deliberately the terms *literary theorist* and *academy*, since they mark the place where post-structuralist theory seems to have situated itself in the West. The situating may be linked, I suggest, to a certain discourse on "action" that seems to emerge from contemporary Euro-American literary theory, a discourse that privileges undecidability and, consequently, the impossibility of action.

2. Derrida, "In Memoriam," trans. Kevin Newmark, *Yale French Studies* 69 (1985): 324.

was 'de Manian,' "³ and recent programmatic essays by Joseph Riddel and Rodolphe Gasche establish de Man's stature as the foremost contemporary American "theorist."⁴ An emergent post-colonial practice of translation attempting to solicit or shake post-structuralism is therefore compelled to read the work of Paul de Man. The compulsion refers to what de Man himself has called the "necessity" of reading.

In the 1969 essay "Literary History and Literary Modernity," de Man writes about Nietzsche's notion of modernity, suggesting that "action" implies a break with the past that involves an "absolute forgetting."⁵ By deconstructing "modernity," de Man also criticizes the theories of periodization proposed by traditional literary history. Since one has to forget in order to be "modern," or to "act," and since absolute forgetting is impossible, action perhaps cannot be seen in de Man's scheme as other than naive or blind.⁶ I would argue that post-colonials, obliged to underwrite certain practices of interpretation and impelled by the urgency for certain types of "action," need to practice a kind of forgetting. This practice, perhaps, can be named translation: a translation that in-

3. Frank Lentricchia, *Criticism and Social Change* (Chicago: University of Chicago Press, 1983), p. 38.

4. See Joseph N. Riddel, "Coup de Man, or The Uses and Abuses of Semiotics," *Cultural Critique* 4 (Fall 1986): 81–109, and Rodolphe Gasche, " 'Setzung' and 'Übersetzung': Notes on Paul de Man," *Diacritics* 11 (Winter 1981): 36–57.

5. Gasche shows how de Man in his later work criticizes the notion of "act" in speech act theory. He quotes de Man to the effect that a deconstruction of the identity principle (a critique of the subject) involves a deconstruction of the possibility of "doing." See Gasche, " 'Setzung' and 'Übersetzung,' " p. 50. I would argue, however, that the "death of the subject" does not necessarily imply the impossibility of "action," which does not always exist in a simple relationship to the fiction of a coherent self. Riddel, "Coup de Man," suggests that de Man's deconstruction of the "performative" does not negate "action" but implies that it must be reconceived outside the speech act theorists' recuperation of the subject.

6. Lentricchia elaborates this point in part 1 of *Criticism and Social Change*. Apart from the perceptive reading of de Man's Nietzsche, however, Lentricchia's critique is often merely denunciatory, and his two-phase division of de Man's career into existential and Derridaean is too schematic to account for the complexity of this thinker's work. This division is proposed in Lentricchia's *After the New Criticism* (Chicago: University of Chicago Press, 1980).

volves "citation" rather than "absolute forgetting," that indicates not a simple rupture with the past but a radical rewriting of it.

Rewriting is necessarily based on the act of reading, as de Man's own work can show us. In chapter 1, I referred to Gayatri Spivak's essay on the Subaltern Studies group of historians, where she speaks of a deconstructive historiography that practices "transactive reading" between past and future.[7] I suggested there that transactive reading might also be called translation. De Man's exemplary emphasis on the act of reading may teach post-colonial theorists a good deal about how to "solicit," how to translate. Since the critique of representation occupies a prominent position in these projects, we could begin our reading of de Man by looking at his concept of allegory.[8]

De Man's notion of allegory offers a valuable interrogation of the idea that a text's reading must be "adequate" to a referent. Besides incorporating the critique of representation, de Man's "allegory" draws our attention to "figure" and the instability of language even in texts that are not overtly liter-

7. Spivak, "Subaltern Studies: Deconstructing Historiography," in *Subaltern Studies IV: Writings on South Asian History and Society*, ed. Ranajit Guha (New Delhi: Oxford University Press, 1985), pp. 330–63. It seems more appropriate to use "present" instead of "future" in this context. Only a simplistic reading would dismiss this emphasis on the present as an indication of the "metaphysics of presence."

8. I use *allegory* in a sense that has little to do with English or German pre-Romantic usage of the term. Fredric Jameson summarizes the significance of allegory for contemporary theory: "If allegory has once again become somehow congenial for us today, as over against the massive and monumental unifications of an older modernist symbolism or even realism itself, it is because the allegorical spirit is profoundly discontinuous, a matter of breaks and heterogeneities, of the multiple polysemia of the dream rather than the homogeneous representation of the symbol. Our traditional conception of allegory—based, for instance, on stereotypes of Bunyan—is that of an elaborate set of figures and personifications to be read against some one-to-one table of equivalences: this is, so to speak, a one-dimensional view of this signifying process, which might only be set in motion and complexified were we willing to entertain the more alarming notion that such equivalences are themselves in constant change and transformation at each perpetual present of the text" (Jameson, "Third-World Literature in the Era of Multinational Capitalism," *Social Text* 15 [Fall 1986]: 73).

ary.[9] De Man performs a thoroughgoing critique of totalizing interpretive models, which he invokes synecdochically with the words *metaphor* and *historicism*. His concept of allegory, while it problematizes adequacy of representation, does not, I shall argue, account for the historicity of the text. What I explore in this chapter is the question of whether it is the neglect of historicity that in fact enables de Man's theory of allegory, and, if so, whether this turning away still allows us to use the strengths of de Man's critique of representation. By historicity, I mean, of course, what Nietzsche would call effective history, history "working" in our times. Also marked by historicity would be those conjunctions of past and present that Walter Benjamin calls "constellations."[10]

Let us attempt to place de Man's "allegory" in the context of his larger project of formulating a notion of "reading." The act of reading crucial to de Man's idea of literary theory is one that, he claims, is being "systematically avoided" by contemporary critics bent on ignoring the tension in the text between "grammar" and "rhetoric." De Man's notion of reading comes out of his concern with allegory, which he would salvage from its devalued position in post-Romantic criticism by suggesting that it undermines the totalizing movement of metaphor, a figure he often equates with the symbol. For de Man, allegory is both "enigmatic and inescapable," a "unique and plural touchstone by which all readings and all literary and philosophical corpuses are measured."[11] Derrida points out that in de Man's work allegory always precludes "any totalizing summary," for it is "not simply one form of figurative language among others; it represents one of language's essential possibilities: the possibility that permits language to say the

---

9. Derrida's argument regarding representation has helped problematize the notion of "adequacy" in the interpretive paradigms of literary criticism and literary historiography. See, in particular, Derrida's essay "Sending: On Representation," *Social Research* 49, no. 2 (Summer 1982): 294–326.

10. For my discussion of Benjamin's work, see chapters 4 and 5.

11. Jacques Derrida, *Memoires: For Paul de Man*, trans. Cecile Lindsay, Jonathan Culler, and Eduardo Cadava (New York: Columbia University Press, 1986), p. 36.

other and to speak of itself while speaking of something else; the possibility of always saying something other than what it gives to be read, including the scene of reading itself."[12]

It is possible to see the Romantic and post-Romantic valorization of the symbol as a privileging of what Derrida would call the "transcendental signified," or as a refusal to accept the impossibility of "immediacy." The desire to arrive at a totalization (manifested, for example, in the New Criticism), to discover an "origin" or an "original," is part of the search for immediacy. The model of literary criticism that depends on a distinction between allegory and symbol, and condemns the former for the purpose of reinforcing the latter, must necessarily concern itself with the "adequacy," not only of the literary representation, but also of theory's re-presentation of the representation. In other words, literary criticism must reckon with the symbol itself, and with the interpretation provided for it by the critical model. This kind of critical model, reminiscent of "hermeneutics" or "historicism" for de Man, would be characterized by him as repressive or "totalizing." De Man's own critical practice tries to deliver literary theory from the constraints of historical and hermeneutical models, which for him are manifestations of "Western metaphysics."[13]

12. Ibid., p. 11.
13. De Man repeats this phrase several times in *Allegories of Reading* (New Haven: Yale University Press, 1979) (henceforth abbreviated as *AR*), notably in the Nietzsche essays. Following my discussion in chapter 1, I continue to use *metaphysics* here to refer to Western philosophy, which, in Derrida's work, is shown to have throughout its history privileged presence over absence, speech over writing, unity of meaning over "dissemination." I do not intend to suggest, however, that de Man's project is identical to Derrida's, although de Man does deal with both "literary" and "philosophical" texts and frequently indicates that the borderline between the two discourses cannot be clearly drawn. In the preface to *AR*, de Man says that he used the term *deconstruction* before Derrida's texts became popular in Anglo-American academia. Of course, de Man's sense of the word is slightly different from Derrida's, but de Man says he will gladly incorporate the meaning the word has come to have. For perceptive discussions of the differences between de Man and Derrida, see Gasche's "Setzung and Übersetzung" and Suzanne Gearhart's "Philosophy before Literature: Deconstruction, Historicity, and the Work of Paul de Man," *Diacritics* 19 (Winter 1983): 63–81. See also Gearhart's analysis

Western philosophy has, according to de Man, repressed or covered up the "aporia" between constative (or referential) and performative (or figural) language. This repression is conducted in the interests of the unity of meaning, a unity that needs to be deconstructed in order to recover figurality. The power of philosophical language can be subverted, thinks de Man, by showing how language itself is "figure," a notion that, he says, destabilizes the thrust toward totalization of meaning. De Man's work suggests further that "literature" is the supreme example of figural language. In an operation he sees as paradigmatic for the critique of metaphysics, de Man mounts an attack on the model of literary history predominant in contemporary criticism (a model he sees as "genetic," and therefore a manifestation of a "totalizing" historicism) and on the kind of literary interpretation that strives for adequacy of representation. His main concern is to develop a literary theory that performs "the methodical undoing of the grammatical construct" and produces the "literariness" of the text.[14] In other words, de Man's "reading" of a text produces its "allegory," but it is one that is always an allegory of its own reading.

According to the parameters he sets up for his project, de Man would claim to be "unreadable." By this token, one can either not read him at all, "read" him in a style approximating his own, or else read him against himself. For expository reasons, I shall follow the third option, undertaking what de Man would criticize as a "genetic" reading to trace his preoccupation with allegory from the relatively early essay "The Rhetoric of Temporality" (1969) to *Allegories of Reading* (1979) and some of the later essays.[15]

---

of the two thinkers' readings of Rousseau in her book *The Open Boundary of History and Fiction* (Princeton: Princeton University Press, 1984), pp. 234–84.

14. De Man, "The Resistance to Theory," in *The Resistance to Theory* (Minneapolis: University of Minnesota Press, 1986), pp. 3–20. Hereafter cited as *ResTh*.

15. De Man had written on Romanticism before 1969: see the essays collected in *The Rhetoric of Romanticism* (New York: Columbia University Press,

I shall also indicate how a rhetorical reading of de Man's work—that is, a search for the "hinges" of his text—would give us a series of what seem to be metacritical statements.[16] These statements, which are usually drawn from the text de Man is examining, merit close attention, since he appears to be using them to support his own readings. My "rhetorical" reading of de Man's essays will attempt to illuminate the complexity of his notion of allegory as well as his strategies for achieving this complexity.

For de Man, the "key to the critique of metaphysics" seems to be a concept of the rhetoricity or figurality of language. His description of allegory or "figure" appears, as I suggested earlier, to depend on a critique of "hermeneutics" and "historicism," and on a series of elaborately conceived, constantly shifting distinctions between terms like *grammar* and *rhetoric*, *truth* and *error*, *metaphor* and *metonymy*, *trope* and *persuasion*, *constative* and *performative* (utterance), *symbol* and *allegory*. As we follow the unfolding of de Man's readings of Wordsworth and Coleridge, Proust, Nietzsche, Rousseau, Hegel, and Benjamin, we see how the critique of historicism, along with the setting up of the paired distinctions, is based on de Man's criticism of a theory of language that accords primacy to perception. De Man seems to suggest that in order to get beyond the latter, we use the linguistic model of literature, and, as Suzanne Gearhart has it, actually *derive* historicity from language.[17]

One of de Man's earliest discussions of allegory is to be found in "The Rhetoric of Temporality," his account of the Romantics' privileging of symbol over allegory. The symbol,

---

1984). But none of the essays deal extensively with the notion of allegory. Some of the essays in *AR*, however, were first written in the early 1970s. I shall use the abbreviation RhT in future references to "The Rhetoric of Temporality," first published in *Interpretation: Theory and Practice*, ed. Charles Singleton (Baltimore: Johns Hopkins Press, 1969).

16. It is not always possible to determine whether de Man is "blind" to the way these statements function in his text.

17. Gearhart, "Philosophy before Literature," p. 72.

according to de Man, appeals to "totality" because it suggests a complete correspondence between sign and meaning:

> This appeal to the infinity of a totality constitutes the main attraction of the symbol as opposed to allegory, a sign that refers to one specific meaning and thus exhausts its suggestive potentialities once it has been deciphered. . . . Allegory appears as dryly rational and dogmatic in its reference to a meaning that it does not itself constitute, whereas the symbol is founded on an intimate unity between the image that rises up before the senses and the supersensory totality that the image suggests.   (RhT, p. 174)

It is the historian of Romanticism, claims de Man, who is attracted by the appeal to totality made by the symbol and who records it as being the supreme Romantic image, in opposition to allegory, which is seen as nonorganic and limited in meaning. A fundamental concept of the aesthetics of Romanticism adopted by Anglo-American critics is the metaphor, which they would define (under the influence of Coleridge) as "a dialectic between object and subject, in which the experience of the object takes on the form of a perception or a sensation" (RhT, p. 178). The metaphor indicates a synthesis, the mode of which is "defined as 'symbolic' by the priority conferred on the initial moment of sensory perception" (p. 178). Writers on Romanticism—for example, M. H. Abrams and Earl Wasserman—privilege the subject's perception, but at the same time they also assert that nature (the object) is seen by the Romantics as having priority over the self (the subject). De Man agrees with those commentators who believe the subject-object tension is part of a "pseudo dialectic." This dialectic comes out of "the assumed predominance of the symbol" in Romantic diction, a predominance that de Man would question.

The "act of ontological bad faith" (RhT, p. 194) that allowed the Romantics as well as the historians of Romanticism to substitute symbol for allegory resulted in their defining the Romantic image as a hierarchical relationship "between subject and object" that gives priority to the subject's "perception." De Man's objection to the Romanticists' "mystification" is couched in terms similar to those he would later use to criticize *Rezeptionsästhetik* and what he calls "hermeneutics."

Putting into question the predominance of symbol over allegory in Romantic/post-Romantic criticism will lead us, suggests de Man, to the Romantics' rediscovery of an allegorical tradition and their "unveiling of an authentically temporal destiny" (RhT, p. 190). In a reading of Wordsworth and Coleridge, de Man indicates that the "asserted superiority" of symbol over allegory is a "defensive strategy" that allows the Romantics to hide from the knowledge of the self's "authentically temporal predicament" (p. 191). But wherever allegory prevails in the work of the Romantics, it "always corresponds to the unveiling of an authentically temporal destiny" (p. 190). There is a suggestion here that allegory could be based on a notion of historicity, but de Man's later work explicitly treats temporality as sequence or succession rather than as history. In fact, his concept of allegory in "The Rhetoric of Temporality" indicates, especially in the reading of Rousseau and Wordsworth, that the figure is "a relationship between signs in which the reference to their respective meanings has become of secondary importance" (p. 190). "It remains necessary," says de Man, "if there is to be allegory . . . [that] the allegorical sign refer to another sign that precedes it" (p. 190).

Having suggested that for the Romantics "the relationship between sign and meaning is discontinuous," de Man then forges a connection between allegory and irony, implying that they—and all figural language—share a similar structure, where "the sign points to something that differs from its literal meaning."[18] Although it is not clear whether de Man is treating allegory as a sign, or as a sequence of signs, this definition does point forward to *Allegories of Reading* and the concept of literature/literariness.[19]

18. De Man seems to be making the reductive assumption that the sign has a literal meaning in the first place.

19. In RhT, de Man elaborates on the parabasis or anacoluthon as figure/trope, a notion that informs his conception of allegory and is, therefore, crucial to his later readings of nineteenth-century writers. Parabasis, according to Schlegel (as de Man quotes him), is a disjunction, a disruption of the con-

The persistence over the years of de Man's concerns and the continuity of their development are remarkable.[20] The central essay in *Blindness and Insight* is on Jacques Derrida's reading of Rousseau,[21] and de Man rehearses here his major ideas regarding the "ambivalence" of literary language, the theory of language as figural, and the difficulty of distinguishing between the discourses of philosophy, criticism, and literature. The differences between de Man's reading of Rousseau and Derrida's have been laid out skillfully by Gearhart, and we need not go into them here. But we do need to note that de Man uses *both* Derrida and Rousseau to make his point about the "literary" text, which is "any text that implicitly or explicitly signifies its own rhetorical mode and prefigures its own misunderstanding as the correlative of its rhetorical nature; that is, of its 'rhetoricity' " (*BI*, p. 136).

Toward the end of his life, de Man wrote approvingly of Hegel's *Aesthetics* and Walter Benjamin's "The Task of the Translator" as exemplary texts that undo themselves. Critics achieve an insight through a negative moment in their thought that "annihilates" the premises leading up to the insight. The vision of criticism, therefore, is "blind." And this blindness is "the necessary correlative of the rhetorical nature of literary language" (*BI*, p. 141), a rhetoricity that also structures the language of criticism and philosophy. De Man even suggests here that although the blindness of a text is what makes it literary, a text without blind spots, like Rousseau's, is more "mature" and more "radical" than Nietzsche's or Derrida's,

---

tinuum—such as the author's persona interrupting a narrative to address the reader—that could also be called irony. The term comes from theory of drama and refers to a choric interference in the action.

20. Suzanne Gearhart is right, to my mind, in emphasizing the continuity of de Man's preoccupations. See also Tilottama Rajan, "Displacing Post-Structuralism: Romantic Studies after Paul de Man," *Studies in Romanticism* 24, no. 4 (Winter 1985): 451–74.

21. De Man, "The Rhetoric of Blindness: Jacques Derrida's Reading of Rousseau," in *Blindness and Insight: Essays in the Rhetoric of Contemporary Criticism* (New York: Oxford University Press, 1971), pp. 102–41. Henceforth cited as *BI*.

since it is able to account fully for its own undoing. As de Man has it in "Literary History and Literary Modernity," literature's specificity "is defined by its inability to remain constant to its own specificity" (*BI*, p. 159); it is "a form of language that knows itself to be mere repetition, mere fiction and allegory" (p. 161). Traditional literary history, according to de Man, cannot account for the literary aporia, literature's simultaneous existence as truth and error.[22]

De Man's continued polemic against the "genetic pattern of literary history" is at the center of the first Nietzsche essay in *Allegories of Reading*, "Genesis and Genealogy." It begins with de Man's criticism of the "flight from language" that allows literary interpreters to approach "questions of literary meaning by ways of nonlinguistic referential models used in literary history" (*AR*, p. 79). De Man expresses surprise that historical rather than "semiological or rhetorical terms" are used in literary studies, when the "historical nature of literary discourse is *by no means an a priori established fact*" and when literature consists "*necessarily* of linguistic and semantic elements" (p. 79; emphasis mine). It is not clear how literature's "linguistic and semantic elements" detract from its historical explanation; on the contrary, the semantic elements in literary discourse would seem to constitute its historicity. De Man presents a curiously monolithic view of "history." He insists that historical explanation is a flight from language; historiography, for him, is always genetic (searching for origins) and teleological (moving toward a closure). For de Man, the genetic principle "*necessarily* underlies all historical narrative" (p. 82; emphasis mine). Even Nietzsche's own denunciation of Romanticism, says de Man, still labors within the genetic, totalizing, teleological pattern of what Nietzsche himself would call monumental history.

Making what he calls a "detour" into the fragments Nietzsche left out of *The Birth of Tragedy*, de Man suggests that a "nonauthoritative secondary statement" derived from a

---

22. De Man defines *aporia* as that which allows for "two incompatible, mutually self-destructive points of view" (*AR*, p. 131).

reading of these fragments will provide a statement that *"will have to be"* one "about the limitations of textual authority" (*AR*, p. 99; emphasis mine). Interestingly, de Man's syntax indicates a legislation of authority. We also witness here the skilled footwork that is a mark of de Man's "technique," permitting him to mimic the movement of the text he is "reading" to such an extent that the "secondary statements" of the text are appropriated into his own discourse, thus providing the basis for further readings of totally different kinds of texts.

We should examine de Man's own metacritical statement as it is presented in "Semiology and Rhetoric," the essay that forms the opening chapter of *Allegories*. Polemicizing against the renewed interest in what he calls the nonverbal "outside" of the text, de Man advocates "semiology" (or a Peircean semiotics) as an interpretive mode, since it "demonstrates that the perception of the literary dimensions of language is largely obscured if one submits uncritically to the authority of reference" (*AR*, p. 5).[23] Grammar, for de Man, enforces the link between sign and meaning; grammar and logic support each other, whereas the "third element in the trivium—rhetoric—dialectically subverts the totalizing impulse of the grammatical pattern." Having in passing mentioned Kenneth Burke's "well-known insistence" on the gap between grammar and rhetoric, de Man then appropriates C. S. Peirce's notion of the sign to reinforce what has now become his own "insistence": "the sign is not the thing but a meaning derived from the thing by a process . . . called representation. . . . The interpretation of the sign is not, for Peirce, a meaning but another sign; it is a reading, not a decodage, and this reading has, in its turn, to be interpreted into another sign, and so on ad infinitum" (p. 8).

23. One wonders in what sense de Man uses the term *perception* here, after his critique of a reading process linked to perception. In "Rhetoric of Blindness," he suggests that Derrida and Rousseau use a "vocabulary of substance and presence" not declaratively but "rhetorically" (*BI*, p. 138). We can assume de Man deliberately uses the language of "presence," but it is not always easy to sense the "self-consciousness" of such an awareness.

De Man suggests that although the object engenders the sign "by representation," the sign does not engender meaning in the same way. Quoting Peirce, de Man calls this process by means of which one sign gives birth to another "pure rhetoric," which unlike pure grammar, does not suggest that meaning is referential and, therefore, unproblematic. Peirce's sign-reproducing process becomes, for Paul de Man, the sign sequence that is allegory. De Man had already suggested in *Blindness and Insight* that allegory, far from being representational, was purely intralinguistic, that it had no referent outside language. De Man is implying, of course, that a concept of allegory dependent on the critique of "metaphysics" has to be intralinguistic, and, consequently, ahistorical.

The emphasis on rhetoric is reinforced in the 1979 essay "The Resistance to Theory," where de Man examines the relationship between grammar, rhetoric, and logic in the medieval trivium and describes "literariness" as being a use of language "that foregrounds the rhetorical over the grammatical and the logical function" (*ResTh*, p. 14). It is important to examine de Man's distinction carefully, since his writing moves toward a notion of allegory that becomes synonymous with literature, with the figurality of "all language." In "Semiology and Rhetoric," as well as in "The Resistance to Theory," de Man equates grammar with logic (since they support each other) to claim that grammar implies reference. Yet he seems to contradict himself on that very point, arguing that "no grammar is conceivable without the suspension of referential meaning" (*AR*, p. 268). He proceeds therefore to conflate grammar and logic by saying that "grammatical logic" can function "only if its referential consequences are disregarded" (p. 269). As far as this statement goes, grammar does not seem to imply reference. Elsewhere, however, he says that grammar does suggest reference, for "a stable cognitive field" extends from grammar to logic, and from logic to the phenomenal world; this is a construct that, according to him, can be undone by "rhetorical analysis." Rhetoric has a disruptive relationship to grammar and logic; it undermines the "claims of the trivium (and by extension, of language)" to be "epistemologically stable" (*ResTh*, p. 17). In order to show how rhetoric subverts grammar and logic, de Man self-confessedly retreats from a theoretical exposition of the problem "into a pragmatic discourse" (*AR*, p. 9). His now famous examples— Archie Bunker and the line from Yeats's poem—are meant to indicate the "tension" between grammar and rhetoric that informs de Man's notions of reading, deconstruction, and allegory.[24]

De Man uses the notion of the tension between grammar and rhetoric throughout *Allegories of Reading* to define his sense, not only of literature itself, but also of allegory and the reading of literature. For de Man, literariness dwells in "the aporia between constative and performative" functions of language. Our acceptance, and our understanding, of this claim depends on an acceptance of de Man's distinction between constative and performative, a distinction that implicitly argues for a notion of the performative as "intralinguistic" (like allegory) and a notion of the constative as "referential."[25] De Man's distinction between performative and constative is analogous to the one between rhetoric and grammar. In aligning rhetoric (which for him is literature) with the intralinguistic, he questions the claim of literature to speak of a world "other" than its own, raising issues of referentiality in language as well, especially because he advocates that philosophical, critical, and literary discourse be seen as continuous

24. In "Semiology and Rhetoric," the first chapter of *AR*, the distinction first made by John Austin between constative and performative utterances is aligned by de Man with the distinction between grammar and rhetoric, or the referential and the nonreferential. It should be pointed out here that de Man does not redefine Austin's concept of *illocution*, and consequently his use of the term (and his use of the performative/constative distinction) seems to contradict Austin's. One wishes de Man would somehow "signal" his points of departure. Riddel, "Coup de Man," suggests that de Man's critical language employs a strategy of paleonymy, using old concepts in "new and not yet defined or definable senses" (p. 89). Gasche, " 'Setzung' and 'Übersetzung,' " sees in *Allegories of Reading* a critique of the notion of the "speech act" itself.

25. For de Man, *performance* is like *figure*, which for him is intralinguistic, and which he sometimes uses as a synonym of *allegory*.

with one another: "Poetic writing is the most advanced and refined mode of deconstruction; it may differ from critical or discursive writing in the economy of its articulation, but not in kind" (*AR*, p. 17).

We must remember that de Man derives these "metacritical" statements from his readings of diverse texts, both "literary" and "philosophical." His method of appropriation is quite unique: he follows the "stuttering" narratives of a Proust, a Nietzsche, or a Rousseau to the point where deconstructed text becomes deconstructor's weapon, where residual statements ("strategies that tended to remain unnoticed") not only undo the text that supports them but are also assimilated into de Man's own arsenal.[26]

If a narrative were capable of containing the contradictions of its own reading, says de Man, it would have "the universal significance of an allegory of reading" (*AR*, p. 72). From a description of Proust's attempt to reassert "the superiority of the 'symbolic' metaphor over the literal, prosaic metonymy," de Man concludes authoritatively that "any narrative is primarily the allegory of its own reading . . . it will *always* lead to the confrontation of incompatible meanings between which it is *necessary but impossible* to decide in terms of truth and error" (p. 76; emphasis mine). The "incompatible meanings," de Man seems to be saying, reside solely in language; allegory is intralinguistic, and therefore in de Man's scheme, ahistorical.

Throughout his work, de Man develops his contrast between the "allegorical" and the "historical." In his discussion of "truth and error" in Nietzsche, de Man states that "the trope is not a derived, marginal, or aberrant form of language but the linguistic paradigm par excellence" and that "the figurative structure . . . characterizes language as such" (*AR*, p. 105). According to de Man, Nietzsche provides the rhetorical awareness that enables us to read him. This awareness also shows us that his "allegory of errors"—which de Man

26. Thus we can, perhaps, equate these "residual" statements with de Man's own "metacritical" statements.

perceives as "an endlessly repeated gesture"—is "the very model of philosophical rigor" (p. 118).[27] What is repeated is the "potential confusion between figurative and referential statement" (p. 116). The "allegorical" pattern is contrasted by de Man to the "historical" one "revelatory of a teleological meaning." The insistent contrast prevents de Man, when faced with a text like Benjamin's "The Task of the Translator," from seeing that the paradoxical patterns present there indicate a *synonymity* between allegory and historicity.

For de Man, the problematization of representation always seems to lead to a privileging of "figure," which is intra-linguistic. Nietzsche's observation that tropes are the truest nature of language leads de Man to the conclusion that language (as rhetoric), rather than seeking adequation to an "extra-linguistic referent," is rooted in "intralinguistic" figures. As always, he is careful to indicate that this affirmation comes from the text he is reading (in this case, Nietzsche) and not necessarily from his own critical discourse. He goes on to suggest that the "necessary subversion of truth by rhetoric" is "the distinctive feature of all language" (*AR*, p. 110). In a series of substitutions, de Man has introduced truth in the place of grammar.[28] The technique of substitution is one he uses to good effect in the essay on Benjamin. Especially because metaphor occupies such a prominently negative position in de Man's thinking (as an analogue of the "symbol" opposed to allegory), it is fascinating to watch him do in his writing exactly what he says is done by Rousseau or by Nietzsche: he performs "'analogical, metaphorical substitutions,'" describing "seductive similarities where they do not exist" (*AR*, pp. 122, 239), thus reproducing what he sees as the "aberrant totalizations characteristic of metaphor."

27. Nietzsche's "allegory of errors" is evident to de Man in that "all the authoritative claims . . . [Nietzsche's *Birth of Tragedy*] seems to make can be undermined by means of statements provided by the text itself" (*AR*, p. 117).

28. Later, he extends the chain of substitutions to include *deconstruction*, which he aligns with rhetoric (and uses in place of the term *allegory* or the term *literature*).

Rousseau's text, de Man claims in his discussion of metaphor as the totalizing figure par excellence, "describes conceptualization as substituting one verbal utterance . . . for another on the basis of a resemblance that hides differences which permitted the existence of entities in the first place" (*AR*, p. 145). In other words, conceptualization is similar to the creation of metaphor, a figure that he characterizes as a disfiguration: "Metaphor is error because it believes or feigns to believe in its own referential meaning" (p. 151). De Man points out that language, ironically, is made possible by the erring metaphor; this observation in turn allows him to substitute for the "double process" of conceptualization the narrative pattern of allegory. From the study of Rousseau's theory of language, de Man derives his own proposition that "conceptual language . . . is a lie superimposed upon an error"; Rousseau's genealogical fable concerning the word *man*, a fable that involves a metonymic substitution (the "naming" of man as "giant"), suggests to de Man that this concept is the result of the "deceitful misrepresentation of an original blindness" (p. 155). It is, therefore, "doubly metaphorical" (AR, p. 154). The "second metaphor," says de Man, is equated *by Rousseau* with "the literary . . . and rhetorical" (p. 153).

The dizzying substitutions de Man carries out have turned "metaphor," which—analogous to the symbol—was the totalizing image par excellence, into " 'second' metaphor" or allegory. In the other Rousseau essays, de Man continues to use in this contradictory sense the figure (that is, metaphor) that he had earlier denounced as involving a sense perception. He speaks of "the curiously unreadable metaphor of reading" and of how "all readings are in error because they assume their own readability" (*AR*, p. 202), thereby concealing the "radical figurality of language."

If the metaphor of reading in Rousseau is a "deconstructive narrative," says de Man, then narratives to the second or third degree can be called allegories: "Allegories are always allegories of metaphor and, as such, they are always allegories of the impossibility of reading" (*AR*, p. 205). Metaphor, which has to decide between symbolization and signification, referentiality and figuration, is used by de Man as a trope that is itself a kind of metonymy for language. Like metaphor, language has to *totalize* in order to arrive at a meaning. De Man, however, makes frequent references to "the aberrant *proper* meaning of metaphors against which the allegory constitutes itself" (p. 210; emphasis mine). It is difficult to see what the "proper" meaning could be in the scheme that de Man derives from Rousseau's linguistics, a scheme in which connotation is "wild" and reference "can never be a meaning."

The themes of allegory and unreadability are carried over by de Man into his reading of Rousseau's *Profession de foi*. He reads the "unreadability" of this text only to find it to be "structured exactly like the *Nouvelle Héloise (Julie)*" (*AR*, p. 247). De Man would make the same statement about Hegel's *Aesthetics* or Benjamin's translation essay, for all the texts that de Man chooses to comment upon seem to share the same structure: "The resulting 'meanings' " or themes, whatever they may be, are "torn apart by the aporia that constitutes [them]" (ibid.). I have already indicated that the "aporia" is, for de Man, the tension—built up by skillful substitution and repetition—between grammar and rhetoric, reference and figure, constative and performative.

In the "Excuses" chapter of *Allegories of Reading*, de Man once again returns to his concern with "parabasis," the figure of allegorical (dramatic) double action that concludes "The Rhetoric of Temporality." Now he describes it in terms of a sudden revelation of the discontinuity between two "rhetorical codes," those of "performative rhetoric" and "cognitive rhetoric"; this distinction seems to replace or allude to or repeat/reproduce the one between performative and constative utterance. The discontinuity between the codes, says de Man, becomes "irony" or "permanent parabasis" when it is "disseminated" over all points of "the figural line" (*AR*, p. 300). Irony, thus accorded the status of a meta-trope, not only "enforces the repetition" of an aberrant tropological system but also undoes allegory, which is itself deconstructive of all "tropological cognitions," and thereby undoes "understanding" itself.

To approach de Man's statement about irony from a different angle, let us consider for a moment his essay on Pascal.[29] Here he declares that "allegory is the trope of irony," though this is to say "something that is *true enough* but not intelligible" (PA, p. 12). Seizing on his own observation that Pascal's text shows how "one is the trope of zero" but zero is not subject to "real definition," de Man uses this notion, in a technique we have seen throughout *Allegories of Reading*, to say that allegory is the trope of irony but irony cannot be defined, except perhaps ironically. The alternative is compulsive repetition of the pattern, insistent and aberrant reading, allegorization of the allegory.

De Man's "readings" consistently derive from a "rhetoric" directed against "literary history," historicism, and "hermeneutics." This attack is closely connected to his "rhetoric" against symbol and metaphor as images of totalization that are tied to "perception." De Man indicts contemporary *Rezeptionsästhetik*, for instance, for being bound to traditional hermeneutical models that support a literary theory rooted in aesthetics, and therefore disallowing a problematization of what he calls "the phenomenalism of reading." De Man's objection to language being assimilated to perception, which has echoes in "Semiology and Rhetoric," the Rousseau essays, and even in the relatively early "Rhetoric of Temporality," is reiterated once more in his introduction to *Toward an Aesthetic of Reception*, a collection of essays by Hans-Robert Jauss.[30] Writing of the "overwhelmingly mimetic" nature of hermeneutic systems, de Man criticizes Jauss's concept of "the horizon of expectations" for setting up an interpretive model for literary understanding that involves a phenomenal experi-

29. De Man, "Pascal's Allegory of Persuasion," in *Allegory and Representation*, ed. Stephen Greenblatt (Baltimore: Johns Hopkins Press, 1969), cited henceforth as PA.
30. Jauss, *Toward an Aesthetic of Reception*, trans. Timothy Bahti (Minneapolis: University of Minnesota Press, 1982), cited henceforth as *TAR*.

ence and thereby "imitates" a perception. "Firmly rooted" in an aesthetics of representation, such a model, according to de Man, fails to account for the rhetorical process (namely, allegory) "by which the literary text moves from a phenomenal, world-oriented to a grammatical, language-oriented direction" (*TAR*, p. xxiii). Of course, de Man is assuming here that allegory is nonreferential and that "language" and "world" are mutually exclusive. While de Man's "displacement" of the notion of reading helps it to bypass perception, it is not clear whether his "theory" has room for the commonplace concept of reading, without which his allegory of reading loses much of its force.

I suggested earlier that although de Man's notion of allegory performs a valuable critique of representation, it does not have any conception of history or historicity. De Man's essays on Hegel may, however, show us a way of salvaging his insights to reinscribe historicity.[31] The allegory that accounts for its own misreading is crucial to the Hegel essays, which also add another pair of terms—*Erinnerung* and *Gedächtnis*, aligned with symbol and sign—to the chains elaborated by de Man throughout his career.[32] I shall focus here on de Man's analysis of allegory in Hegel. As Derrida points out, Hegelian allegory becomes for de Man "that allegory which constitutes the grand final figure of philosophy and of the philosophy of history . . . the figure of every *disjunction* between philosophy and history" (*Memoires*, p. 36). Derrida also suggests that Hegelian philosophy as allegory in the de Manian sense is not historical.

From a post-colonial perspective that recognizes the persistence of Hegelian constructions of the non-Western other, it seems urgent to dismantle a philosophy of history that has

31. See de Man, "Hegel on the Sublime," in *Displacement: Derrida and After*, ed. Mark Krupnick (Bloomington: Indiana University Press, 1983), pp. 139–53, and "Sign and Symbol in Hegel's Aesthetics," *Critical Inquiry* 8, no. 4 (Summer 1982): 761–75. My discussion focuses on the second of these essays, which I cite as SSH.

32. *Erinnerung* is interiorizing memory, and *Gedächtnis* is thought, writing, *technē*.

shored up these fables. De Man's insight that Hegelian philosophy is not historical may be of use here in showing up the "constructed" nature of the Orient or the non-West. In another sense, however, we have to recognize the *historicity* of Hegel's conceptions: we need to understand the material force these conceptions have acquired in shaping contemporary Western attitudes to the non-West and non-Westerners' attitudes toward themselves.[33]

Closely analyzing a section from Hegel's *Encyclopaedia of the Philosophical Sciences*,[34] de Man shows how Hegel's valorization of the symbol is actually supported by allegory, which is the "defective cornerstone of the entire system" (SSH, p. 775). It is the defective cornerstone that enables the construction of Hegel's mammoth philosophical system, which is shown in conventional interpretations of it to privilege *Erinnerung* (recollection, remembrance) over *Gedächtnis* (memory, a tool of the intellect), poetry over prose, and symbol over sign. De Man's reading reverses the usual positioning of symbol and sign in the *Aesthetics* by linking Hegel's terms with a problematics of the self. Hegel's assertion about art belonging to the realm of the symbolic, suggests de Man, comes from the distinction between symbol and sign, the latter being characterized, unlike the former, by an *arbitrary* relationship between "sensory component" and "intended meaning" (p. 766). The sign, for Hegel, is "great" because, being "citational," it "touches upon the question of the relationship between subject and predicate in any declarative sentence" (p. 767). From the problem of the sign we come to the problem of the subject or the self.

The difficulty that Hegel is grappling with, says de Man, is that the sign or the "I" is on the one hand "*singular* in its independence from anything that is not itself" and on the

33. De Man observes that "[whether] we know it, or like it, or not, most of us are Hegelians and quite orthodox ones at that" (SSH, p. 763).

34. Paragraph 23 of the *Encyclopaedia of the Philosophical Sciences* (1817), 1: 80, de Man's translation, from Hegel's *Werke in zwanzig Banden* (Frankfurt am Main, 1979). De Man claims this paragraph is one of the "defective cornerstones" of Hegel's *Aesthetics* of 1830.

other hand appears in logic as "the most inclusive, plural, general, and impersonal of subjects" (SSH, p. 768). As de Man points out, Hegel assumes that "meaning" is assimilated to "me," or to an "I," since thought implies the appropriation of the world by the subject. So what does Hegel suggest in the remarks that de Man cites? "Since language states only what is general, I cannot say what is only my opinion [*so kann ich nicht sagen was ich nur meine*]" (ibid). *Meinung*, which is German for "opinion," has, as de Man suggests, the connotation of *meinen*, "to mean," and *meinen* in turn can be read as the "verbalization of the possessive pronoun *mein* ("my"). Hegel's sentence is made to mean: " 'I cannot say what I make mine' or, since to think is to make mine, 'I cannot say what I think,' and since to think is fully contained and defined by the I . . . what the sentence actually says is 'I cannot say I' " (ibid.).

De Man's relentless troping of Hegel's phrase results in a "disturbing proposition," since for Hegel "the very possibility of thought depends on the possibility of saying 'I' " (SSH, p. 768). "What the allegory narrates," says de Man, "is . . . in Hegel's own words, 'the separation or disarticulation of subject from predicate *(die Trennung von Subjekt und Prädikat).*' For discourse to be meaningful, this separation has to take place, yet it is incompatible with the necessary generality of all meaning. Allegory functions, categorically and logically, like the defective cornerstone of the entire system" (p. 775). The stability of the *cogito*, or the subject, in Hegel is thus shown by de Man to be always already disarticulated.

What are the implications of de Man's reading for an emergent post-colonial discourse? As I indicated in chapter 1, both Hegel's *Aesthetics* and his *Philosophy of History* have for their cornerstones an "othering" of the non-West, especially India and China, and a denial of subjectivity and agency to the people of these continents. This denial, which manifests itself as the bestowal of subjecthood on the "West," enables Hegel's texts to function as sites where idioms of domination are fashioned, sites emblematic of the technologies of colonial power. De Man's perceptive discussion of Hegel helps us see how the repression of the *cogito's* disarticulation makes possible not only the constitution of the Western subject but also the construction of the non-Western other. If the Hegelian subject is a "defective" cornerstone, the other, too, has to be seen as far from coherent or homogeneous. Since the other endorses and is produced by the articulation of the Western self, the disarticulation or deconstruction of the latter, as performed, for example, by de Man, must necessarily lead to the dismantling of the non-Western other and the discourses of domination it authorizes.

4

Politics and Poetics: De Man, Benjamin, and the Task of the Translator

Historical materialism conceives historical "understanding"
as an after-life of that which is understood, whose pulse
can still be felt in the present.
—Walter Benjamin,
"Eduard Fuchs, Collector and Historian"

"Reading" and "translation" occupy as significant a place in
the work of Walter Benjamin as they do in that of Paul de
Man. As I have indicated in chapter 1, the act of reading for
Benjamin is propelled by a "critical, dangerous impulse," since
it both challenges the tradition and intervenes in changing it.[1]
Benjamin's critique of historicism is as powerful as de Man's,
but whereas de Man subsumes all "historical" approaches
under "historicism," Benjamin's critique is employed in the
service of a new materialist historiography. Benjamin's conception of allegory, unlike de Man's, suggestively brings together the task of the allegorist (and the reader of allegory)
with the task of the historian and the translator.[2]

1. Benjamin, "Theoretics of Knowledge, Theory of Progress," trans. L.
Hafrey and R. Sieburth, *Philosophical Forum* 15, nos. 1–2 (Fall–Winter 1983–
84): 1–40.
2. For Benjamin, the historian or allegorist retrieves and temporalizes the
allegorical images. In *The Origin of German Tragic Drama* (London: New Left
Books, 1977), Benjamin problematizes genetic concepts like "origin" while
writing a history of baroque allegorical drama. His practice of *citation* ("quoting" history) suggests a link between the function of the historian and that
of the allegorist, as well as the reader of allegory. Benjamin, like de Man, is
obviously using a concept of allegory quite different from that rooted in the
tradition of biblical exegesis.

I would like to suggest that de Man's notion of allegory
needs to be extended in a direction he would perhaps have
resisted. To do this, we might draw upon the work of Benjamin, whose conception of allegory is intimately linked to
"history," which it shows to be an irreversible process of decay that can be comprehended only from the perspective of
some possible "redemption."[3] In this chapter and the next, I
analyze two exemplary post-structuralist readings—de Man's
and Derrida's—of Benjamin's famous essay on translation,
showing how each "swerves" from the concern with "history" in Benjamin's text.

Like de Man, though from very different premises (com-
bining a Kabbalistic philosophy of language with a historical
materialist view of social revolution), Benjamin launches an
attack on essentialism and empirical historicism. Benjamin
claims that while historicism "presents an eternal image of
the past," historical materialism shows "a specific and unique
engagement with it," since "it has recourse to a consciousness of the present that shatters the continuum of history."[4]
For Benjamin, this destruction of continuity is characterized
by the allegorical image, in which "the past and the now flash
into a constellation," making possible, perhaps, what Spivak
would call "transactive reading" and what I have called
"translation."

Of late, a good deal of attention has been paid to Benjamin's texts by post-structuralist theorists. The early texts on
language and translation seem, however, to occupy a privileged position, to the near-exclusion of the important essays
on historiography.[5] In spite of the post-structuralist emphasis

3. In this chapter and the next, I show how Benjamin "figures" the realm
of redemption in his writings on historiography.
4. Benjamin, "Eduard Fuchs: Collector and Historian," in *One-Way Street
and Other Writings*, trans. E. Jephcott and K. Shorter (London: New Left Books,
1979), p. 352. Cited hereafter as EF.
5. The key texts are "On the Mimetic Faculty" and "On Language as
Such and the Language of Man," both in *Reflections*, ed. Peter Demetz, trans.
Edmund Jephcott (New York: Harcourt Brace Jovanovich, 1978); "The Task
of the Translator," in *Illuminations*, ed. Hannah Arendt, trans. Harry Zohn
(New York: Schocken Books, 1969), cited hereafter as TT; "Theses on the

on intertextuality, Benjamin's essays are seldom read by contemporary theorists in a manner that brings out the persistent nature of his concerns and his preoccupation with "history." This refusal to read the figure of "history" in Benjamin, I would argue, marks even the interpretive strategies of Paul de Man's fascinating essay on "The Task of the Translator."[6]

De Man's reading of "Task" for the most part does not refer to the later texts of Benjamin, and it does not, therefore, engage with the questions of historicity these texts raise.[7] Nor does de Man signal his awareness of the passages in "Task" that find their resonance in the later Benjamin who directly addresses the problem of "writing history." In fact, the attempt to formulate a nontraditional concept of history preoccupied Benjamin from the start of his intellectual career, and is present, I would argue, as a subterranean current even in the translation essay. Benjamin's writings on the concept of history are inseparable from his work on translation, and any attempt to describe the latter must necessarily account for the force of the former concern. It appears that de Man's preoccupation with the *linguistic* supplementarity of the act of translation leads him either to ignore or to dismiss the references to "history" in Benjamin's text. Another strategy he seems to employ is to address the passages that resonate in the later work, but then interpret them in ways that negate the significance of the resonance. I would like to claim that "Task" not only foreshadows some of Benjamin's most important concerns with historiography and the function of "remembrance," but does so in a manner that is almost impossible to overlook. Let me elaborate on these remarks by first surveying Benjamin's essay and isolating some significant

---

Philosophy of History," in ibid., cited hereafter as TH; and "Eduard Fuchs, Collector and Historian," in *One-Way Street and Other Writings.*

6. De Man, " 'Conclusions,' Walter Benjamin's 'The Task of the Translator,' " in *The Resistance to Theory* (Minneapolis: University of Minnesota Press, 1986), pp. 73–105. Cited hereafter as C.

7. "The Task of the Translator" was published in 1923, and Benjamin was an extremely productive writer until his death in 1940.

passages, and then by reading de Man reading Benjamin's "Task."

For the sake of convenience, I shall cite the 1969 English translation by Harry Zohn, and make occasional reference to the German text.[8] Not surprisingly, de Man refers not only to Benjamin's "original" essay but also to Zohn's translation into English and Maurice de Gandillac's translation into French in order to make a point or two about "fidelity" and "betrayal." Benjamin's essay is itself an introduction to his translation into German of Baudelaire's *Tableaux Parisiens*.

Benjamin begins by saying that "in the appreciation of a work of art or an art form, consideration of the receiver never proves fruitful. . . . No poem is intended for the reader, no picture for the beholder, no symphony for the listener" (TT, p. 69). He has to emphasize his notion that art does not transmit or "communicate" anything in order to set up his notion of translation of the art work: "any translation which intends to perform a transmitting function cannot transmit anything but information—hence, something inessential. This is the hallmark of bad translations" (ibid.). Since a literary work contains something "unfathomable" in addition to information, a bad translator would be transmitting "inessential content" in an "inaccurate" fashion. Since the "original does not exist for the reader's sake," neither can the translation. It is possible, of course, to read this passage as a negation of the historicity of the art work; however, it can also be seen as a move of Benjamin's that is later transformed into a critique of historicism. In Benjamin, unlike in de Man, the critique of historicism does not involve a corresponding negation of historicity.

In the very next paragraph, Benjamin swings—and this is typical of his style—from an ostensible negation of "history" to a complex affirmation of it. He speaks of translation as a

8. Zohn's translation is in *Illuminations*, ed. Arendt, pp. 69–82. The German text is in Benjamin, *Gesammelte Schriften*, ed. Rolf Tiedemann and Hermann Schweppenhauser (Frankfurt am Main: Suhrkamp Verlag, 1974), 4: 9–21.

mode,[9] and of how, in order to comprehend this notion, one has to refer to the *translatability* of the text: "The question of whether a work is translatable has a dual meaning. Either: Will an adequate translation ever be found among the totality of its readers? Or, more pertinently: Does its nature lend itself to translation and, therefore, in view of the significance of the mode, *call for it?*" (TT, p. 70; emphasis mine). Benjamin suggests that the second question can be decided "apodictically." Even if a work is not translated by men, it represents only a *claim* unfulfilled. What is important is its *translatability*—that which is essential to certain works if one can see translation as a *mode*. This is not to indicate, says Benjamin, that it is essential such works be translated. "It means rather that a specific significance inherent in the original manifests itself in its translatability" (p. 71).

The notion of a work calling for its translation, and that translatability represents a *claim* on humankind, shows up repeatedly in Benjamin's writing. In the 1940 "Theses on the Philosophy of History," these figures are clearly connected to "historical materialism": "There is a secret agreement between past generations and the present one. . . . Like every generation that preceded us, we have been endowed with a *weak* Messianic power, a power to which the past has a claim. That claim cannot be settled cheaply. Historical materialists are aware of that" (TH, p. 254). In juxtaposing these passages, I am suggesting that in Benjamin's later work the task of the translator becomes the task of the historical materialist or the critical historian. As he moved increasingly closer to Marxism, the concerns of which he translated into the lan-

9. For Benjamin, translation, poetry, and criticism are "modes." But the "mode of intention" should be distinguished from the "intended object" before we can comprehend the "basic law of a philosophy of language" (TT, p. 74). De Man says that even if the meaning-function is intentional, it is not a priori certain that the mode of meaning, the way in which I mean, is intentional in any way. The latter is dependent on linguistic properties perhaps not even created by humans at all. This allows de Man to conclude, ultimately, that translation can be a purely linguistic problem.

guage of his own obsessions, Benjamin's notion of translation was "figured" into his conception of historiography.

The claim on humankind is linked in Benjamin's text to questions of "survival" and "living on." [10] He suggests that "a translation issues from the original—not so much from its life as from its afterlife. . . . translation marks their [the works'] stage of continued life" (TT, p. 71). The idea of an afterlife seems to be neither theological nor vitalist; for in the same paragraph Benjamin insists that "the range of life must be determined by history rather than by nature" and that "the philosopher's task consists in comprehending all of natural life through the more encompassing life of history" (ibid.). I shall explore this passage's implications in chapter 5; we should, however, note here that Benjamin's ostensibly Hegelian conception of the relationship between nature and history actually points to his profoundly anti-Hegelian critique of historicism.

At this point in the essay, Benjamin suggests that the purpose of translation is to express "the central reciprocal relationship between languages": to bring out the "kinship of languages" (TT, p. 72). Again, it may not be entirely appropriate to see this as the expression of a theological hope, given the use of the redemption metaphor in Benjamin's later work, and given that Benjamin continually uses theological metaphors and imagery to describe essentially secular processes. [11] I suggest that although "The Task of the Translator" draws heavily on Judaic conceptions of language, it is at the same time pointing forward to a secular notion of redemption as the function of translation. Benjamin indicates here that lan-

10. See my discussion of this notion in chapter 5, where I read Derrida's reading of Benjamin. Derrida's essay in the landmark volume *Deconstruction and Criticism* (London: Routledge & Kegan Paul, 1979) is called "Living On: Border Lines." *Survivre* is French for "live on." The essay, in a "message" to its translators, suggests a notion of "reada-translatability."

11. Tiedemann, "Historical Materialism or Political Messianism? An Interpretation of the Theses 'On the Concept of History,' " *Philosophical Forum* 15, nos. 1–2 (Fall–Winter 1983–84): 71–104.

guages are "interrelated in what they want to express." The kinship of languages is therefore demonstrated by a translation that conveys "the form and meaning of the original as accurately as possible." Traditional theory of translation, however, "would be hard put to define the nature of this accuracy and therefore could shed no light on what is important in a translation" (TT, p. 72). Perhaps this *accuracy* could also refer to the translator/historian's capacity to recognize what it is in the "text" that *claims* us.

The text undergoes changes in its afterlife, but "to seek the essence of such changes . . . in the subjectivity of posterity rather than in the very life of language and its works, would mean—even allowing for the crudest psychologism—to confuse the root cause of a thing with its essence. More pertinently, it would mean denying . . . one of the most powerful and fruitful historical processes" (TT, p. 73). This denunciation is of a piece with Benjamin's opening remarks about the reception of an art work. His emphasis on historical process, however, indicates that this comment is not a negation of the work's historicity but an attack on psychologism, for Benjamin considers the changes in a language crucial to a reading (or translation) of a work's historicity.

Returning to the notion that translation expresses the kinship between languages through grasping "the intention underlying each language" (TT, p. 74), Benjamin suggests that this intention is a striving toward a "pure language" *(reine Sprache)*. Every translation, in taking the text further from its origins, raises it spiritually into a realm where it can approximate the *reine Sprache* more closely. Julian Roberts compares Benjamin's notion of translation to the Romantic concept of *Kritik*, which was supposed to "raise the power" of a work by creating a fuller universe of meanings through intense contemplation. For Benjamin, suggests Roberts, *Kritik* could be a paradigm for intellectual activity other than that which is purely poetic.[12] Writers on Benjamin's work usually insist that Ben-

12. Roberts, *Walter Benjamin* (Atlantic Highlands, N.J.: Humanities Press, 1983), p. 121.

jamin's theory of translation is rooted in a divine language of "names" that becomes the theological foundation of the kinship between languages.[13] Without denying the theological impulses in "The Task of the Translator," I would like to suggest that we are not reading rigorously enough if we stop at this juncture. We will not then be accounting for the innumerable "translations" (transformations that never reproduce the "original" propositions) Benjamin carried out in the course of his career. "Pure language" in the later work becomes the realm of history, flawed, dispersed, where "all translation is . . . somewhat provisional" (TT, p. 75), where the historical materialist / critic / translator catches at "sparks of hope in the past" before they disappear (TT, p. 255).

A constant troping, we have seen, is characteristic of Benjamin's work. The tropes reappear again and again in his writings, as if his changing political-theoretical concerns continually clustered around his favorite motifs and drew the strength of their articulation from the obsessive, repetitive nature of his style. The concern with "accuracy" surfaces again when Benjamin states that "the task of the translator consists in finding that intended effect [*Intention*] upon the language into which he is translating which produces in it the echo of the original." Translation, unlike a literary work, "does not find itself in the center of the language forest but on the outside facing the wooded ridge; it calls into it without entering, aiming at that single spot where the echo is able to give, in its own language, the reverberation of the work in the alien one" (TT, p. 76). Compare this with a passage from the 1930s, from "Eduard Fuchs, Collector and Historian": "[A] critique of history . . . [must] become aware of the critical constellation in which precisely this fragment of the past is found with precisely this present"; as before, the concern with the translator's *accuracy* appears as "figuring" the historian's desire for "an engagement with history original to every new present" (EF, pp. 351, 352).

13. See ibid., and also Richard Wolin, *Walter Benjamin: An Aesthetic of Redemption* (New York: Columbia University Press, 1982).

The critique of representation that Benjamin says a historical materialist must employ is prefigured in the notion that
the "language of truth" is the "true language" concealed in
translations. This essentialist vocabulary undercuts itself in
its insistence that "reproduction of the sense" is not significant, although translation needs to ripen "the seed of pure
language" (TT, p. 77). How does Benjamin arrive at this statement? Viewed in the light of his earlier suggestion that translation strives to capture the original's *mode of intention* and not
the *intended object*, the attack on traditional translation theory
seems justified: "The traditional concepts in any discussion
of translations are fidelity and license—the freedom of faithful reproduction and, in its service, fidelity to the word. These
ideas seem to be no longer serviceable to a theory that looks
for other things in a translation than reproduction of meaning" (p. 78). The critique of representation implied here pre-
pares the way for the critique of historicism in the later writings.

Searching for a strategy that "completely demolishes the
theory of reproduction of meaning," Benjamin comes up with
the notion that a translator must provide a "literal rendering
of the syntax" (TT, p. 78). Since the case for literalness cannot
be made on the basis of an appeal for reproducing the "sense,"
another context must be found for this discussion. Here the
metaphor of the vessel—or, as Derrida suggests, the amphora—comes in:

> Fragments of a vessel which are to be glued together must
> match one another in the smallest details, although they need
> not be like one another. In the same way a translation, instead
> of resembling the meaning of the original, must lovingly and
> in detail incorporate the original's mode of signification, thus
> making both the original and the translation recognizable as
> fragments of a greater language, just as fragments are part of
> a vessel. . . . [The] work reflects the great longing for linguis-
> tic complementation [and] . . . a literal rendering of the syntax
> . . . proves words rather than sentences to be the primary ele-
> ment of the translator. For if the sentence is the wall before
> the language of the original, literalness is the arcade.
>
> (TT, p. 79)

Benjamin's emphasis on the "word" can be understood as indicating his disregard for the "reproduction of meaning." As he suggests earlier, "a literal rendering of the syntax completely demolishes the theory of reproduction of meaning and is a direct threat to comprehensibility" (TT, p. 78). Whereas the self-contained sentence, with its unity and coherence, does not call for translation, the word—a fragment or shard of the "vessel"—reflects the "longing for linguistic complementation." Literalness as a translative technique necessarily privileges the word over the coherence of the sentence, since a "literal rendering of the syntax" splinters the linearity and symmetry of the sentence. The arcade was to be the central "figure" of Benjamin's great unfinished *Passagen-Werk,* also known as the Arcades Project. In this massive work, Benjamin planned to write a new kind of history of Paris in the nineteenth century. The literal translator of "Task" was to become the literal historian of the arcades. The translator's practice of *citation* would inform the historian's project.

For Benjamin, a translation's success as a mode is "determined objectively by the translatability of the original"; he also suggests that "the higher the level of a work, the more . . . [it remains] translatable" (TT, p. 81). He returns at the conclusion of the essay to this notion of translatability, perhaps a figure for the past charged with "Messianic time" that recurs in his later writings. Only if a text is translatable can it demand that its *claim* be fulfilled. Only if a past image possesses "now-time" *(Jetztzeit)* is it redeemed. The notion of "now-time," the constellation of past and present, shatters the continuity of teleological history.

Benjamin emphasizes that his attack on the reproduction of meaning is not a call for "free translation" in the old sense. There is a new justification for free translation, and it "does not derive from the sense of what must be conveyed, for the emancipation from this sense is the task of fidelity." By fidelity Benjamin means here, of course, literalness. Free translation, he says, should "base the test on its own language. It is the task of the translator to release in his own language that pure language which is under the spell of another, to liberate the language imprisoned in a work in his re-creation of the work. For the sake of pure language he breaks through decayed barriers of his own language" (TT, p. 80).

"Release," "liberate," "breaks"—the vocabulary used here appears with increasing frequency in Benjamin's writings on the task of the historical materialist. The concern with accuracy, combined with the critique of the reproduction of sense, points to a critique of historicism. In the new historiography, the "powerful forces that lie bound in the 'once-upon-a-time' of historicism are set free. The task of historical materialism is to set to work an engagement with history original to every new present. It has recourse to a consciousness of the present that shatters the continuum of history" (EF, p. 352).

In a manner that reminds us of Derrida's use of quotation to "interrupt" his text, Benjamin often inserts a few significant lines into the essay on translation, like the passage from Rudolf Pannwitz's *Die Krisis der europäischen Kultur*, a text he ranks among the best writing in translation theory published in Germany. Pannwitz says the translator must allow his language to be "powerfully affected by the foreign tongue" instead of preserving the state of his own language. Benjamin's citation indicates how he values heterogeneity over homogeneity, and the contamination of translation over the purity of the original. The translator who must allow the "foreign" text to affect her language does so by a literalness that produces a translation "between the lines":

> Translation must be one with the original in the form of the interlinear version, in which literalness and freedom are united. For some degree all great texts contain their potential translation between the lines; this is true to the highest degree of sacred writings. The interlinear version of the Scriptures is the prototype or ideal of all translation. (TT, p. 82)

The text therefore exists in both languages at the same time; it is inscribed perhaps as a text that is already "double."

Reading Paul de Man reading Benjamin and his translators, I shall attempt to show that the model of literature or of reading proposed by de Man leaves out historicity as I have defined it; I speculate as to the inevitability of this neglect in de Man's scheme, and suggest what significance it might have for post-colonial readers. I choose de Man's text on Benjamin, not because it is one of the last things he ever prepared for an audience, but because in turning toward "translation" de Man shows more clearly than ever the nature of his preoccupations and the strategies he employs in inscribing them into his readings. In discussing this unedited, unrevised essay, I mimic a de Manian practice that makes "detours" into fragments, to catch texts at unguarded moments.

A preliminary comment that may not be irrelevant: de Man's tone in this "lecture" is informal, engaging, witty, "reasonable." The talk was transcribed without any attempt on the part of the editors to smooth it out. Since this text lacks the more authoritarian voice of de Man's other published work, it is harder for a reader not to be persuaded by the almost intimate, conversational style to accept even the most startling of de Man's interpretations.

In the very first paragraph de Man makes an extremely skillful move: "I want to stay pretty close to this particular text, and see what comes out. If I say stay close to the text, since it is a text on translation, I will need . . . translations of this text; because if you have a text which says it is impossible to translate, it is very nice to see what happens when that text gets translated. And the translations confirm, brilliantly, beyond any expectations which I may have had, that it is impossible to translate" (C, p. 74). On the one hand, de Man suggests that nothing is determined yet, that the text is as yet "unread" in a sense; on the other hand, after this disarming gesture, he presents a description of this text that is yet unread, indicating that it says "it is impossible to translate." Although he has not, at this point, provided any evidence from Benjamin's text to show this is indeed what it is saying, he has already given us a powerful restatement of one of his "conclusions." In a characteristic move, de Man has first of all substituted "translation" for "reading"; he has then pre-

sented his own preoccupation with the impossibility of reading as Benjamin's statement about the impossibility of translation.

De Man then proceeds to offer "a framework which is historical" for the discussion of Benjamin's essay. He says he
feels obliged to do this "since the problems of history have
come up frequently" (C, p. 74). In this context, de Man mentions the problem of *modernity*, a "recurrent problem in history and historiography" (p. 74), which he himself addresses,
as we have seen, in the Nietzsche essays and in "Literary
History and Literary Modernity." He refers to a 1965 essay by
Hans-Georg Gadamer, "The Philosophical Foundations of the
Twentieth Century," [14] which asks if it is possible to speak of
"modernity" with regard to contemporary philosophical
thought. According to de Man, Gadamer suggests that "modern" philosophy is characterized by a decreased naiveté.
Compared to Hegel and Kant, we have gone beyond the naiveté of positing, of reflection, and of the concept. Contemporary philosophy has developed a critique of the subject and
does not any longer believe that the subject controls its discourse. Also, individual self-reflection has given way to the
possibility of a "historicity of understanding." Here de Man
allies Gadamer with the later reception aesthetics and says
that his contribution is "historicizing the notion of understanding, by seeing understanding . . . as a process between
author and reader in which the reader acquires an understanding of the text by becoming aware of the historicity of
the movement that occurs between the text and himself" (C,
p. 75). Hegel, still concerned with the subject, was not historical enough. Overcoming the third kind of naiveté, that of the
concept, involves an understanding of how even philosophical discourse uses metaphors and of how philosophical language is dependent on ordinary language. De Man thinks
Gadamer's analysis belongs to a Hegelian model even though
it displays a critical outlook that is Kantian. For Gadamer,

14. Available in English in Gadamer, *Philosophical Hermeneutics*, trans. David
E. Linge (Berkeley and Los Angeles: University of California Press, 1976).

says de Man, modernity is defined "as a Hegelianism which has concentrated more on linguistic dimensions" (C, p. 76).

To make sense of de Man's polemics here, we must reflect on why he uses Gadamer's essay at all. Firstly, Gadamer belongs roughly to the same philosophical tradition as Benjamin and might be presumed to share both a vocabulary and a set of problems with him, and it is in de Man's interest to show that this is not the case. Since de Man obviously privileges Benjamin's remarks on language as being close to his own thinking, he is using the translation essay as a foil to Gadamer's ideas—ideas he has attacked elsewhere (in his introduction to Jauss) as inspiring a model of literary interpretation caught up in the aesthetics of representation, a model still phenomenal rather than linguistic. The criticism of Gadamer is part of de Man's general criticism of "historicism" and "hermeneutics." [15] De Man seems to be using the words *historicizing* and *historicity* without attempting to indicate to the reader what they connote, although it is clear they do not have any privileged position in his discourse. We have to ask if the meaning he appears to assign to the terms is comprehensive for our purposes, and whether it accounts for the significance they have for Benjamin.

Although it appears to explore the "historicity" question, de Man's outlining of Gadamer's position does not really attempt to do this. As I suggested in chapter 1, the term *historicity* could incorporate the *Wirkung* of the text in the present, and help us, without falling into the traps of essentialist discourse, ask questions about *who* is using or interpreting the text, and *how* or *why* they are using it. By this token, not only does de Man not take into account *why* or *how* he himself is using Benjamin's text, he also appears to indicate that such questions of "historicity" do not necessarily belong in a poststructuralist model that has language as its most important

15. However, Gadamer himself initiates a critique of "historicism," and his philosophical hermeneutics is much more sophisticated than de Man seems to give him credit for. See Gadamer's *Truth and Method*, trans. Garrett Barden and John Cumming (1975; reprint, New York: Crossroad, 1975).

paradigm. My argument, on the other hand, is that these questions must increasingly and more urgently be posed in post-structuralist criticism to prevent its assimilation into, and undermine its complicity with, hegemonic and universalist discourses.

Given that de Man never clarifies his use of *historicity*, we may be justified in suggesting, for the time being, that he intends the word in its dictionary meaning of "historical authenticity"—that is, being "adequate" to some past event. Note how the striving for *adequatio* is thereby implicitly attached by de Man to Gadamer's use of the term, and, by extension, to any use of the term. As I suggested earlier, this definition of *historicity* does not allow for Benjamin's notion of historical materialism or for his formulation of the historian's task.

In contrast to Gadamer's "pragmatic" notion of modernity, says de Man, Benjamin's notion of language would appear "highly regressive," because it would seem "messianic, prophetic, religiously messianic" (C, p. 76). De Man in fact repeats the words *messianic* and *sacred* several times in the course of this paragraph and the next. Although we must allow for this essay's having been delivered as a talk, the repetition is reminiscent of de Man's writing elsewhere, in which he goes over certain phrases or words in almost incantatory fashion, strengthening his argument by sheer force of the repetition. I am not saying de Man projects Benjamin as a prophetic or messianic writer; I am, however, suggesting that he emphasizes one reading of Benjamin for the following reason: to show that an ostensibly "essentialist" text subverts itself by putting forward a nonrepresentational notion of language that is ultimately non-Hegelian as well,[16] thereby also pointing to the "naiveté" of Gadamer's Hegelian model, a model that depends on what de Man calls the "historicity" of the text. This move of de Man's suggests that the debate about historicity marks the site of another conflict—the one between "politics" and "poetics," which is addressed at a crucial point in de Man's

16. As I indicate in chapter 5, Benjamin's conception of history, too, is non-Hegelian.

essay. I call the moment crucial because it is where de Man conclusively "appropriates" Benjamin's concerns by likening them to his own (C, pp. 92–93).

Before he can do that, however, he must firmly establish his critique of the concern with "historicity." One dimension of this critique is the polemic against the proponents of *Rezeptionsästhetik*, who "analyze the problem of poetic interpretation from the perspective of the reader," and for whom Benjamin's opening sentences in "Task" are "absolutely scandalous" (C, p. 77). The reference is, of course, to the passage asserting the art work's disregard for its audience. De Man suggests that the reception theorists would like to dismiss this as a "regression to the messianic conception of poetry which would be religious in the wrong sense" (p. 78). We might speculate here as to what de Man means by "religious in the wrong sense"; it could be that he is contrasting this attitude toward Benjamin's work with the one formulated by Geoffrey Hartman, who, according to de Man, "praises him [Benjamin] precisely for the way in which he combines a complex historical pattern with a sense of the sacred" (p. 78). Before he quotes Hartman, de Man implies, in what is for me a problematic passage, that Benjamin would be opposed to Gadamer's notion of modernity and therefore to "historicity":

> Benjamin is also frequently praised as the one who has returned the dimension of the sacred to literary language, and who has thus overcome, or at least considerably refined, the secular historicity of literature on which the notion of modernity depends. If one can think of modernity as it is described by Gadamer as a loss of the sacred, as a loss of a certain type of poetic experience, as its replacement by a secular historicism which loses contact with what was originally essential, then one can praise Benjamin for having re-established the contact with what had there been forgotten. (C, p. 78)

First of all, we will have to ask again whether Gadamer's essay provides an entrance into Benjamin's "Task," or whether de Man is using it to deemphasize "historicity" both in Benjamin's text and as an interpretive problem. Gadamer's "secular historicism" and "secular historicity" are presented as that which is overcome (or "considerably refined") by Benjamin's theory of language. This suggestion allows de Man to deny categorically that what Benjamin is actually putting forward in his later work is a secularized notion of "redemption"; it also blinds him to the possibility that Benjamin's theory of language (and the critique of representation it implies) is actually the early formulation of his—Benjamin's—later notions of historical materialism and historicity.

Geoffrey Hartman's thesis that it is a political act to remember the past, and his comment that Benjamin sees this as the duty and function of the critic as well as the historian, is met with gentle raillery by de Man, who thinks it is having one's cake and eating it too if one can combine the "apocalyptic" mode (or "sacred revelation") with "nihilistic rigor" (C, p. 79). Since de Man also sees this as a seductive way of "marrying history with the sacred," we have to ask, first, what he means by history in this phrase, and, second, if he is suggesting a parallel between "nihilistic rigor" and the concern with "history." The latter suggestion, combined with the fuzziness of the concept of history, makes for an extremely scrambled commentary indeed.

Meanwhile, "what does Benjamin say?" (C, p. 79). De Man's "reasonable" and genuinely puzzled tone at this juncture in his text is winning. So when he complains that Benjamin's translators don't have a clue as to what Benjamin is saying, we are led to sympathize with his exasperation rather than question his move. Discussing key passages of Benjamin's "Task" in German, French, and English, de Man attempts to gather evidence for his initial assertion that it is impossible to translate, a statement he claims is borne out by the muddled efforts of the translators, as well as by Benjamin's text itself. In order to assert the impossibility, however, de Man needs to retranslate crucial phrases of the Benjamin essay.

Strangely enough, suggests de Man, Harry Zohn (the translator into English) and Maurice de Gandillac (the French translator) end up turning positives into negatives and conveying the opposite of what Benjamin is saying. For example,

where Benjamin has, "Wo der Text unmittelbar, ohne ver-
mittelnden Sinn . . . der Wahrheit oder der Lehre angehört,
ist er übersetzbar schlechthin," de Man's translation has
"Where the text pertains directly, without mediation, to the
realm of truth and of dogma, it is, without further ado, translatable." And Gandillac comes up with "Là où le texte, im-
médiatement, sans l'entremise d'un sens . . . relève de la vér-
ité ou de la doctrine, il est purement et simplement
*in*traduisible." De Man narrates an anecdote about Derrida's
use of the Gandillac translation in a seminar where part of his
reading was based on the "*in*traduisible." It was pointed out
to him that it was in fact "translatable." De Man comments:
"I'm sure Derrida could explain that it was the same—and I
mean that in a positive sense, it *is* the same, but still, it is not
the same without some additional explanation" (C, p. 80). Let
us see whether de Man provides this additional explanation
to support his claim that Benjamin's text is about the impossibility rather than the possibility of translation.

Here de Man asks a question to which he already seems to
know the answer, a question confirming the "secondary
statements" he has obtained from readings of other texts: Why
is the translator the exemplary figure? "Why is the translator
held up in relation to the very general questions about the
nature of poetic language which the text asks?" (C, p. 80). The
translator, says de Man, is chosen by Benjamin because he
fails "per definition." "The translator can never do what the
original text did. Any translation is always second in relation
to the original, and the translator as such is lost from the very
beginning" because "*Aufgabe*, task, can also mean the one who
has to give up. . . . The translator has to give up in relation
to the task of refinding what was there in the original" (ibid.).
The context of de Man's remark indicates that the translator
has to give up something, if not to give up altogether. Could
de Man also be implying that we have to give up on the translator?[17] We should note here that Benjamin's "translator" does

17. De Man's misleading phraseology is obviously owing to the im-
promptu nature of the lecture.

not really have to *give up*, because he is not even *trying* to
"refind" the essence of the original. What is the strategy de
Man uses to limit what the text is saying? By suggesting that
the central concern of the text is "the nature of poetic language," de Man can suggest not only that Benjamin's text is
essentialist in that it reverts to the fidelity versus freedom
debate of traditional translation theory; he also adds another dimension to the portrait of Benjamin as a saturnine,
melancholic thinker preoccupied with "failure." I could not
agree more with de Man's suggestion that Benjamin's use
of the translator points to a critique of representation; but
to limit Benjamin's critique to a concern with "language"
is to neglect the most problematic parts of the translation
essay.

Having made the move that puts translation squarely within
the realm of language, de Man reformulates his question: "Why
[is] this failure with regard to an original text, to an original
poet . . . for Benjamin exemplary? The question also becomes
how the translator differs from the poet; and here Benjamin
is categorical in asserting that the translator is radically unlike, differs essentially from the poet and from the artist" (C,
p. 80). Since this notion goes so much against common sense,
argues de Man, one of Benjamin's translators refuses to see
it. Instead of saying that translation is "unähnlich der Kunst"
or *unlike* art, Gandillac presents it as "n'est pas sans ressem-
blance avec l'art" (*not unlike* art). Another failure of the translator.

In de Man's deft reading, Benjamin's distinction between
poet and translator is described thus:

> The poet . . . has to say something . . . he has to convey a
> meaning which does not necessarily relate to language. The
> relationship of the translator to the original is *the relationship
> between language and language*, wherein the problem of meaning
> or the desire to say something, the need to make a statement,
> *is entirely absent*. Translation is a relation from language to lan-
> guage, not a relation to an extralinguistic meaning that could
> be copied, paraphrased, or imitated . . . poetry is certainly not
> . . . a copy in that sense." (C, pp. 81–82; emphasis mine)

The distinction between an inside and outside of language is one that de Man has set up in this text. Benjamin suggests that translation expresses the kinship between languages (TT, p. 72); it does not necessarily follow that translation is "a relation from language to language." In indicating that the translator is not trying to say anything, de Man cuts us off from a possible way of explaining a particular translator's *interpretive choices*. To put it somewhat differently, in making translation a relation of language to language, de Man may be preempting any attempt to bring the political or historical dimension into a discussion of translation. Instead, he will suggest, as he does at the end of his essay, that *politics* in Benjamin actually means *poetics*.

Surprisingly, de Man seems to have ignored, in the previous paragraph of Benjamin's text, the insistence on the notion of afterlife: "a translation issues from the original—not so much from its life as from its afterlife," says Benjamin. "In the final analysis, the range of life must be determined by history" (TT, p. 71). It is in passages like this one about "living on" that Benjamin seems to be circling around what would later become a major concern: a new kind of historiography, modeled after the translation process, that incorporates the critique of representation as well as a desire to engage "the present." Benjamin's concern with history's being able to comprehend "nature" is part of a powerful critique of origins that also contributes to his thinking on translation.

Since at least two essays on translation are circulating in the space of this chapter, it may not be inappropriate to draw attention to de Man's own translative practice. Suggesting that in Benjamin translation resembles philosophy and also theory of literature (rather than poetry), de Man gives his own translation of a passage where *Erkenntniskritik* is mentioned. The German *die Unmöglichkeit einer Abbildstheorie* becomes for de Man "the impossibility of a theory of simple imitation"; the supplement here is, of course, the word *simple*, which shows that de Man's notion of the impossibility of translation is not a seamless one. His case would be weakened, in one sense, if he had to admit that he was concerned with "simple imitation" rather than "imitation" in general. Curious, then, how he first adds the qualifying adjective in his translation and then represses it in order to construct a coherent narrative about the "impossibility" of translation.

Both translation and criticism, says de Man, "are caught in the gesture which Benjamin calls ironic, a gesture which undoes the stability of the original by giving it a definitive, canonical form in the translation or the theorization" (C, p. 82). Let us juxtapose this with the relevant passage from "The Task of the Translator": "Thus translation, ironically, transplants the original into a more definitive linguistic realm since it can no longer be displaced by a secondary rendering. The original can only be raised there anew and at other points of time" (TT, p. 75). The "ironic gesture" seems to be, actually, "It is ironic that. . . ." Again, de Man unerringly points to the presence of a critique of representation (the unstable "original"); again, he also neglects to consider the sentence with which Benjamin follows the first statement about the definitive linguistic realm. Once again, the sentence repressed by de Man's commentary seems to foreshadow the way in which the critique of representation will be brought into the service of a historical materialist who will retranslate for every present.

The notion that translation gives a "canonical" form to the original work signals another characteristic move made by de Man: "The translation canonizes, freezes, an original and shows in the original a mobility, an instability, which at first one did not notice" (C, p. 82). After presenting this insight, de Man tells us in the very next sentence that this function of translation is not a *canonization* but a *de-canonization:* "The act of critical, theoretical reading . . . performed by literary theory in general—by means of which the original work is not imitated or reproduced but is to some extent put in motion, *de-canonized*, questioned in a way which undoes its claim to canonical authority—is similar to what a translator performs" (C, pp. 82–83; emphasis mine). De Man might argue that the two words, ostensibly opposites, are "the same" (as in the anecdote about Derrida's seminar), but without "additional explanation" it is hard for us to see how this might be the case.[18] This kind of almost imperceptible move in de Man's text is suggestive of how he will turn "politics" into "poetics," and possibility of translation into its impossibility.

Now we come to de Man's reading of what he concedes is the most complex passage in Benjamin's text. According to de Man, translation for Benjamin is "like history" (C, p. 83). The passage that bears the closest resemblance to what de Man is describing does not mention translation as being like history at all: "In the final analysis, the range of life must be determined by history rather than by nature. . . . The philosopher's task consists in comprehending all of natural life through the more encompassing life of history" (TT, p. 71). We need to look closely at de Man's explication of this passage:

> We are not supposed to think of history as ripening, as organic growth, or even as a dialectic, as anything that resembles a natural process of growth and of movement. We are to think of history rather in the reverse way; we are to understand natural changes from the perspective of history, rather than understand history from the perspective of natural changes. If we want to understand what ripening is, we should understand it from the perspective of historical change.   (C, p. 83)

"To understand this historical pattern would be the burden of any reading of this particular text," de Man notes, perceptively enough (C, p. 83), but even if we grant that *historical* is used rather loosely in the context, it is hard to see how he can derive from his explanation the idea that "the perspective of historical change" is the perspective of "a pure language." Nonetheless, he has to make this connection in order to prove that the writing of history, like critical philosophy and literary theory, is "interlinguistic." (We shall return to the emphasis on *ripening*.)

18. The "additional explanation" would need to elaborate on how the unstable original produces variants—translations—that *canonize* one sense of the work, but how by doing so the variants actually *de-canonize* the "original."

Before stating this position, which he attributes to Benjamin, de Man attempts to show how the text is structured by a paradox. Since "translation" is not a natural process, de Man suggests it is not an imitation or a copy. He points to Benjamin's insistence that the model of its derivation is "not that of resemblance" (C, p. 83). From this de Man concludes that translations are not metaphors. Earlier, he uses *history* to mean "writing history" and collapses *metaphorize* into *metaphor*. Now he adds that "the German word for translation, *übersetzen*, means metaphor. *Übersetzen* translates exactly the Greek *meta-phorein*, to move over, *übersetzen*, to put across. *Übersetzen*, I should say, *translates* metaphor—which, asserts Benjamin, is not at all the same" (ibid.).

The German word for translation is, of course, *Übersetzung*, and we can grant that it bears the traces of the verb's translation from the Greek. But it is one thing to say that the activity of translating is the same as "metaphor" and another to say that translation itself is metaphor. Benjamin does say that the idea of life and afterlife "should be regarded with an entirely unmetaphorical objectivity" (TT, p. 71); but other than this, there is no mention of "metaphor" in his text. Perhaps de Man alludes here to his own redefinition of "second metaphor" or allegory/figure, which for him structures all "literary" texts. Perhaps he is stressing the transformative nature of translation. Even so, he seems to imply that the emphasis on metaphor is proof of Benjamin's focus on the interlinguistic and suggests that the blindness of Benjamin's translators is owing to the amazing paradoxes in the translation essay, which is saying that translation is not translation, metaphor is not metaphor.

In determining what paradoxes structure Benjamin's text, de Man is preparing the ground for the moment when he will suggest that even when Benjamin explicitly mentions "history" or "historical process," he really means that which is "interlinguistic." This kind of reading, I argue, fails to account for the force of Benjamin's growing concern with "writing history" and for the continuity, however jagged, of his development as a theorist.

At the very moment when de Man seems to be recognizing that critical philosophy, literary theory, and history[19] resemble each other in utilizing a critique of representation, he reiterates that these are all "intralinguistic" activities. "They disarticulate, they undo the original, they reveal that the original was always already disarticulated. . . . They reveal that their failure . . . reveals an essential failure, an essential disarticulation" (C, p. 84). De Man suggests that a reading of the original from the perspective of the *reine Sprache*, a language that is "pure form," brings to light the "disarticulated" nature of the text being read. Perhaps he is on the verge of recognizing that it is translation's historicity that permits us to uncover in detail the instability of the original.

Would de Man want, however, to consider the historicity of translation? He has declared that Benjamin's notion of translation "has little to do with the empirical act of translating, as all of us practice it on a daily basis," a statement of a piece with the following one: "Translation, to the extent that it disarticulates the original, to the extent that it is pure language and is *only concerned with language*, gets drawn into . . . the bottomless depth" (C, p. 84; emphasis mine). Nowhere does Benjamin indicate that translation is *identical* with "pure language." Also, to equate the disarticulation of the original and the preoccupation with language is to miss the thread of Benjamin's discourse that subverts what de Man sees as the "interlinguistic" nature of the translator's task. To remove translation from the realm of the mundane and the "empirical" and to place it squarely within language is also to take it away from the world of historical process that Benjamin is so concerned about.

The realm of historical process is figured in the translation essay by the image of *Nachreife*. De Man's discussion of this image brings us to another "blunder" of Benjamin's translators. This one concerns the notion of *Wehen* in the following passage about translation: "Dass gerade unter allen Formen ihr als Eigenstes es zufallt, auf jene Nachreife des fremden

---

19. We can assume here that by *history* he means historiography.

Wortes, auf die Wehen des eigenen zu merken." Zohn translates this as: "Translation . . . of all literary forms . . . is the
one charged with the special mission of watching over the
maturing process of the original language and the birth pangs
of its own" (TT, p. 73). De Man objects to Zohn's translation
of *Nachreife* as "maturing process" and *Wehen* as "birth pangs,"
contending that *Nachreife* belongs to the "afterlife" of the original and not to its "life," because the original is already dead.
Although de Man does not suggest an alternative translation
here (for to do so would be to undermine his own theory that
the text is untranslatable), he does insist that *Nachreife* in Benjamin's text refers to something that happens *after* maturation
has taken place, and is not the maturation process itself.[20]
Actually, what Benjamin seems to be implying in speaking of
an afterlife is "the continued life" of the text rather than a life
to *follow* its death. This idea is echoed in his later conception
of how a past era is a *Jetztzeit* brought into a constellation with
our own, a spark of hope seized from the past.

Having said that *Nachreife* has to come after the life of a
text, de Man adds that *Wehen* can mean suffering in general
and not merely "birth pangs" as Zohn translates it. Bringing
the meanings of the two terms *(Nachreife* and *Wehen)* together,
de Man suggests that, in the context, *Wehen* could also stand
for "death pangs," the stress being "perhaps more on death
than on life" (C, p. 85). Although this marks another extraordinary sleight-of-hand in de Man's essay, it is not clear how
Benjamin's *Nachreife des fremden Wortes* and *die Wehen des eigenen* are one and the same thing. The move is reminiscent of
the substitutions carried out in texts de Man himself has "read"
and analyzed as "blind" to the way in which they achieve
their insights. Here, this move allows de Man to suggest that
if "birth pangs" really refers to "death pangs," the notion of
the possibility of translation could actually refer to its impossibility: "The reasons for this pathos, for this *Wehen*, for this
suffering, are specifically linguistic. They are stated by Benjamin with considerable linguistic structural precision. . . . The

20. Perhaps we can use *after-ripening* or *after-ripeness* to match *afterlife*.

text about translation is itself a translation, and the untrans-latability which it mentions about itself inhabits its own tex-ture. . . . The text is untranslatable, it was untranslatable for the translators who tried to do it, it is untranslatable for the commentators who talk about it, it is an example of what it states, it is a *mise en abyme* in the technical sense, a story within the story of what is its own statement" (C, p. 86).

De Man has finally presented a version of Benjamin's text that most closely resembles his own concern with the figure of allegory and the unreadability of texts it embodies. Alle-gory always presents an allegory of its own reading; and the allegory of reading always says that it is impossible to read. We have seen in the previous chapter how de Man arrives at this position by an emphasis on the intralinguistic nature of texts and the disjunction between "grammar" and "rhetoric." Here, de Man enlists Benjamin's theory of language to sug-gest that translation is purely linguistic.

Claiming that Benjamin puts forward three kinds of dis-junction in language—between the hermeneutic and the po-etic, grammar and meaning, and now symbol and what is being symbolized—de Man goes on to suggest that they in-dicate "a disjunction on the level of tropes between the trope as such and the meaning as a totalizing power of tropological substitutions. There is a similar and equally radical disjunc-tion, between what tropes (which always imply totalization) convey in terms of totalization and what the tropes accom-plish taken by themselves" (C, p. 89).

This, for de Man, is the "main difficulty" of the translation essay. While it is true that Benjamin's tropes are not what they seem to be, it is hard to see how one can extract the statement from Benjamin's text itself. In the relevant passage, Benjamin appears to be saying that "pure language" is what "seeks to represent" as well as to "produce itself" in the evo-lution of languages. In other words, pure language is both symbol and symbolized, and "to turn the symbolizing into the symbolized, to regain pure language fully formed in the linguistic flux, is the tremendous and only capacity of trans-lation" (TT, p. 80). The translation, then, is a particular realization of the general structure of the "original," which can be said to be "pure language," since the "original" is only a translation of the *reine Sprache*. We have come to realize that de Man makes the moves he does in order to show that the text he is reading is "an example of what it states" and a technical *mise en abyme*. The obsession with tropes and totalization runs throughout de Man's writings and to a large extent determines what he will read in most texts.

Not surprisingly, therefore, one of the passages whose translation de Man contests has for its central metaphor an image that might be read as one of "totalization." This metaphor is the "vessel" or "amphora," what Derrida calls the "ammetaphor." De Man claims that Zohn's English translation suggests a totality of fragments brought together, whereas Benjamin seems to insist the final outcome is still broken parts: "All you have to do, to see that, is translate correctly, instead of translating like Zohn" (C, p. 90). The offending translation reads:

> In the same way a translation, instead of resembling the meaning of the original, must lovingly and in detail incorporate the original's mode of signification, thus *making both the original and the translation recognizable as fragments of a greater language, just as fragments are part of a vessel* [um so beide wie Scherben als Bruchstück eines Gefässes, als Bruchstück einer grösseren Sprache erkennbar zu machen].[21]
>
> (TT, p. 78; emphasis mine)

The translation that de Man advocates as the "correct" one is by Carol Jacobs:

> So, instead of making itself similar to the meaning, to the Sinn of the original, the translation must rather, lovingly and in detail, in its own language, form itself according to the manner of meaning [Art des Meinens] of the original, to *make both recognizable as the broken parts of the greater language, just as fragments are the broken parts of a vessel.*
>
> (C, p. 91; emphasis mine)

21. Benjamin, *Gesammelte Schriften*, 4:18.

The contested words in Benjamin are *Bruchstück* (which Jacobs translates as "broken parts," and Zohn leaves out of his translation), and *scherben* (translated by both as "fragments"). I suggest yet another version, which would perhaps avoid the repetitiousness of the Jacobs translation and reinscribe Benjamin's emphatic concern with lack of "wholeness": "to make both recognizable as fragments of the greater language, just as shards are the fragments of a vessel" (my translation).

Zohn's neglect of the crucial word *Bruchstück* (shards, broken parts) and Jacobs's collapsing of *Bruchstück* and *Scherben* deemphasize Benjamin's preoccupation with fragmentation. De Man is right in pointing out that Benjamin is emphasizing what is *fragmented* and not a unified, reconstituted whole, and "least of all is there something like a *reine Sprache*" (C, p. 92). One cannot in de Man's reading reassemble that which is fragmented, because the "broken parts" are themselves always already broken, the amphora is fractured to begin with. Benjamin seems to use the fiction of a pure language toward which all translations move, but the "vessel" of the original either breaks constantly or was never whole in the first place. A "free" translation, therefore, reveals what de Man would call "the instability of the original." This description of translation as a critique of re-presentation is not incompatible with the theory of historiography developed in the writings of the later Benjamin. The "theory" in fact depends on a critique of the striving for *adequatio*. In the essay on translation, however, contrary to what de Man is suggesting, Benjamin does not seem to present the distinction between "symbol" and "symbolized" as crucial, for both are for him manifestations of the pure language. This distinction of Benjamin's indicates, for de Man, "the unreliability of rhetoric as a system of tropes which would be productive of a meaning" (C, p. 91). Reading the passage in this way permits de Man to add that the instability of the original revealed by translation is "the linguistic tension between trope and meaning" (p. 92). This statement describes the instability as "purely linguistic," preempting any suggestion that a critique of origins might be used for purposes other than textual analysis.

Having established the purely linguistic nature of translation in his reading of Benjamin's essay, de Man goes on to make one of the most startling assertions in his piece:

> This errancy of language which never reaches its mark . . . this illusion of a life that is only an afterlife, [is what] Benjamin calls history. As such, history is not human, because it pertains strictly to the order of language; it is not natural, for the same reason; it is not phenomenal, in the sense that no cognition, no knowledge about man, can be derived from a history which as such is purely a linguistic complication.
>
> (C, p. 92)

Now this equation between history and language is not one that Benjamin makes in his essay. While I am not questioning de Man's right to establish such a connection, I am interested in knowing what that claim *excludes*.

It is at this juncture that de Man refers to Benjamin's supposed opposition of poetic language to sacred language, an opposition that for de Man reinforces the claim about history being "purely a linguistic complication." The Benjaminian text "Theologico-Political Fragment," which de Man quotes here, does oppose the sacred to the profane, if not to the poetic: "Nothing that is truly historical can want to relate by its own volition to the messianic. Therefore the kingdom of God is not the *telos* of the dynamics of history, it cannot be posited as its aim; seen historically it is not its aim but its end [Historisch gesehen ist es nicht Ziel, sondern Ende]; therefore the order of the profane cannot be constructed in terms of the idea of the sacred."[22] De Man's problem here is that the English word *aim* can also mean "end," so *end* can mean *Ziel* as well as *Ende*. The translation would then become "seen historically it is not its end but its end" (C, p. 93). This is a substitution Benjamin would not want to make, says de Man, because he wants to keep apart *Ziel* and *Ende*.

22. "Theologico-Political Fragment," in *Reflections*, ed. Demetz, pp. 312–13. Cited hereafter as TpF. The German text is in *Gesammelte Schriften*, 2: 203–4.

The insight should allow de Man to see Benjamin's point: the messianic kingdom is the termination of history; *"therefore theocracy does not have a political but only a religious meaning"* (TpF, p. 312; emphasis mine). Benjamin is arguing here for a secular notion of "history," with the messianic realm posited not as an "aim" but as an "end," as a *figure* for "the idea of happiness." But since de Man has turned "history" into a purely linguistic phenomenon, he has to oppose the *linguistic* to the messianic. The sacred/profane distinction becomes for him a sacred/poetic distinction. Poetic language has a negative knowledge of its relation to sacred language; and this is "a necessarily nihilistic moment that is necessary in any understanding of history" (C, p. 92). So if history is not messianic, it is linguistic; and Benjamin says this, according to de Man, in the "Theologico-Political Fragment." As we shall see shortly, this reading, while referring obliquely to the idea of nihilism in the crucial last sentence of the fragment, ignores Benjamin's conception of "world politics" in the same passage.

Finally, de Man suggests: "Since . . . what is here called political and historical is due to purely linguistic reasons, we can in this passage replace 'political' by 'poetical' in the sense of a poetics. For we now see that the nonmessianic, nonsacred, that is the *political* aspect of history is the result of the *poetical* structure of language" (C, p. 93).[23] Since for de Man theology is replaced by rhetoric in the text of Benjamin, the nonmessianic and nonsacred nature of our condition is equated with the poetical and the linguistic, whereas Benjamin would instead set up the political and the historical on this side of the equation. It is not that de Man is unaware of Benjamin's emphasis. But he alters its significance considerably by saying that the political and the historical are the same as the

23. Curiously enough, de Man suggests on p. 34 of his essay that it is translation that is linguistic—operating within the realm of language—and that it is opposed to poetry. Here he seems to collapse poetry and poetics as well.

poetical and the linguistic—an insight he derives ostensibly from the essay on translation.

Let us look briefly at a couple of other key passages in "Theologico-Political Fragment." "The order of the profane," says Benjamin, "should be erected on the idea of happiness. The relation of this order to the Messianic is one of the essential teachings of the philosophy of history" (p. 312); "nature is Messianic by reason of its eternal and total passing away. To strive after such passing, even for those stages of man that are nature, is the task of world politics, whose method must be called nihilism" (p. 313). It may not be relevant here to discuss nihilism as a political strategy. But there is enough evidence even in this fragment to suggest that Benjamin is working out another version of his theory of "history" and how it should be read. There seems to be no nostalgia here for an edenic and original prelapsarian state; nature's "passing away" is somehow final. By the same token, the messianic, which Benjamin identifies with nature, is merely a figure for the idea of "happiness." The task of "world politics" is to bring about the passing away of nature and to reveal the realm of history. As Benjamin indicates in "The Task of the Translator," the "more encompassing life of history" must help comprehend the "life of nature" (TT, p. 71).

Although de Man's reading of Benjamin suggests that the concern with translation is a version of the concern with history, it cannot account for the connotations *history* assumes in Benjamin's writing. De Man ends up telling a story in which the stuttering of Benjamin's text remains unexplained and "history" becomes just a "linguistic complication." I have shown how de Man makes a series of metaphorical substitutions that allow him to turn history into language and the political into the poetical. The inevitability of the results in de Man's version of post-structuralism may hinder rather than help our attempt to use the critique of representation as a strategy for a practice of translation that is a "transactive reading."

5

Deconstructing Translation and History: Derrida on Benjamin

> The political problem, which seems to me inevitable and
> real, has a very complex strategy. All of its terms must be
> laid out again; one must rethink translation.
>
> —Jacques Derrida,
> *The Ear of the Other*

Elliptical, cryptic, and convoluted as they are, Benjamin's works
are remarkable for the passion with which they engaged in
the intellectual and political struggles of the first half of the
century. His "Theses on the Philosophy of History," written
shortly before his suicide in 1940 while fleeing from Nazi Germany, touch upon and strike sparks off almost all the preoccupations that structure his *oeuvre* (an unlikely word for writings as scattered and fragmentary as Benjamin's).

The reflections on "history" and historiography are especially interesting because they often seem to be displaced and
transfigured versions of Benjamin's early writings on language and translation. In fact, the parallels are so striking that
one wonders why they have remained, by and large, unex-
plored.[1] Yet another puzzle: the post-structuralist emphasis
on *intertextuality* should have ensured at least an internally
interleaved reading of Benjamin's work. Although the fa-

---

1. Benjamin's commentators mention the continuity in his thought, but
seldom pick up on the similarities between his notion of translation and his
"theses" on history. The exceptions are Irving Wohlfarth and Julian Roberts.
See Wohlfarth's insightful articles in *Glyph* and *Diacritics*, especially "On the
Messianic Structure of Walter Benjamin's Last Reflections," *Glyph* 3 (1978):
148–212; and Roberts, *Walter Benjamin* (Atlantic Highlands, N.J.: Humanities
Press, 1983). Even these critics, however, draw the occasional illuminating
parallel but do not present exhaustive comparisons.

mous essay on translation was published in 1923, Benjamin wrote copiously for the next seventeen years, and his thoughts returned obsessively to the same concerns. As Rolf Tiedemann points out, Benjamin kept using the metaphors and images from his earlier writing throughout his life.[2]

In my reading of Paul de Man's essay on Benjamin's "The Task of the Translator," I argued that for de Man the critique of representation informing his notion of allegory implies a turning away from "history." De Man's re-figuring of politics into poetics in the reading of Benjamin suggests a valorizing of the rhetoricity of the text over what I have called its historicity (that which enables the constellation of past and present in the act of reading).

I propose now to examine another post-structuralist version of Benjamin's translation essay, Jacques Derrida's "Des Tours de Babel."[3] My attempt will be once again to make the reading an intertextual one: I shall go back and forth not only over Derrida's essay and Benjamin's but also over the other writings of the two thinkers, showing how the texts on translation carry the traces of different texts within them. My reading traces the "turns" made by Derrida's commentary that deflect it from Benjamin's concern with writing history.

The title of Derrida's essay already evokes the passage from *Of Grammatology* on "the turn" of writing.[4] The translator had noted there that *tour* refers in French to trope as well as to trick, so that the turn of writing was actually to be read as the turning/trope/trick of writing. The translator of "Babel" sug-

2. Tiedemann, "Historical Materialism or Political Messianism? An Interpretation of the Theses 'On the Concept of History,' " *Philosophical Forum* 15, nos. 1–2 (Fall–Winter 1983–84): 71–104. Another writer who is clearly aware of the metaphorical continuity of Benjamin's thought is Terry Eagleton. Eagleton's *Walter Benjamin, or, Towards a Revolutionary Criticism* (London: Verso Editions and NLB, 1981), which contains a perceptive discussion of the theory of allegory and tragic drama, is, however, rather too quick in aligning Benjamin's concerns with those of post-structuralism. I have in mind especially the comments on "writing" on p. 4 and p. 32 of Eagleton's text.

3. Derrida, "Des Tours de Babel," trans. Joseph F. Graham, in *Difference in Translation*, ed. Graham (Ithaca, N.Y.: Cornell University Press, 1985), pp. 165–207. Cited hereafter as Babel.

4. *OG*, p. 216.

gests that the title "can be read in various ways. *Des* means 'some'; but it also means 'of the,' 'from the,' or 'about the.' *Tours* could be towers, twists, tricks, turns, or tropes, as in a 'turn' of phrase. Taken together, *des* and *tours* have the same sound as *detour*, the word for detour." The economy of language here points to a possible strategic economy of translation (Babel, p. 206).

Why does Derrida begin his essay on Benjamin with a detour that is a parable of a *tour*? In homage, I suggest, to a thinker who himself constantly works through detours and secret paths, through translations into parables (like that of the dwarf inside the chess-playing automaton introducing the "Theses on the Philosophy of History") of what Derrida would call "ammetaphors." Also because the story of Babel, an interrupted narrative, is "the translation of a system in deconstruction" (Babel, p. 166). Babel is an ammetaphor, not just one figure among others; it is "the metaphor of metaphor, the narrative of narrative, the translation of translation" (Babel, p. 165). This Judeo-Christian myth, for Derrida, tells "of the inadequation of one tongue to another" and "of the need for figuration, for myth, for tropes, for twists and turns, for translation inadequate to compensate for that which multiplicity denies us" (Babel, p. 165).

The myth of Babel, in short, crystallizes a number of Derrida's preoccupations over the years into what Benjamin would call a "monad." The concern with the myth of *adequatio* and the nostalgia for presence, with an always already deferred and divided origin, with phallogocentrism and the name of the Father, with *différance*—these "themes" of deconstruction come together in the name of this tower that never was. In fact, Babel is the name of *différance*, "the movement by which language, or any code, any system of reference in general, becomes 'historically' constituted as a fabric of differences."[5] *Différance*, with its silent *a*, refers to "differing, *both* as spac-

5. Derrida, "Differance," in *Speech and Phenomena, and Other Essays on Husserl's Theory of Signs*, trans. David B. Allison (Evanston, Ill.: Northwestern University Press, 1973), p. 141.

ing/temporalizing and as the movement that structures every dissociation."[6] It speaks therefore of what Derrida would call the possibility-impossibility of translation. *Différance*, like Babel, "opens up the very space in which onto-theology—philosophy—produces its system and its history."[7]

The gift of tongues, both present and poison (the German *Gift*—Benjamin, or Paul Celan, would agree) is given to men by God. But as he imposes his name, which is that of the Father, he "confounds the lip of all the earth," "breaks the lineage," inaugurates the tower's deconstruction, and simultaneously "imposes and forbids translation" (Babel, p. 170). It is easy to see why this story is, for Derrida, exemplary: "It recounts, among other things, the origin of the confusion of tongues, the irreducible multiplicity of idioms, the necessary and impossible task of translation, its necessity *as* impossibility" (Babel, p. 171). Curiously, Derrida also suggests that in interrupting the Babelian project of universal transparency, God "interrupts also the colonial violence or the linguistic imperialism" of this project. Curious, because in another sense, it would appear as if the interruption *initiated* colonial violence.

The Babelian performance, says Derrida, could serve as an introduction to the problematic of translation. It is a problematic that he would place at the heart of metaphysics; for the notion of the transcendental signified, which is at the "origin" of philosophy, takes shape "within the horizon of an absolutely pure, transparent, and unequivocal translatability."[8] Derrida has often suggested that the program of translation is the passage into philosophy. The notion of translatability in the common sense, "as the transfer of a meaning or truth from one language to another without any essential harm being done," is the "thesis of philosophy," which finds itself defeated when it is unable to "master a word meaning two

---

6. Ibid., p. 129.
7. Ibid., p. 134.
8. Derrida, *Positions*, trans. Alan Bass (Chicago: University of Chicago Press, 1981), p. 20.

things at the same time." Hence the importance of *das Gift* and of the *pharmakon* (both remedy and poison) in Derrida's work of deconstruction.[9] Hence the significance of translation, and the attention paid to Benjamin's writing.

For Benjamin, on the other hand, translation—in a project that seems at first glance to be absolutely essentialist and nostalgic—is to point toward the realm of reconciliation of languages. This realm of reconciliation or redemption later appears in Benjamin's work as the "end" (*Ende*, not *Ziel*) that guides the translations of the materialist historiographer. It has been suggested by Julian Roberts that Benjamin makes a connection between translation and philosophy. Translation is Benjamin's answer to the Romantic notion of *Kritik*, defined by Roberts as a principle that, used for the in-depth contemplation of the art work, could "raise the power" of the work and create "a fuller universe of meanings." Although Benjamin felt that *Kritik* was "an attractive paradigm for intellectual activity," he thought Romantic theory was conceptually weak, whereas translation, which would take the text away from its "origins" and closer to the realm of pure language, retained the strengths of *Kritik* while "converting its conceptuality."[10] Benjamin's theory of language and translation, says Roberts, was meant to be the groundwork for a critique of contemporary philosophy. Perhaps his affinities with the project of deconstruction are even closer than they appear.

Benjamin's philosophical program does not, however, seem to have survived the turmoil of World War I, the October Revolution, and the years before war broke out once more. The theory of translation was eventually re-figured into the theory of "mortification" in the book on baroque allegory, and in the later work into Benjamin's version of historical ma-

9. Derrida, "Roundtable on Translation," in *The Ear of the Other* (New York: Schocken Books, 1985), p. 120. For an extended discussion of the *pharmakon*, see the essay "Plato's Pharmacy," in Derrida, *Dissemination*, trans. Barbara Johnson (Chicago: University of Chicago Press, 1981).

10. Roberts, *Walter Benjamin*, p. 121.

terialism. Benjamin's practice as a translator seems to have led to his practice of radical historiography.

Perhaps it was Benjamin's insight into translation, the awareness that "the Babelian performance" could not be dominated by what Derrida calls "theorization," that led him gradually to change the contours of his projects. It is a similar awareness that prompts Derrida to abandon the "theoretical mode" and "translate in my own way the translation of another text on translation" (Babel, p. 175). Derrida is, of course, using the French translation of Benjamin's essay by Maurice de Gandillac.

Translation after God's interruption of the Babelian project "becomes law, duty and debt, but the debt one can no longer discharge" (Babel, p. 174). Now Derrida translates the first noun of Benjamin's German title, which is *Die Aufgabe der Übersetzers*.[11] *Aufgabe*: the task, "the mission to which one is destined (always by the other), the commitment, the duty, the debt, the responsibility" (Babel, p. 175). To which we can add: problem, question, placing, insertion, handing in (a letter, *Postsendung*, sending or *Sendung* being a problem of representation, as in Derrida's discussion of Heidegger's sequence of epochs, or *Zeitalter*, which are "grouped under the unity of a destiny of Being as fate," *envoi* or *Geschick*).[12] The dictionary does not give Derrida's *debt*. But Derrida is perhaps anticipating. One of Benjamin's most important comments about translation is that it is a *claim*. Similarly, he will say of historical materialism that it records the agreement between a past generation and the present one.

Among the meanings that, according to Derrida, *Aufgabe* connotes are those that stand for restitution. Derrida, whose *The Truth in Painting* includes a major chapter called "Resti-

11. Benjamin, "The Task of the Translator," in *Illuminations*, ed. Hannah Arendt, trans. Harry Zohn (New York: Schocken Books, 1969). The original German essay is in Benjamin's *Gesammelte Schriften*, 4:9–21.

12. Derrida, "Sending: On Representation," trans. Peter and Mary Ann Caws, *Social Research* 49, no. 2 (Summer 1982): 306.

tutions,"[13] suggests that for Benjamin this restitution of meaning is impossible. Insolvency, therefore, is something the translator has to take for granted, and the scene of insolvency in Benjamin, says Derrida, is a genealogical one.[14] The swerve toward the genealogical debt is made possible by Derrida's use of the French translation of Benjamin's essay, which, in English reads: "[of the task of ripening the seed of pure language in translation] it seems impossible ever to acquit oneself" (Babel, p. 177). The German, "scheint niemals losbar," suggests "never soluble" or "insoluble" (as Zohn has it), while the French has "il semble impossible de jamais s'acquitter." By virtue of what Gandillac inserts into the French version—namely, a subject, "oneself"—and on the authority of Benjamin's title, which refers to the "translator," Derrida can speak of the "indebted subject, obligated by a duty, already in the position of heir, entered as survivor in a genealogy, as survivor or agent of sur-vival" (Babel, p. 179). For Derrida, alluding to Benjamin's connection between the translation of a work and its afterlife, the translation essay circulates among life, seed, and survival, since *überleben* (to live on, survive) would seem to be "essentially" related to *übersetzen* (to translate). Derrida does not seem to use the term *genealogy* in the sense that Nietzsche or Foucault would.[15] He refers to the "geneticist metaphor" in Benjamin's essay (the maturation of a "seed") and its support of a "genealogical and parental code" presiding over translation, a notion Benjamin inverts, so that we start from translation in order to understand "what life and family mean." The "turn" toward

13. Derrida, *The Truth in Painting*, trans. Geoff Bennington and Ian McLeod (Chicago: University of Chicago Press, 1987).

14. For Derrida's preoccupation with the family romance and the marriage "contract," see *The Post Card: From Socrates to Freud and Beyond*, trans. Alan Bass (Chicago: University of Chicago Press, 1987).

15. In "Nietzsche, Genealogy, History," in *Language, Counter-Memory, Practice*, ed. Donald Bouchard (Ithaca, N.Y.: Cornell University Press, 1977), Foucault says that genealogy tries to "dispel the chimeras of the origin" (p. 144) so as to comprehend the "play of dominations" and "systems of subjection" (p. 148).

the parent and the family performed by Derrida deemphasizes one of Benjamin's significant obsessions, that which links survival to historiography.

In a landmark essay published in the volume *Deconstruction and Criticism*, Derrida wrote, "A text lives only if it lives *on [sur-vit]*, and it lives *on* only if it is *at once* translatable *and un*translatable."[16] The possible-impossible task is the translator's, and, for the later Benjamin, the critical historiographer's. And because it becomes the task of the historian, the concern with "afterlife" does not seem to be a concern with the "survivor in a genealogy" (Babel, p. 179), as Derrida would have it, but with that of the revolutionary potential of the past. The historical materialist, according to Benjamin, approaches configurations of past and present on recognizing "a revolutionary chance in the fight for the oppressed past." A specific age is "blasted" out of the homogeneous continuum of history so that it can live *on*.[17]

Although he recognizes Benjamin's "metaphoric catastrophe" that inverts the order of genealogy and translation, Derrida turns from the implications of comprehending "the life of history" even as he embeds the passage in his text. For Benjamin, says Derrida, survival "gives more of life" (Babel, pp. 178–79), since we gain access to notions of family and life only through the idea of a language and its living on in translation. In Benjamin's essay we find: "The concept of life is given its due only if everything that has a history of its own, and is not merely the setting for history, is credited with life. In the final analysis, the range of life must be determined by history rather than by nature. . . . The philosopher's task consists in comprehending all of natural life through the more encompassing life of history" (TT, p. 71). Although the Hegelian appearance of this notion of history has been touched upon by Derrida, we cannot disregard the long debates about

16. Derrida, "Living On: Border Lines," in *Deconstruction and Criticism* (London: Routledge & Kegan Paul, 1979), pp. 75–176.

17. Benjamin, "Theses on the Philosophy of History," in *Illuminations*, ed. Arendt, trans. Zohn, pp. 253–64. For convenience, I use Zohn's version of the title. It has also been translated as "On the Concept of History."

the relationship between nature and history in the writings of the Frankfurt School thinkers, especially Theodor Adorno, who was deeply influenced by Benjamin's proposal for a new historiography.[18] These debates point quite clearly toward a *critique* of Hegelian history.

Let us assume that Derrida refuses to engage with the Benjaminian passage he cites because for him the word *history* carries with it "the theme of a final repression of difference"[19] and can be meaningful "only within a logocentric epoch."[20] Adorno, in a lecture given in 1931, suggested that "[the] adequacy of thinking about Being as totality . . . has decomposed itself"; the concept of history, a bourgeois invention, could no longer provide anything like "truth."[21] In *The Dialectic of Enlightenment*, which Adorno wrote with Max Horkheimer during World War II, the critique of history as "progress" is persuasively outlined. Adorno argued that the idea of history as a regulative concept and "historical reality" were not identical. History-as-progress was unacceptable because of the violence it did to "nature." Present nature, however, was not a founding concept any more than history was; nature itself was historically produced. The concepts of history and nature had a double character that permitted their critical use; the unchanging side of both notions indicated a rationalization of the status quo and human suffering, while the transitory side enabled action for change. The critical theorist had *"to grasp historical being in its most extreme historical determinacy, there where it is most historical, as itself natural being, or . . . to grasp nature there where it appears to harden most profoundly within itself, as historical being."*[22]

---

18. For extensive documentation regarding the Benjamin-Adorno friendship, see Susan Buck-Morss, *The Origin of Negative Dialectics* (New York: Macmillan, 1977).
19. Derrida, "Differance," p. 141.
20. *OG*, p. 4.
21. Quoted in Buck-Morss, *Origin of Negative Dialectics*, p. 46.
22. Adorno, "Die Idee der Naturgeschichte," *Gesammelte Schriften*, 1:354–55; emphasis in original. Quoted in Buck-Morss, *Origin of Negative Dialectics*, p. 55.

Adorno's comment is remarkably evocative of Derrida's analysis, in *Of Grammatology*, of the metaphysical concepts surrounding the notion of "arbitrariness." Derrida mentions how the nature/culture opposition as well as the one between *physis* and *technē* function to "*derive* historicity; and paradoxically, not to recognize the rights of history, production, institutions, etc., except in the form of the arbitrary and in the substance of naturalism."[23]

This is the gesture that, for Derrida, rules philosophy; it is the same gesture that he says informs the concept of history. But history as Hegelian may not be what Benjamin refers to in the sentences where he talks about the philosopher's *Aufgabe* being the comprehension of all life starting from the life of history. In the same passage, he goes on to mention the *afterlife* of art works, and the fact that translation is more than mere "transmission" of content. The ideas of *überleben* (as afterlife) and *übersetzen* (as *Übertragung*, or displacement), I argue, undermine the Hegelianism or totalizing force of the mention of history. Unmetaphorically *(in völlig unmetaphorischer Sachlichkeit)*, history "follows" nature, and translation, which comes from the afterlife or sur-vival of a work, displaces the work into the realm of history, revealing therefore its instability at the "origin." The meditation on translating provides a basis—although not unproblematically—for a critique of historicism.

Carefully, Benjamin teases out the nature-history problematic in *The Origin of German Tragic Drama,* his book on baroque allegory, which stands midway between the translation essay and the theses on history (as does the Eduard Fuchs essay)[24] in terms of the development of Benjamin's critique of traditional history-writing. The allegorical tragic drama *(Trauerspiel)* of the seventeenth century is distinguished by Benjamin from symbolic classical tragedy: "Whereas in the symbol de-

---

23. *OG*, p. 33.
24. "Eduard Fuchs, Collector and Historian," in *One-Way Street and Other Writings,* trans. E. Jephcott and K. Shorter (London: New Left Books, 1979), pp. 349–86.

struction is idealized and the transfigured face of nature is fleetingly revealed in the light of redemption, in allegory the observer is confronted with the *facies hippocratica* of history as a petrified, primordial landscape." For Benjamin, this mortification of objects and events is "the heart of the allegorical way of seeing"; it is "the baroque, secular explanation of history as the Passion of the world."[25] Unlike tragedy, therefore, *Trauerspiel* is not mythical, religious, and symbolic but historical, secular, and allegorical.

The allegorical image is fragmented, runelike; it "extinguishes" the "false appearance of totality" and appears in the form of "script" or writing.[26] History takes shape as the "ruin," as "irresistible decay." Criticism refers to mortification, to the process of preparatory decay. This decay or transitoriness, at the limits of *Trauerspiel*, is not represented allegorically; it is itself "displayed as allegory. As the allegory of resurrection." Baroque allegory is a "faithless" leaping away from contemplation of decay to "the idea of resurrection."[27] The parallels with the faithless translator and the materialist historian are striking. The allegorist wakes up under the eyes of heaven, in the realm of history. The motif of waking is repeated in the theses on history and in the unfinished *Passagen-Werk*. The new method of writing history would be "the art of experiencing the present as the waking world to which that dream which we call the past in truth relates."[28] The notion that by its translatability the text represents a claim on coming generations is another motif that recurs in Benjamin's work. "The past," he says in "Theses on the Philosophy of History," "carries with it a temporal index by which it is referred to redemption. There is a secret agreement between past generations and the present one. . . . we have been endowed

25. Benjamin, *The Origin of German Tragic Drama*, trans. John Osborne (London: New Left Books, 1977), p. 166.

26. Ibid., p. 176.

27. Ibid., p. 232.

28. Benjamin, *Passagen-Werk* (K 1, 3), quoted in Susan Buck-Morss, "Benjamin's Passagen-Werk: Redeeming Mass Culture for the Revolution," *New German Critique* 29 (Spring–Summer 1983): 225.

with a *weak* Messianic power, a power to which the past has a claim. That claim cannot be settled cheaply" (TH, p. 254). The claim's historicity would prevent us from seeing it as a "strange debt" that "does not bind anyone to anyone" (Babel, p. 182). The translator or materialist historian is doubly committed: to the dead in the oppressed past and to the revolutionary class with whom s/he is allied. Even the dead, said Benjamin, would not be safe from the "victors," who have not stopped being victorious, since their interpretation of history goes unchallenged. It is hard not to see in this sentiment the plight of a hunted minority in the age of fascism. To take this fact of Benjamin's text into account is to read in the translation essay and the notion of translatability a prefiguring of the claim on humankind that the historical materialist recognizes.[29]

Recognizing and representing the claim does not, however, involve the repetition of an "original" text. Translation is concerned with the mode or form of signification that it must reproduce. There is no "sense" of the original work to which the translator is bound; s/he need not *communicate* anything. As Derrida points out, even in the earliest essays, Benjamin was formulating a critique of the "bourgeois conception" of language in suggesting that what language communicates is not any content but its own communicability. In a perceptive essay on Benjamin's theory of language, Rodolphe Gasche suggests that translatability is "that structure that points away from its still natural linguistic unity and weblike quality, toward language itself," or toward the totality of language in all its purity, *die reine Sprache*.[30] The differ-

---

29. I hesitate to use the term *Marxist* here, because Benjamin himself avoids it, perhaps to distance his practice of writing history from the totalizing narrative of a more orthodox Marxism. Note also that he uses the terms *historical materialist* and *materialist historian* interchangeably. H. D. Kittsteiner argues that whereas Marx can properly be called a historical materialist, Benjamin ought to be described as a materialist historian. See Kittsteiner, "Walter Benjamin's Historicism," *New German Critique* 39 (Fall 1986): 179–215.

30. Gasche, "Saturnine Vision and the Question of Difference: Reflections on Walter Benjamin's Theory of Language," *Studies in Twentieth Century Literature* 11, no. 1 (Fall 1986): 69–90.

ence made by translatability, says Gasche, is determined by the intention toward the work's afterlife, toward "what is thoroughly on the other side of natural life and its connections."[31] The connection Gasche fails to make here is not neglected by Benjamin, who quite clearly indicates that what is "beyond" nature is the life of history. Translation, or critical historiography, shows up the arbitrariness and "constructed" nature of what is presented as natural.

Translation for Benjamin is "neither reception, nor communication, nor representation," as Derrida so pithily formulates it (Babel, p. 180). The absence of the addressee and its implications for a critique of representation are discussed in Derrida's "Signature Event Context,"[32] an essay whose pretext is Etienne Bonnot de Condillac's *Essay on the Origin of Human Knowledge* (1746). Condillac, according to Derrida, imagines writing to be born out of a desire to communicate with *absent* persons; and the idea of absence indicates to Derrida a breach or break in the totalizing history. Writing, however, will represent or "supplement" the true language of action. The notion of representation therefore cannot be dissociated from that of communication.

Since "[one] writes to communicate something to those who are absent," writing is always already structured by absence, although Condillac does not examine this (Signature, p. 313).[33] The notion of absence would displace the thinking of writing so that it would cease to be a kind of communication. It would, therefore, cease to come under those concepts of meaning, sign, and idea that preserve the authority of logocentrism. When Benjamin declares that "any translation which intends to perform a transmitting function cannot transmit anything but information—hence, something inessential," he deemphasizes communication and outlines a critique of representation (TT, p. 69).

31. Ibid., p. 78.
32. In Derrida, *Margins of Philosophy*, trans. Alan Bass (Chicago: University of Chicago Press, 1982), pp. 307–30. Cited hereafter as Signature.
33. In *Post Card*, Derrida speculates on *Sendung* and representation in a series of *envois* written to an absent addressee.

The *différance* (delay and distance) that structures writing suggests that it no longer re-presents a presence. For writing to function as writing, though, it must be *iterable*. Even if addressees do not exist, writing must continue to be legible, or repeatable (Signature, p. 315). Legibility is also a major concern of Benjamin's: "The translatability of linguistic creations ought to be considered even if men should prove unable to translate them," for to speak of an "unforgettable" moment even when everyone had forgotten it would be, not to utter a falsehood, but to refer to a *claim* unfulfilled (TT, p. 70). Similarly, the materialist historiographer in Benjamin's later work breaks with a "historicist view of the past" by recognizing the translatability or historicity of past moments that are iterable and can, therefore, be brought to legibility.

Writing, once it is separated from the notion of communicating presence or consciousness, is able to disqualify the idea of "context": "A written sign carries with it a force of breaking with its context, that is, the set of presences which organize the moment of its inscription. This force of breaking is not an accidental predicate, but the very structure of the written" (Signature, p. 317). The structure of writing is the structure of the trace or of iterability, and it is to this structure rather than to any semantic richness that Derrida refers when he indicates that meaning cannot be determined out of context, although "no context permits saturation."[34] Benjamin, who saw the allegorical (that is, the historical, as he shows in *The Origin of German Tragic Drama*) as "script" or as writing, spoke of the allegorist as quoting out of context. Likewise, the historical materialist tears epochs away from their contexts, from a reified "historical continuity." In constructing "a specific and unique engagement" with the past, the materialist historian breaks with the set of presences organizing it—with the " 'once-upon-a-time' of historicism"—and "shatters the continuum of history."[35]

---

34. Derrida, "Living On: Border Lines," p. 81.
35. Benjamin, "Eduard Fuchs," p. 352.

The practice of quotation or citation is part of the technique of the radical historian. As Derrida points out, every mark or sign or "writing," whether linguistic or nonlinguistic, "can be *cited*, put between quotation marks." This trait of the sign suggests that it need not be bound to an "original" context capable of saturation. Instead, it can "engender infinitely new contexts" (Signature, p. 320). As Derrida's *Glas* so skillfully demonstrates, words "are citations, already, always."[36] Since translation marks the continued life of the sign, the text, the past, historical understanding is concerned with this afterlife out of which translation comes. Derrida's *citationality* bears a family resemblance to Benjamin's translatability.

Citing or quoting is in turn akin to *literalness* in translation. For, instead of being concerned with reproducing the meaning of the original, a translation must "lovingly and in detail incorporate the original's mode of signification," thus holding back from communicating. Words rather than sentences are the true element of the translator, who must provide "a literal rendering of the syntax." "For if the sentence is the wall before the language of the original, literalness is the arcade" (TT, p. 79). Derrida rightly recognizes this "passage" as being crucial to the *economy* of translation. He suggests that while the wall supports and conceals the original, the arcade supports while letting light through (Babel, p. 188). The image of the arcade brings us close to the great unfinished materialist history of nineteenth-century Paris, the *Passagen-Werk*, the "Paris passages" as Derrida calls them. The priority of word *(Wort)* over sentence *(Satz)* marks a displacement from syntagmatic to paradigmatic level. It suggests another version of the attack against the continuity imposed by historicism, and the advocacy of the discontinuous construction of "dialectical images."

The ammetaphor of the amphora structures the passage in "The Task of the Translator" about literalness in translation

---

36. Derrida, *Glas*, trans. John P. Leavey and Richard Rand (Lincoln: University of Nebraska Press, 1986), p. 1.

being able to make both original and translation "recognizable as fragments of a greater language, just as fragments are part of a vessel" (TT, p. 78). My discussion of Paul de Man's reading of Benjamin has tried to show the multiplicity of translators' choices for the German: "um so beide wie Scherben als Bruchstück eines Gefässes, als Bruchstück einer grösseren Sprache erkennbar zu machen." I suggested that the English translator's neglect of the crucial word *Bruchstück* (shards, broken parts) or the collapsing of *Bruchstück* and *Scherben* deemphasizes Benjamin's concern with fragmentation. My argument is that although Benjamin used the fiction of a pure language toward which all translations are aimed, the amphora or vessel of the original work is either shattered continually or was never "whole" to start with. Thus, the task of the translator is to reveal the original's instability. The critique of re-presentation implied here is echoed in Benjamin's theory of historicity, which depends on the critique of *adequatio*, on the shattering of the continuum.

What are the consequences of demolishing the need for reproduction of meaning in translation? The translator has to show how each language is a translation of all the others. Aiming at the totality of language, the translator must make the work "reverberate" in her/his own tongue. But, as Benjamin firmly indicated as early as 1916, translation means a "removal from one language into another through . . . transformations. Translation passes through continua of transformation, not abstract areas of identity and similarity."[37] As Derrida suggests, translation does not restore or reproduce an original, because the original transforms itself. Translation as transformation "will truly be a moment in the growth of the original," and if the original needs supplementation, it is "because at the origin it was not there without fault, full, complete, total, identical to itself" (Babel, p. 188).

---

37. Benjamin, "On Language as Such and on the Language of Man," i *Reflections*, trans. Edmund Jephcott (New York: Harcourt Brace Jovanovicl 1978), p. 325.

The amphora of the original is always already in fragments, and for Benjamin translation shows how the fragments are part of a pure language. What Derrida calls linguistic supplementarity brings languages together in a totality that is not a totality but a "harmony" (Babel, p. 202). In the translation process, the pure language is announced rather than presented. This insight of Derrida's leads us to another one: that pure language is a fiction, a metaphor for the realm of messianic redemption or the messianic end of history in Benjamin's writings. The realm of redemption is also a figure; it functions as an "end" for Benjamin, rather than as a "goal" (*Ende* rather than *Ziel*). Translations are "aimed" at the *reine Sprache* but they will never reach their destination. For the claim of the past (the claim of the work) cannot be settled cheaply, as the historical materialist knows, although "our image of happiness is indissolubly bound up with the image of redemption" (TH, p. 254).

The unforgettable moment that we may speak of even if human beings have forgotten it points to the claim not fulfilled. It refers also to "a realm in which it *is* fulfilled: God's remembrance" (TT, p. 70). Although Derrida would say the notion of divinity is complicitous with metaphysics, this should not blind us to the place of sacred or messianic fictions in Benjamin's text. The idea of *remembrance*, which the "Babel" essay does not explore,[38] plays a significant part in Benjamin's conception of historicity.[39]

In essays on Nikolai Leskov ("The Storyteller"), Proust, Baudelaire, and Eduard Fuchs (the collector as historian), as well as in "Theses on the Philosophy of History," Benjamin returns again and again to the notion of remembrance, which he always links to his theory of experience. The two forms of

---

38. See, however, Derrida's meditation, in a different context, on the function of remembrance, in *Memoires: For Paul de Man*, trans. Cecile Lindsay, Jonathan Culler, and Eduardo Cadava (New York: Columbia University Press, 1986).

39. For a careful analysis of the meanings of "remembrance" in Benjamin, see Wohlfarth, "Messianic Structure."

memory, *Eingedenken* and *Gedächtnis*, both related to storytelling, are associated for Benjamin with the novel and the epic respectively. *Eingedenken* is remembrance, linked with *Erlebnis* or "fallen" experience, demanding an attentiveness to the past; *Gedächtnis* evokes the common memory, and is linked with *Erfahrung*, or the experience that becomes part of the collective. Benjamin thought that both kinds of remembrance were in danger of being forgotten. The historical materialist has to learn to use memory: "To articulate the past historically does not mean to recognize it 'the way it really was' (Ranke). It means to seize hold of a memory as it flashes up at a moment of danger" (TH, p. 255). Remembrance is therefore intimately connected with the critique of historicism. Rather than being concerned merely with what once happened and is now past, the historical materialist focuses on what has happened in "a universe which is *still here, now*."[40] In grasping the constellation of the past and the present, the deconstructive historian relies on the notion of "now-time," of *Jetztzeit*, that "grounds a relation between historiography and politics that is identical to the theological interrelation between remembrance and redemption."[41]

The critical historian is like the allegorist (for example, Baudelaire) who, in conjuring forth images of the past from the debris of modern life, suggests *correspondances*, evokes *Jetztzeiten*. Similarly, the translator "breaks through decayed barriers of his own language" to "liberate the language imprisoned in a work" by recreating it (TT, p. 80). As Richard Wolin has it, Benjamin wants to resurrect "traces of utopian potential" that are in danger of disappearing, so as to provide some hope for a "redeemed" life.[42] That this projected future is what Benjamin seeks in the past is indicated by the image of the angel of history (from Paul Klee's painting *Angelus Novus*) he embeds in the "Theses." He was fond of Schlegel's statement

40. Roberts, *Walter Benjamin*, p. 206.
41. Benjamin, *Gesammelte Schriften*, 1, pt. 2:1248, quoted in Wohlfarth, "Messianic Structure," p. 158.
42. Richard Wolin, *Walter Benjamin: An Aesthetic of Redemption* (New York: Columbia University Press, 1982), p. 215.

that the historian is a prophet facing backwards. For Benjamin, the past is never "over and done with."[43] The angel of history is caught in a violent storm blowing from Paradise: "This storm irresistibly propels him into the future to which his back is turned, while the pile of debris before him grows skyward. This storm is what we call progress" (TH, p. 258). The historical materialist treats the idea of progress with great caution, because every document of "civilization" is at the same time a document of "barbarism." "He regards it as his task to brush history against the grain" to recover the sparks of hope in the oppressed past (TH, pp. 256–63). The materialist historian would construct a "future perfect" tense, for in a sense the future is also that which is past.[44]

The future perfect, however, is not a goal but an end. It seems impossible to ripen "the seed of pure language in a translation." As the quotation from Mallarmé in "Task" suggests, languages are "imperfect" and plural (TT, p. 77). Translation is belated, always comes after the original, is always a supplement. But the "original" lives on only in translation. As Benjamin remarks in his book on baroque allegory, "that which is original is never revealed in the naked and manifest existence of the factual; its rhythm is apparent only to a dual insight. It . . . is related to its history and subsequent development."[45] The life in history and the life in translation both follow the passing away of nature. Benjamin's notion of history involves a penetrating critique of what Derrida would call the metaphysical concept of history, "associated with a linear scheme of the unfolding of presence, where the line relates the final presence to the originary presence according to the straight line or the circle."[46] The histor-

---

43. Benjamin, "Eduard Fuchs," p. 360.

44. Peter Szondi, "Hope in the Past: On Walter Benjamin," *Critical Inquiry* 4, no. 3 (Spring 1978): 491–506.

45. Benjamin, *Origin of German Tragic Drama*, trans. Osborne, pp. 45–46. Interestingly, Benjamin appends these sentences as a footnote to his essay on Eduard Fuchs, which proposes a critique of historicism. See "Eduard Fuchs," p. 352.

46. OG, p. 85.

ical materialist, however, emphasizes discontinuity and disrupts continuums.

The language of a translation, says Benjamin, envelops the content "like a royal robe with ample folds" (which Derrida adds as his own cape to Benjamin's notion of translation). The translation's distance from the original makes the language of translation *unangemessen, gewaltig* and *fremd*—"unsuited to its content, overpowering and alien" (TT, p. 75), or as Derrida (or his translator) has it, inadequate, violent and forced, and foreign (Babel, p. 195). The adjectives seem suited to a notion of *reading* that no longer strives to be adequate to an original presence, that is aware both of its inadequacy and of its necessity. Reading is here the supplement marked by what Benjamin has called the critical and dangerous impulse.[47] It is the allegorist, or historical materialist, who reads images "uncertainly" and makes them "highly significant."[48]

Since my concern has been to weave in and out of those metaphors of translation that Derrida's text either does not address or only addresses in passing, I will not go into his "Babel" meditation on genealogy, family, marriage, contract, signature, and proper name, which is in any case more elaborately worked out in *Glas*. But there is one aspect of the signature that, in its conjunction with the interlinear text that is the model for all translation, must be mentioned here. The signature, says Derrida, is an event that is absolutely singular; at the same time, its structure is that of pure reproducibility. For the signature to be possible, its purity must be impossible. In order to be "legible," the signature must be iterable, repeatable, but it must also be singular (Signature, p. 328). Proper names, like signatures, are untranslatable, Derrida remarks in "Babel." A proper name like Babel can therefore mark the very possibility or impossibility of translation itself. Babel "lays down the law it speaks about, and from abyss to

47. Benjamin, "Theoretics of Knowledge, Theory of Progress," trans. L. Hafrey and R. Sieburth, *Philosophical Forum* 15, nos. 1–2 (Fall–Winter 1983–84): 8.

48. Benjamin, *Origin of German Tragic Drama*, trans. Osborne, p. 225.

abyss it deconstructs the tower, and every turn, twists and turns of every sort, in a rhythm" (Babel, p. 204).

Suggesting that in the "Task" essay there is no translation of translation, Derrida claims that this makes Benjamin repeat the foundation of the "law" regarding translation, which makes copyright and authorship possible. Benjamin's gesture is compared to those of Rousseau and Husserl, who, in Derrida's analysis, are both trapped in the very metaphysics whose critique they think they are undertaking. In Benjamin's case, however, it may not be fair, given the powerful critique of historicism in his later work, to accuse him of a nostalgia for presence. It is at our own risk that we ignore the persistent concern with history and historicity that textures Benjamin's writing.

A project like the deconstruction of Western metaphysics should not turn out to be "an ethnocentrism *thinking itself* as anti-ethnocentrism."[49] The possibilities of post-structuralism need not be cut short "by a gesture neither witting nor unwitting" (Derrida on Rousseau); the interventionist, critical edge of deconstruction need not be blunted by the refusal to read the historicity of texts or the concern with "history" they manifest. Derrida has often spoken of the need to *reinscribe* the notion of history by revealing its discontinuous and heterogeneous nature. In the essay on Benjamin, however, he seems to pay attention only to certain kinds of "claim-subverting" statements (those using the vocabulary of contract and debt) while swerving from the statements that modify Benjamin's essentialist positions in the direction of the later writings on materialist historiography.

The intertwining of the "translation" and "history" problematics is crucial to post-colonials who must find a way of accounting for the force of representations while taking into account the post-structuralist critique of representation in general. Perhaps Derrida himself would commend the strategies appropriate to such an enterprise. After all, already in "Differance" he had emphasized that "the efficacy of this the-

49. Derrida on Lévi-Strauss, *OG*, p. 120.

matics of differance very well may, and even one day must, be sublated . . . lend itself, if not to its own replacement, at least to its involvement in a series of events which in fact it never commanded."[50] Perhaps it is the post-colonial situation that escapes the thematics of *différance*, in spite of or because of its existence "in translation."

In the "Theses," Benjamin quotes Nietzsche on the nature of historicity: "We need history, but not the way a spoiled loafer in the garden of knowledge needs it" (TH, p. 260, quoted from *The Use and Abuse of History*). We have learned from deconstruction how one of the most powerful of all systems of totalization—logocentric metaphysics and its concept of *epistēmē*—can be breached by *writing*. Benjamin's notion of historicity may help us to deconstruct the totality of history that Derrida sees as a founding metaphor of logocentrism. The nonrepresentational theory of translation and the historiography that is no longer concerned with recovering the past as it really was suggest a notion of reading that is not epistemological but political—in the sense of being deliberately interventionist and strategic. It is this kind of reading of Benjamin's own work on translation that can uncover the figure of historicity as a translation (*metapherein* or *Übersetzung*) of translation.

50. Derrida, "Differance," p. 135.

6

Translation as Disruption: Post-Structuralism and the Post-Colonial Context

Historical materialism . . . blasts open the homogeneity of
the epoch. It saturates it with *ecrasite*, that is, the present.
. . . The events surrounding the historian and in which he
takes part will underlie his presentation like a text written
in invisible ink.

—Walter Benjamin,
Passagen-Werk

Looking again into Charles Trevelyan's *On the Education of the
People of India*, from which I took the epigraph that inaugurates my first chapter, I find the colonizing gesture performed
repeatedly by a move that translates as it inscribes history.
Describing the benefit derived by the Indians from the British, Trevelyan presents a bizarre analogy whose paradoxically inverted structure betrays the overdetermination of the
field of translation. Trevelyan's narrative of colonialism suggests that the precursors of India and England (standing in
for Asia and Europe) are Greece and Rome: a cradle of civilization, once glorious and mighty but now fallen and deca-
dent, is conquered by a younger, more vigorous race, which
proceeds to imitate and translate the literature of its subjects
as well as take over the leadership of the world. In its crude
lineaments, this narrative is of a piece with William Jones's
construction of an Indian Golden Age and its subsequent decline. The origin story of the "founding" of the West functions in Trevelyan's text as an analogy for, and therefore as a
justification of the inevitability of, the British conquest of India.

Here Trevelyan runs into a problem. He has to account in his book not just for the British desire to learn Indian languages but for what he sees as the native clamor for "English knowledge." So he inverts the analogy, turning Greeks into Romans and Romans into Greeks. The Indians who demand to be taught English are like the Romans who learned the language of those they had conquered in order to become "modern." The "English book" displayed to the boys from Comercolly by the gentlemen on the boat was, after all, Plato's *Republic*. The "profound speculations" of the Greeks drove out the "doting superstition" of the Etruscans, whose language the Romans used to employ. A similar revolution, argues Trevelyan, is taking place in India (*Education of the People of India*, p. 38). England now takes its place in colonialism's narrative as the mother country, the "place" of civilization.[1] India, through the English language, draws strength from it to be able to turn away from "useless knowledge" and reenter the story of humankind. The colonized are wrenched from "history" in order to be inserted into history-as-progress.

The curious shuffling between "Greeks" and "Romans" reveals an incoherence at the very center of the discourse of improvement. It is an incoherence that marks a simultaneous recognition and disavowal of *difference*, which also makes possible the double inscription of the colonial encounter in a homogenizing universal history—as a version of Greeks-and-Romans, and as a necessary moment in history-as-imperialism. The universalizing move, which is, after all, part of the West's constitution of itself as subject, contributes to erasing the violence of colonialism. Non-Western peoples attain to maturity and subject-hood only after a period of apprenticeship in which they learn European languages and thereby gain a "voice."

Inserting the encounter with the language of the colonizer into universal history permits Trevelyan to imply that a knowledge of this history promotes the widespread use of

1. Trevelyan, *On the Education of the People of India* (London: Longman, Orme, Brown, Green & Longmans, 1838), ch. 2.

English. The order of mimesis presiding over the notion of translation that enables Trevelyan's text helps domesticate the colonized and repress their heterogeneity by dismissing it as "fantastic" and "barbaric." The material for Trevelyan's dismissal comes not just from what he calls his "experience" as an administrator in India but, more important, from the discourse on "the Hindoos"—evoked by such proper names as William Jones, William Ward, and James Mill—which provides a matrix for the "experience" of nineteenth-century colonialists, and allows translation to function as translation-into-history.

As Derrida points out, "History and knowledge, *istoria* and *episteme* have always been determined (and not only etymologically or philosophically) as detours *for the purpose of* the reappropriation of presence" (*OG*, p. 10). *Istoria* and *episteme* claim to "represent," and the idea of translation circulating in Trevelyan's treatise on education proposes representation as adequate to a pre-given "reality," as being transparent in its providing of knowledge. This is a concept of translation that functions as an originary philosopheme, for, according to Derrida, the notion of a transcendental signified takes shape "within the horizon of an absolutely pure, transparent, and unequivocal translatability."[2] Translation, as I have contended, is thus brought into being in the colonial context in a complex field structured by law, violence, and subjectification, as well as by determinate concepts of representation, reality, and knowledge.

To see the overdetermined nature of translation is to complicate our response to the construction of the "Hindoo." Under the sign of Western liberalism, a certain kind of moral indignation has condemned colonial representations as simplistic and demanded "better" representations in their place. This kind of response, although partially aware of the intersections of power/knowledge, can be seen, in its argument for a simple reversal, to be as much a response to a "com-

2. Derrida, *Positions*, trans. Alan Bass (Chicago: University of Chicago Press, 1981), p. 20.

mand" as that of Trevelyan's "natives" asking to be given history.

The call for reversal also informs the discourses of nationalism and nativism that circulate in the colonial and post-colonial situations, and that participate in what Said calls a "politics of blame," a politics of lamentation for a lost precolonial past combined with a denunciation of the colonizers. The nationalist and the nativist, whose class provenance is usually that of the indigenous elite created in part by colonialism, often end up colluding in the denial of history and the occlusion of heterogeneity. In the interests of constructing a unified national identity that will challenge colonial domination, the discourse of nationalism suppresses marginal and non-elite peoples and struggles. Claiming to counteract Western domination, nativism (or its more familiar and frightening face, religious revivalism and fundamentalism) advocates a return to lost origins that completely obscures the violent history of the colonial encounter. Fanon points out that the "passionate search for a national culture which existed before the colonial era finds its legitimate reason in the anxiety shared by native intellectuals to shrink away from that Western culture in which they all risk being swamped."[3] Confronted by European descriptions of a history of decline, degradation, and bestiality, the "native intellectual" attempts to discover a counter-history of a "wonderful past" that will provide the basis for a post-colonial national culture. However, to quote Fanon again, "the attitude of the native intellectual sometimes takes on the aspect of a cult or of a religion,"[4] and the tendency is to forget that the creation of culture in colonized space often involves techniques and languages "borrowed" from the colonizer.[5] The reformist native response, on the other hand, is to accept the story of the fall

3. Fanon, *The Wretched of the Earth*, trans. Constance Farrington (Harmondsworth: Penguin Books, 1967; New York: Grove Press, 1968), p. 168.

4. Ibid., p. 175.

5. Ibid., p. 180.

into barbarism and to put forward programs that will turn the colonized into "civilized" imitators of the colonizers. Both the nationalist and the nativist discourses converge, therefore, in an acceptance of the paradigm of representation provided by the colonizing culture.

They accept thereby the incoherent analogy with Greeks and Romans provided by Trevelyan, whose liberal discourse makes room for a period of learning or apprenticeship as a time of imitation necessary in the history of nations. The Indians will imbibe, along with the English language, models of national culture: "We must . . . give a liberal English education to the middle and upper classes, in order that we may furnish them with both the materials and models for the formation of a national literature."[6]

The post-colonial translator must be wary of essentialist anticolonial narratives; in fact, s/he must attempt to deconstruct them, to show their complicity with the master-narrative of imperialism. This is a crucial task, especially at a time when the myths of nationalism—secularism, tradition, nationhood, citizenship—are invoked to suppress heterogeneity in a decolonizing country like India, for example. The translator must participate in what Fanon spoke of as "a complete calling in question of the colonial situation," and this includes the reexamination of liberal nationalism as well as the nostalgia for lost origins, neither of which provides models of interventionist practice or "grounds" for ideological production that challenges hegemonic interpretations of history.[7] As Homi Bhabha, using the model of literary criticism, maintains, when nationalism takes over "universalist" criticism's "mimetic view of the text's transparent relationship to a pre-constituted reality," it "represses the ideological and discursive construction

6. Trevelyan, *Education of the People of India,* p. 175. We must remember here that the notion of culture itself evolved into a tool for nation-building during the period of European imperialism.
7. Gayatri C. Spivak, "Can the Subaltern Speak?" in *Marxism and the Interpretation of Culture,* ed. Cary Nelson and Lawrence Grossberg (Urbana: University of Illinois Press, 1987), pp. 271–313. Cited hereafter as CSS.

of difference, reducing the problem of representing difference to the demand for different and more favorable representations."[8]

The political and theoretical discussion of nonessentializing representation must, therefore, avoid replicating the moves
of Western imperialism and metaphysics. It might be useful
to remember here Walter Benjamin's remark that "the state
of emergency in which we live is not the exception but the
rule. We must attain to a concept of history that is in keeping
with this insight,"[9] as also Bhabha's suggestion that "the state
of emergency is also always a state of *emergence*."[10] The state
of emergency/emergence that is the post-colonial condition
demands a disruptive concept of history that, by problematizing the striving for *adequatio* in the ways shown by Derrida,
de Man, and Benjamin, will also contribute to formulating a
notion of representation/translation to account for the dis-
crepant identities of the post-colonial "subject."

Analyzing the collusion of *istoria* and *episteme*, I have emphasized the need to examine the political aspects of representation along with the linguistic. We ought to keep in mind
both these notions of representation, as Gayatri Spivak suggests in "Can the Subaltern Speak?" In Marx's *The Eighteenth
Brumaire*, for example, the need to keep the two notions together shows how "both in the economic area (capitalist) and
in the political (world-historical agent), Marx is obliged to
construct models of a divided and dislocated subject whose
parts are not continuous or coherent with each other" (CSS,
p. 276). This is because Marx takes representation to mean,
on the one hand, *Darstellung* or the philosophical concept of
representation as "staging" or "signification," which, "com-
puted as the sign of objectified labor," is related to the production of value, and, on the other hand, *Vertretung*, which
for Marx is representation in the political context (p. 278). Spi-

8. Benita Parry's account of Bhabha's position in "Problems in Current
Theories of Colonial Discourse," *Oxford Literary Review* 9, nos. 1–2 (1987): 46.
9. Benjamin, quoted in Bhabha's foreword to the 1986 English edition of
Fanon's *Black Skin, White Masks*, p. xi.
10. Bhabha, in ibid., p. xi.

vak sees these related notions of representation ("representation or rhetoric as tropology and as persuasion") being run together by certain post-structuralists (her targets are Michel Foucault and Gilles Deleuze) in the interests of "an essentialist, utopian politics" that would require that "oppressed subjects speak, act, and know *for themselves*" in a situation beyond representation (p. 276). Spivak's position is that we cannot afford to overlook the double meaning of representation if we are to account for the "micrological texture" of the geopolitical and economic dimensions of neocolonial domination: "[We] must note how the staging of the world in representation—its scene of writing, its *Darstellung*—dissimulates the choice of and need for 'heroes,' paternal proxies, agents of power—*Vertretung*" (p. 279). Here Spivak sounds a useful cautionary note against a nationalist discourse that arrogates to itself the position of proxy (representative and speaking *for*) after constructing itself as portrait (representative and speaking *as*), erasing thereby the heterogeneity of the post-colonial subject.

But the problem remains. How does one represent difference without privileging the role of the Western intellectual or the post-colonial intellectual? How can we extend the meaning of representation while calling it into question? Meditating on the translation of *repraesentatio* into *Vorstellung, Darstellung*, representation, *representation*, and *Repräsentation*, Derrida points out that before we know "how and what to translate by 'representation,' we must interrogate the concept of translation and of language which is so often dominated by the concept of representation" or a "presupposition or the desire for an invariable identity of sense."[11] Derrida asks if translation is "of the same order as representation," or whether "the so-called relation of translation or of substitution" escapes "the orbit of representation."[12] I have argued throughout the previous chapters, and will demonstrate in the sec-

11. Derrida, "Sending: On Representation," *Social Research* 49, no. 2 (Summer 1982): 302–3.
12. Ibid., pp. 297–98.

ond section of this chapter, that to rethink a practice of translation regulating and regulated by the horizon of metaphysics involves a use of translation that shatters the coherence of the "original" and the "invariable identity of sense." This coherence is constituted in part, as I have shown, through the operation of history and knowledge in the colonial context. To deconstruct these essentializing discourses, therefore, is to disrupt history in the Benjaminian sense. The Derridaean critique of "representation" combines *Darstellung* and *Vertretung* in "translation," not in any simple collapsing of the economic and the political but in a practice in which we constantly interrogate ourselves and our right to speak *as* and/ or speak *for*.

The problematic of translation exists uneasily on the interface between the post-colonial context and post-structuralist theory.[13] For some, this is also a version of the decolonization debate, and to use "Western" theory in deconstructing colonial texts is to reproduce the conditions of neocolonialism. This attitude, which can be seen to be part of a nativist discourse,[14] seems to me to deny history in at least two ways: first, in arguing for a return to a lost purity, it not only employs a discredited realist epistemology but also ignores the pervasiveness of a colonial violence that renders impossible even the positing of a mythical uncontaminated space; second, in denouncing post-structuralism as "Western," the nativist does not realize the extent to which anti-colonial struggles have intervened in changing the trajectory of "Western" thought by demanding a nonexploitative recognition of dif-

---

13. For stimulating explorations of this idea, see Vivek Dhareshwar, "The Predicament of Theory," in *Theory between the Disciplines,* edited by Martin Kreiswirth and Mark A. Cheetham (Ann Arbor: University of Michigan Press, 1990), pp. 231–50; Susie Tharu, "Tracing Savitri's Pedigree," in *Recasting Women,* edited by Kumkum Sangari and Sudesh Vaid (New Delhi: Kali for Women, 1989), pp. 254–68; and Kumkum Sangari, "The Politics of the Possible," *Cultural Critique,* no. 7 (Fall 1987): 157–86.

14. The suspicion of post-structuralist theory also marks the responses of sections of the non-nativist "left" which do not want to give up their versions of the history-as-progress narrative.

ference.[15] To accept the need for "theory" in the post-colonial setting is not to accept uncritically the totalizing narrative of global capitalism but to make the best use we can of the tools available for deconstructing that narrative and showing the infinitely varied inflections of the post-colonial condition. As I argued in chapter 3, the Western subject is constituted not only through a repression of the non-Western other but also through a marginalization of its own otherness. Post-structuralism's attempt, therefore, to dismantle the hegemonic West from *within* is congruent with post-colonial praxis.

Literary theory contributes to that praxis through its focus on the rhetoric of representation. In "The Resistance to Theory," Paul de Man emphasizes that "what we call ideology is precisely the confusion of linguistic with natural reality, of reference with phenomenalism. It follows that, more than any other mode of inquiry, including economics, the linguistics of literariness is a powerful and indispensable tool in the unmasking of ideological aberrations, as well as a determining factor in accounting for their occurrence."[16] De Man's meticulous unraveling of literary and philosophical texts, and his serious engagement with questions of ideology, representation, and history, provide to the post-colonial intellectual, even when s/he may not agree with de Man's conclusions, an important reminder of the salience of rhetorical structures in hegemonic discourses.

Walter Benjamin writes: "An image is that in which the past and the present moment flash into a constellation. . . . The image that is read, I mean the image at the moment of recognition, bears to the highest degree the stamp of *the crit-*

15. Vincent Descombes, *Modern French Philosophy*, translated by L. Scott-Fox and J. M. Harding (Cambridge: Cambridge University Press, 1980), p. 137. Descombes suggests that the 1960s talk in France about the end of philosophy indicated a "philosophical examination of conscience" that was "contemporaneous with the disappearance of the European colonial empires (1962, the end of the Algerian war)."

16. De Man, "The Resistance to Theory," in *The Resistance to Theory* (Minneapolis: University of Minnesota Press, 1986), p. 11.

ical, dangerous impulse that lies at the source of all reading."[17]
Reading, because it is interventionist, is both critical and dangerous. Taking a cue from Derrida, I have argued that postcolonial interpretations or readings "will not be readings of a hermeneutic or exegetic sort, but rather political interventions in the political rewriting of the text and its destination."[18] I have shown in previous chapters how Benjamin troped his theory of translation into a theory of writing history; the deferred epistemological desire of translation, the attempt to reach a realm of "pure" language, was re-figured as the need for political intervention, in the realm of world history. Reading, then, is a model for the historian as well as for the translator who chooses to read certain past "texts" over others. The choices of the translator/historian, I have suggested, are prompted by the *historicity* of these texts: they are constellations or conjunctures of past and present, they lay claim to us, as Benjamin would put it. They may also be especially emblematic of technologies of colonial power.

The post-colonial desire to *re-translate* is linked to the desire to *re-write history*. Re-writing is based on an act of reading, for translation in the post-colonial context involves what Benjamin would call "citation" and not an "absolute forgetting." Hence there is no simple rupture with the past but a radical rewriting of it. To read existing translations against the grain is also to read colonial historiography from a post-colonial perspective, and a critic alert to the ruses of colonial discourse can help uncover what Walter Benjamin calls "the second tradition," the history of resistance.[19] This act of *remembering*, as

17. Benjamin, "Theoretics of Knowledge, Theory of Progress," trans. L. Hafrey and R. Sieburth, *Philosophical Forum* 15, nos. 1–2 (Fall–Winter 1983–84): 1–40; emphasis added.
18. Derrida, "Otobiographies," in *The Ear of the Other*, trans. Peggy Kamuf (New York: Schocken Books, 1985), p. 32.
19. See, e.g., Ranajit Guha's "The Prose of Counter-Insurgency," in *Subaltern Studies II: Writings on South Asian History and Society* (New Delhi: Oxford University Press, 1983), which demonstrates brilliantly how a post-colonial historiographer can construct a tale of resistance through a new reading of texts by British officials engaged in suppressing uprisings by Santal tribals in northeastern India in the early part of the nineteenth century.

Bhabha has pointed out, "is never a quiet act of introspection or retrospection." Rather, it is "a painful re-membering, a putting together of the dismembered past to make sense of the trauma of the present."[20] This is not to say that the past can, simply, be made whole again. As Benjamin suggests in his ammetaphor of the amphora, the fragments that are pieced together in translation were fragments to begin with. Deconstructive practice shows us that we need, as Spivak indicates, "provisional and intractable starting points in any investigative effort."[21] It insists that "in disclosing complicities the critic-as-subject is herself complicit with the object of her critique," and also acknowledges "that its own discourse can never be adequate to its example."[22] The use of post-structuralism in the decolonizing world, although fraught with the anxieties and desires of representation, brings to legibility areas of contradiction, difference, and resistance.

Just as Benjamin's awareness that the Babelian performance could not, perhaps, be dominated by what Derrida calls "theorization" appears to motivate his troping of translation into historiography, I turn from theorizing to a translation of translations. To be able to reject the signifying systems of imperialism, we need "a cartography of imperialist ideology more extensive than its address in the colonialist space."[23] I turn, therefore, to an analysis of two post-colonial translations that, in very different but related ways, participate in the production of the Orient. I initiate here a practice of translation that is speculative, provisional, and interventionist.

I shall provide here the "original" in transliteration, and three translations, the last one being my own. The exemplary poem or *"vacana"*[24] is a fragment from a lengthy spiritual text "produced" in South India in the twelfth century but codified only in the fifteenth century. One of the reasons I choose a

20. Bhabha, foreword to Fanon's *Black Skin, White Masks*, p. xxiii.
21. Spivak, translator's foreword to "Draupadi," by Mahasweta Devi, in *In Other Worlds: Essays in Cultural Politics* (London: Methuen, 1987), p. 180.
22. Ibid.
23. Parry, "Problems in Current Theories of Colonial Discourse," p. 45.
24. Pronounced *vachana*.

"sacred" poem to re-translate is to emphasize that what Benjamin would call a "profane" reading is of great significance in a context dominated by nationalist and nativist discourses that, in seemingly opposed but related ways, essentialize religions and thereby endorse communal violence. As Benjamin puts it, "In every era the attempt must be made anew to wrest tradition away from a conformism that is about to overpower it" (TH, p. 255).

TRANSLITERATION

> nimma tējava nōḍalendu heresāri nōḍuttiralu
> śatakōti sūryaru mūḍidantirdudayyā!
> miñcina baḷḷiya sañcava kaṇḍe;
> enagidu sōjigavāyittu!
> Guhēśvarā, nīnu jyōtirliṅgavādare
> upamisi nōḍaballavarillayyā.[25]

TRANSLATION A

> As I stepped back and looked
> To see Thy light,
> It seemed a hundred million suns
> Came into sight;
> A cluster of creeping lightnings I
> With wonder saw.
> O Guhēśvara, if Thou become
> The effulgent Linga, there be none
> Thy glory to match![26]

TRANSLATION B

> Looking for your light,
> I went out:
>
> it was like the sudden dawn
> of a million million suns,
> a ganglion of lightnings
> for my wonder.
>
> O Lord of Caves,
> if you are light
> there can be no metaphor.[27]

---

25. From the *Śūnyasampādane*, ed. and trans. S. C. Nandimath, L. M. A. Menezes, and R. C. Hiremath (Dharwar: Karnatak University, 1965), 1:240. Reprinted by kind permission of Karnatak University.
26. Ibid., 1:240–41.
27. From *Speaking of Śiva*, trans. A. K. Ramanujan (Harmondsworth: Penguin Books, 1973), p. 168.

TRANSLATION C

Drawing back
to look at your radiance
I saw
the dawning of a hundred million suns.

I gazed in wonder
at the lightning's creepers playing.
Guhēśvara, if you are become the *liṅga* of light
Who can find your figuration.[28]

A brief introduction to the proper name that is usually des-
ignated as the author of this text: Allama Prabhu was a twelfth-
century saint born in Balligāvé (in present-day Karnataka State),
a small village in one of the kingdoms of South India. Allama
was one of the "founders" of what became (and still is) a
powerful sect devoted to the worship of the god Śiva. Vīraśaivism launched an attack on the Vedic tradition of orthodox
Hinduism, demanding the abolition of caste and gender distinctions in the access to worship. Its saint-poets disregarded
Sanskrit, the traditional religious language of Hinduism, in
favor of the local language, Kannada. In addition, the *vacana*-
poets used for the first time the local "nonstandard" dialects
of the areas they came from, whereas others poets of the time
employed "a highly stylized archaic language."[29] For more
than two hundred years, the *vacanas* circulated as part of a
strong oral literature, until the Vijayanagar Empire revived
Vīraśaivism in the fifteenth century and underwrote the codification of its sacred texts. So the text comes to us (even in
Kannada) always already disarticulated, en-coded.

The Vīraśaiva movement, commonly known in Karnataka
as the *vacana* movement, has been examined primarily by students of religion or of literature. Very little material exists on
the sociocultural history of the period, and even that which
is available is a welter of contradictory assertions.[30] What ap-

---

28. My translation.
29. Ramanujan, introduction to *Speaking of Śiva*, p. 46.
30. By far the most thought-provoking Kannada book on *vacana* poetry is
Basavaraja Kalgudi's *Madhyakaaleena Bhakti matthu Anubhaava Saahitya haagoo
Charitrika Prajne* (Bangalore: Kannada Sahitya Parishat, 1988). See also M.

pears certain, however, is that the Vīraśaivas or Lingayats came from different castes and occupations, and successfully challenged both priest and king, or temple and palace—the traditional centers of power. Although the influence of Jainism, Buddhism, and Islam on the Vīraśaiva movement has been remarked upon, some writers see the Vīraśaiva movement as resulting in a reformed Brahminism strengthened by the adherence of different castes.[31] The *bhakti* movement (to give it its pan-Indian name) in general is seen by some historians as not really anti-Vedic, and ultimately as performing the function of incorporating the non-Brahmin, non-Aryan population into the Vedic hierarchy.[32] However, a re-translation of the *vacanas* can show, for example, that *bhakti*, or Vīraśaivism, was neither monolithic nor homogeneous.

Given the lack of material on medieval Karnataka, we can only ask a series of questions: Why is it that the *vacana* movement did not come into being until the twelfth century in spite of Śaivism being a strong religious current for four centuries before? Did the movement present a radical challenge to the established religious and economic order, or did it actually strengthen feudalism and the Vedic tradition? What was the significance of the participation of people from different castes? How did this undermine existing notions of caste bound-

---

Chidananda Murthy, *Vacana Saahitya* (Bangalore: Bangalore University Press, 1975).

31. See Romila Thapar, *A History of India* (Harmondsworth: Penguin Books, 1966), 1:216, for the influences on Vīraśaivism, and Louis Dumont, *Homo Hierarchicus: The Caste System and Its Implications*, trans. Mark Sainsbury, Louis Dumont, and Basia Gulati (Chicago: University of Chicago Press, 1980), p. 190, for the notion of Brahminism being strengthened by a movement like that of the Vīraśaivas. The problem with Dumont's theory is that it seems to rest on the same kind of essentialized and unchanging Hinduism and Brahminism that we find depicted in Orientalist texts.

32. M. G. S. Narayanan and Veluthat Kesavan, "Bhakti Movement in South India," in *Indian Movements: Some Aspects of Dissent, Protest and Reform*, ed. S. C. Malik (Simla: Institute for Advanced Study, 1978), pp. 45, 53. I am grateful to Gauri Dharampal for pointing out that the images of light, the void, and the cave, which are crucial to an understanding of Vīraśaiva poetry, are typical images in Vedic texts as well.

aries? Why was the notion of ritual purity and impurity abandoned by the Vīraśaivas? Did a great number of women really take part in religious discourse, or was it just a highly visible minority? What is the relationship between the Vīraśaiva movement and social transformation in the twelfth century? What does the Lingayat consolidation of caste and socioeconomic power in later centuries tell us about the Vīraśaiva tradition's impulses? How do questions like these inform our contemporary translations of the *vacanas*? My inability to provide even provisional answers forces me to devise other strategies of interpretation. These strategies, however, are marked profoundly by the questions I have just raised.

The parameters of my reading/translation of Allama's text are provided, on the one hand, by the consistent and disarticulated imagery of Śaivite mystic poetry and, on the other, by my "theorization" about translation in the post-colonial context. That is to say, on the one hand by the notion of *figure* in Śaivite poetry, which undoes the insistence on *linga*, meaning, and representation; and on the other hand, by a consideration of the afterlife, the *living on* of a text, and the task of the translator.

In his attempt to assimilate the religious experience into everyday life, in his concern with propagating the new path to salvation, Allama emerges in this fragment and others as a poet deeply interested in issues of articulation and representation. The fragment comes from the *Śūnyasampādane* (achievement/ attainment of nothingness). A work written around Allama's life, the *Śūnyasampādane* incorporates Allama's *vacanas* as well as those composed by the other Vīraśaiva saints, and is presented as Allama's dialogue with those saints. It was first compiled by Sivagana Prasādi Mahadēvayya in the early decades of the fifteenth century, and included 1,012 *vacanas*. The edition in use today is based on the fourth compilation, made by Gūlūra Siddhavīranārya, including 1,543 *vacanas*.[33]

33. For more information about the different editions, see the translators' preface to the *Śūnyasampādane*, ed. and trans. Nandimath, Menezes, and Hiremath, 1:xi.

The fragment we read belongs to Allama's "spiritual autobiography." It is part of a dialogue with a saint-to-be in which
Allama tries to convey a sense of the "ultimate" experience,
the experience of the "void," or *śūnya*. The eye of the god
(Śiva) has opened up the eye of fire in the sole of Allama's
foot, and Allama sings the praises of this eye, calling it "radiance," "lightning," "a hundred million suns."

If we are to have a privileged "figure" for this text, it is the
liṅga, which in fact offers itself as "originary" figure for the
entire corpus of Śaivite poetry. The *liṅga* is / is not Śiva or
god; it is a form for formlessness, a shape for shapelessness.
It is an attempt to articulate that which cannot be articulated
in the mystic experience, and in the poem-fragment it eventually turns out to be an articulation of a disarticulation.[34]

The thematization of light in Allama's poetry is always
bound up with the possibility of articulation. And images of
light are always connected here to those of sight. In the short
space of six lines, Allama uses *look* or *see* three times; and light
appears five times (radiance, suns, dawning, lightning, the
liṅga). In Allama's spiritual biography there is a description
of his meeting with the saint Animiśa (literally, "one who
does not blink," that is, a god; one who, therefore, *sees* stead-
ily). Animiśa *trans*mits the unutterable experience to Allama's
heart through his eye alone. A single look *trans*forms Allama,
and the *liṅga* on Animisa's palm is *trans*ferred to Allama's.

Allama has now experienced the "void," and is in a state
of *Jīvanmukta* (free from life), which means to live in the world
and be out of it at the same time, like "light in a crystal bowl."
There are a number of light images in this part of the *Śūnyasampādane*: burning charcoal, lighted camphor, lamps, fire,
the refractive crystal. Allama has become form, though formless; he is body, though bodiless. He is *śūnyamūrthi*, void taken
on form, image or figure of the void. *Jaṅgama*, the saint, is

34. Although Western commentators have suggested that the *liṅga* is a
phallic symbol, there is no indication in any of the surviving *vacanas* that this
was the case. Ramanujan explains that the *liṅga* is "the only symbol of Śiva"
and is "to be worn inseparably on his body by the devotee" (introduction to
Speaking of Śiva, p. 32). Female devotees of Śiva wear the *liṅga* too.

himself *liṅga*, proclaims Allama. *Nōdi kūdi saiveragāda / sukha-vanēnendupamisuvenayyā, guhēśvara?* asks Allama. How can I *figure* this joy of looking at and mingling with you? He adds: *Nimma suḷuhina sogasanupamisabāradu!* I should not / ought not to *figure* the splendor of your passing. *Suḷuhu* can mean "motion," "turning," "going," or "passing." It shades off into "glimpse," "transitory perception," and eventually into "trace." I ought not to figure the splendor of your trace. *Suḷuhu* can also mean *sign*.

The traces left by Allama's experience are always already there in the conception of this kind of experience in the *bhakti* or devotional tradition. The failure to find figures is an expected failure of language, a failure of articulation because of the disarticulation at the center of what demands articulation. Allama cannot finally believe that his figures *represent* his experience. "The undoing of the representational and iconic function of figuration by the play of the signifier"[35] is indicated by the *liṅga* (neither signified nor signifier, but that which can move with ease from one position to the other), which makes mockery of all attempts to figure its glory. These attempts are seductive insofar as they lead us to believe we have somehow captured in language the shadows of the cave (Guhēśvara, Allama's god, is lord of the cave). But the movement of Allama's poem is a step beyond "traditional conceptions of figuration as modes of representation," and is therefore a movement toward "the undoing and erasure of the figure."[36] The arrest of articulation (recalling Derrida's speculations on Maurice Blanchot's *L'Arrêt de mort*) is actually a triumph of articulation, for the *jaṅgama* is shown to be the *liṅga*, and death (or Benjamin's *mortification*) or attainment of the void is seen as survival or a living on.

Let us return to the different translations of Allama's poem, keeping in mind Derrida's comment that any translation contaminates the text with meanings, which it imports in turn

---

35. Paul de Man, "Shelley Disfigured," in *Deconstruction and Criticism*, edited by Harold Bloom et al. (New York: Seabury Press, 1979), p. 61.
36. Ibid.

and which rework the text. As he suggests, a text in translation trails more than one language behind it.[37] Because the
poem has what Benjamin calls translatability, because it is not
untranslatable, although it presses for constant deformation
and disfiguration, there is an economy of translation—which
does not exclude the political—that regulates the flow of medieval Kannada into modern English.[38]

My contention is that Translations A and B fail to comprehend the economy of translation in this poem because they
fail to understand "the specific significance inherent in the
original which manifests itself in its translatability."[39] Attempting to assimilate Śaivite poetry to the discourses of
Christianity or of a post-Romantic New Criticism, these translators reproduce some of the nineteenth-century native responses to colonialism. Accepting the premises of a universalist history, they try to show how the *vacanas* are always
already Christian, or "modernist," and therefore worthy of
the West's attention. Their enterprise is supported by the
asymmetry between English and Kannada created and en-
forced by colonial and neocolonial discourse. This is an asymmetry that allows translators to simplify the text in a predict-
able direction, toward English and the Judeo-Christian tradition
and away from the multiplicity of indigenous languages and
religions, which have to be homogenized before they can be
translated.

The first Western-style dictionary of Kannada was prepared in 1817 by William Carey, the polyglot colleague of William Ward and one of the most prolific of the Serampore missionaries.[40] The first translators of the *vacanas* were Christian

37. Derrida, "Living On: Border Lines," in *Deconstruction and Criticism,*
edited by Harold Bloom et al. (New York: Seabury Press, 1979), p. 76.
38. Medieval Kannada is comprehensible to a speaker of modern Kannada. A discussion of this, and of how the punctuation, syntax, and vocabulary of present-day Kannada have been affected by English, is beyond the
scope of this chapter.
39. Walter Benjamin, "The Task of the Translator," in *Illuminations,* trans.
Harry Zohn, ed. Hannah Arendt (New York: Schocken Books, 1969), p. 71.
40. Carey, *A Grammar of the Karnata Language* (Serampore: Mission Press,
1817).

missionaries in the 1860s,[41] attracted to Śaivite poetry, according to Ramanujan, by its "monotheism," which "lashes out in an atmosphere of animism and polytheism."[42] This is, by the way, the same paradigm that allows James Mill to differentiate Islam, which he calls monotheistic, from the barbaric polytheism of Hinduism. The missionaries are said to have made sarcastic references to the failure of the Vīraśaiva saints' prophecies that they would return from the "west," for *they,* the Christians, had arrived instead. Even according to the terms of the Śaivites' own texts, they argued, the Christians represented a more evolved religion. We see here one of the typical moves of a colonial discourse that translates indigenous religious texts, castigates the natives for not being faithful to the tenets of their (translated) religion, then claims that the native religion is incapable of sustaining its devotees, and proposes "conversion" as a path to salvation. The missionaries even speculated that *"bhakti* attitudes were the result of early Christian influence,"[43] another move that seamlessly accommodates the idea of a former Golden Age and the present fallen, degraded state of the "Hindoos."

Both European and Indian commentators persist in discussing Vīraśaivism in terms of Puritanism and Protestantism, suggesting that the poems of the Vīraśaiva saints are part of a Pilgrim's Progress. Speaking of the fact that the Vīraśaiva saints came from all classes, castes, and trades, Ramanujan adds in parenthesis "like Bunyan, the tinker."[44] Ramanujan's version of the *vacanas* emphasizes that they are "deeply personal" poems, that they use the language of "personal conversation," that they embody the conflicts of "real persons." There is a corresponding stress on the similarities between Vīraśaivism and European Protestantism: the privileging of "individual," "original," and "direct" experience; "monothe-

41. I have not been able to locate these early translations of the *vacanas.* It would be interesting to speculate what direct or indirect influence they might have had on the diction of Translation A.
42. Ramanujan, introduction to *Speaking of Śiva,* p. 27.
43. Ibid., p. 27 n. 4.
44. Ibid., p. 54.

ism" and "evangelism"; and distrust of "mediators" like priests.[45] This combination of emphases allows Ramanujan to produce a post-Romantic translation of Allama's *vacana* that presents it as a "quest for the unmediated vision,"[46] a project deconstructed so skillfully in Paul de Man's "The Rhetoric of Temporality." This reading of Ramanujan's, I argue, cannot account for the instability of the "original."

Translations A and B both translate *tēja*, the first significant noun in the *vacana*, as "light." I translate the word as "radiance," because the poem is a movement *toward* the ostensible simplicity of light: Allama goes from "radiance" to "hundred million suns" and "lightning" before he approaches *jyōtis* or "light" in the fifth line. The word *effulgent* in Translation A is superfluous for this reason. We cannot, however, gloss over the fact that *jyōtis* is a Sanskrit word embedded in the Kannada poem, and that *jyōtirliṅga* refers to a special kind of *liṅga*, functioning therefore as a figure of condensation. Translation B has "light" for both *tēja* and *jyōtis*, since Ramanujan claims that Allama begins with a traditional metaphor of light and denies it at the end of the *vacana*. In the first place, the "original" does not suggest any such denial of light. Secondly, it seems to be in Ramanujan's interests to confer on the *vacana* a circularity of movement, or rather to suggest that the Śaivite poets tell cyclical stories like those narrated by Ramanujan himself when he writes of protest against the "establishment" followed by its ultimate institutionalization, which is in turn followed by a new protest. This kind of narrative appears to have for its premise a metaphysical concept of history, associated, as Derrida points out, "with a linear scheme of the unfolding of presence, where the line relates the final presence to the originary presence according to the straight line or the circle."[47] The concept of representation underwriting this notion of history participates, as I have argued, in colonial practices of subjectification.

45. Ibid., pp. 53–55.
46. Ibid., p. 52.
47. *OG*, p. 85.

Heresāri in the first line is translated as "stepped back" by A, and as "went out" by B. The dictionaries do not list the meaning provided by B, but add "drew back" or "drawing back" to "stepped back." I use "drawing back" since it seems to indicate more clearly the context where Allama looks at the eye on the sole of his foot. Why does B use "went out," almost completely contradicting the sense of *heresāri?* One possibility is that B mistakes *here* (back) for *hora* (outside).[48] Or else the translator is playing a variation on the theme of the linear "unfolding of presence," suggesting that it is only by a "going out" that Allama can see the figurative suns and lightning; in fact, the poet is made to go out "looking for your light." The notion of "drawing back" *in order to see* goes so much against his sense of what the poem means that he refuses to grant to the poem what it is saying.

Balli refers to "creeper," as in flowering vine, so the "cluster" in A is superfluous and the "ganglion" in B improbable. *Miñcina* qualifies *balli,* and is adjectival, referring to the lightning. A key word that both A and B leave out of their translations here is *sancu* (as in *miñcina balliya sancu:* the lightning's creeper's play), "flash" or "play." The play of signifiers sets in motion all the images of light in the *vacana,* and B responds by removing the verbs *gazed* and *playing* from the English version, setting in their place the word *ganglion,* taking the "play" from the realm of meaning and placing it firmly within the nervous system of the individual body.

Guhēśvara is the name of Allama's god, and remains untranslated in A as well as in C. It is a name that recurs in every *vacana* that Allama wrote, and force of repetition allows it to function as a unique proper name that is not obscured by simple translation. Given that colonialism's violence erases or distorts beyond recognition (as witnessed in innumerable colonial texts) the *names* of the colonized, it seems important *not* to translate proper names in a post-colonial or decolonizing practice. Ramanujan's rationale for translating Guhēśvara is

48. One of the Kannada versions available has *herasāri* for *heresāri;* this could be one source of the confusion.

oddly significant. He argues that since the god's names are "partly Sanskrit" (interestingly, both *Guhē* and *eśvara* would be of Sanskrit origin), and since "the transparent Kannada" ensures that the Sanskrit is "never opaque or distant for long," the etymologies quicken in the poem and demand the translation of "attributive proper names into literal English."[49] In attempting to smooth over the heterogeneous text, Ramanujan assigns to Kannada, and by implication to English, the ability to make and be "transparent."

I have already suggested that Translation A's use of an adjective in place of a noun, *effulgent* instead of *light*, does not work within the economy of the poem. B's version—"if you are light"—ignores the conception of *liṅga*, which is not only crucial to this *vacana* but also to the entire Vīraśaiva tradition. Ramanujan's refusal to translate or inscribe the *liṅga* is, therefore, a refusal to interrogate the most significant image in Allama's text. My version translates *jyōtis* as "light" and retains *liṅga* to complicate the notion of light as signification, since *liṅga* may be said to function in the *vacana* as the figure of dissemination that authorizes the use of "figuration" in the last line.

Translation B's trick of making verbs disappear is matched by its habit of constantly reducing and simplifying them. In the penultimate line, for example, *ādare* ("if . . . are," in the sense of "to be," and also "if . . . to become") is turned into "are," and in the last line, *nōdaballa* ("find," "to be capable of") is translated simply as "be." Translation A, on the other hand, retains only the sense of "become." In comparison, my version uses a somewhat archaic phrase—"if you are become"—in order to be able to translate both meanings, "be" and "become."

Trying to find a suitable translation for the structuring statement in the *vacana*, *nīnu jyōtirliṅgavādare / upamisinōḍaballavarillayyā*, A takes the easy way out by turning *upama* into a negation *(an-upama)* to mean "incomparable," or "matchless," so that "there be none / Thy glory to match!" This misses the problem entirely, for the question is not one of finding other gods or mortals to "match" the glory of *Guhēśvara*, but one of finding someone capable of *representing* the *liṅga*. *Upama* is figure of speech, simile, metaphor, never merely or simply "metaphor," as Translation B has it. B in fact turns the last line (which I translate as "Who can find your figuration") into "there can be no metaphor," thereby reinforcing its conception of the circularity of the *vacana*: "Sometimes in the vacana-kara's [the author of the *vacana*'s] quest for the unmediated vision, there comes a point when language, logic and metaphor are not enough; at such points, the poet begins with a striking traditional metaphor and denies it at the end."[50] Ramanujan refuses to acknowledge that the poet-saint *does not deny* the need for figuration. He merely recognizes its ineffectualness, marking thereby its possibility/impossibility, like that of representation or translation.

The deliberate roughness of my version of the *vacana* allows the text to "affect," as Benjamin would have it, the language into which it is being translated, interrupting the "transparency" and smoothness of a totalizing narrative like that of Ramanujan. Seeing "literalness" as an "arcade," I privilege the word over the sentence, marking thereby what Derrida calls in "Des Tours de Babel" a "displacement" from the syntagmatic to the paradigmatic level, and inserting my translation into the attack against homogenizing and continuous narratives.

The strategies of containment typical of colonial discourse operate in Translations A and B through the diction and "absences" of the former, and the insistence on the "light" motif and metaphor in the latter. The emphasis on metaphor seems to be "interpreted and overdetermined" here as "a representation of representation."[51] The use of "figuration" and the reinscription of *liṅga* in my version is part of an attempt to resist containment, to re-mark textuality, to dislodge or disturb the fixation on any one term or meaning, to substi-

50. Ibid., p. 52.
51. Derrida, "Sending: On Representation," p. 299.

tute *translation* for representation in the strict sense. The *liṅga* functions as a "supplement" in my translation, exposing polysemy to what Derrida has called the law of dissemination, and the last line—"Who can find your figuration"—is neither a question nor an affirmation but both at the same time.

The *vacanas* "claim" the post-colonial translator by problematizing the issue of representation, which is crucial in a context where nationalist myths of identity and unity are collapsing. It seems more urgent than ever to be aware of the instability of the "original," which can be meticulously uncovered through the practice of translation. The arbitrariness of what is presented as "natural" can be deconstructed by the translator or her/his alter ego, the critical historiographer. The drive to challenge hegemonic representations of the non-Western world need not be seen as a wish to oppose the "true" other to the "false" one presented in colonial discourse. Rather, since post-colonials already exist "in translation," our search should not be for origins or essences but for a richer complexity, a complication of our notions of the "self," a more densely textured understanding of who "we" are. It is here that translators can intervene to inscribe heterogeneity, to warn against myths of purity, to show origins as always already fissured. Translation, from being a "containing" force, is transformed into a disruptive, disseminating one. The deconstruction initiated by re-translation opens up a post-colonial space as it brings "history" to legibility.

Bibliography

Abrams, M. H. "The Deconstructive Angel." *Critical Inquiry* 3, no. 3 (Spring 1977): 425–38.

Achebe, Chinua. *Morning Yet on Creation Day: Essays*. Garden City, N.Y.: Anchor Press; London: Heinemann, 1975.

Ahmad, Aijaz. "Jameson's Rhetoric of Otherness and the 'National Allegory.' " *Social Text* 15 (Fall 1986): 3–25.

Althusser, Louis. "Ideology and Ideological State Apparatuses." Translated by Ben Brewster. In *Lenin and Philosophy, and Other Essays*, 127–88. New York: Monthly Review Press, 1971.

Arberry, A. J. *Oriental Essays: Portraits of Seven Scholars*. London: George Allen & Unwin, 1960.

Arrowsmith, William, and Roger Shattuck, eds. *The Craft and Context of Translation: A Critical Symposium*. Austin: University of Texas Press for the Humanities Research Center, 1961.

Asad, Talal, ed. *Anthropology and the Colonial Encounter*. New York: Humanities Press, 1973.

———. "The Concept of Cultural Translation in British Social Anthropology." In *Writing Culture*, ed. Clifford and Marcus, 141–64.

———. "Two European Images of Non-European Rule." In *Anthropology and the Colonial Encounter*, ed. Asad, 103–18.

Asad, Talal, and John Dixon. "Translating Europe's Others." In *Europe and Its Others*, ed. Barker et al., 170–77.

Attridge, Derek, Geoff Bennington, and Robert Young, eds. *Post-Structuralism and the Question of History*. New York: Cambridge University Press, 1987.

Bahti, Timothy. "History as Rhetorical Enactment: Walter Benjamin's Theses 'On the Concept of History'." *Diacritics* 9, no. 3 (Fall 1979): 2–17.

Barker, Francis, et al., eds. *Europe and Its Others: Proceedings of the Essex Conference on the Sociology of Literature, July 1984*. 2 vols. Colchester: University of Essex, 1985.

Bassnett-McGuire, Susan. *Translation Studies*. London: Methuen, 1980.

Beattie, John. *Other Cultures: Aims, Methods and Achievements in Social Anthropology*. New York: Free Press of Glencoe, 1964.

Belloc, Hilaire. *On Translation*. London: Oxford University Press, 1931.

Belsey, Catherine. *Critical Practice.* London: Methuen, 1980.

Benjamin, Walter. "Eduard Fuchs, Collector and Historian." In *One-Way Street, and Other Writings,* trans. Edmund Jephcott and Kingsley Shorter, 349–86. London: New Left Books, 1979.

———. *Gesammelte Schriften.* Edited by Rolf Tiedemann and Hermann Schweppenhauser. 6 vols. Frankfurt am Main: Suhrkamp Verlag, 1974– .

———. *Illuminations.* Translated by Harry Zohn. Edited by Hannah Arendt. New York: Schocken Books, 1969.

———. *The Origin of German Tragic Drama.* Translated by John Osborne. London: New Left Books, 1977.

———. *Passagen: Walter Benjamins Urgeschichte des XIX Jahrhunderts.* Munich: Wilhelm Fink Verlag, 1984.

———. *Reflections: Essays, Aphorisms, Autobiographical Writings.* Translated by Edmund Jephcott. Edited by Peter Demetz. New York: Harcourt Brace Jovanovich, 1978.

———. "Theoretics of Knowledge, Theory of Progress." From Konvolut N of the Arcades Project. Translated by L. Hafrey and R. Sieburth. *Philosophical Forum* 15, nos. 1–2 (Fall–Winter 1983–84): 1–40.

Bhabha, Homi. "The Other Question." *Screen* 24, no. 6 (November–December 1983): 18–36.

———. "Signs Taken for Wonders: Questions of Ambivalence and Authority under a Tree outside Delhi, May 1817." *Critical Inquiry* 12, no. 1 (Autumn 1985): 144–65.

Bloch, Ernst, Georg Lukács, Bertolt Brecht, Walter Benjamin, and Theodor Adorno. *Aesthetics and Politics.* With an Afterword by Fredric Jameson. London: New Left Books, 1977.

Bloom, Harold, et al., eds. *Deconstruction and Criticism.* New York: Seabury Press, 1979.

Boman-Behram, B. K. *Educational Controversies in India: The Cultural Conquest of India under British Imperialism.* Bombay: D. B. Taraporevala, 1944.

Bourdieu, Pierre. *Outline of a Theory of Practice.* Translated by Richard Nice. Cambridge: Cambridge University Press, 1977.

Brower, Reuben, ed. *On Translation.* Cambridge, Mass.: Harvard University Press, 1959.

Buck-Morss, Susan. "Benjamin's Passagen-Werk: Redeeming Mass Culture for the Revolution." *New German Critique* 29 (Spring–Summer 1983): 211–40.

———. *The Origin of Negative Dialectics: Theodor W. Adorno, Walter Benjamin, and the Frankfurt Institute.* New York: Macmillan/Free Press, 1977.

Chinweizu. *The West and the Rest of Us: White Predators, Black Slavers, and the African Elite.* New York: Random House, Vintage Books, 1975.

Chinweizu, Onwuchekwa Jemie, and Ihechukwu Madubuike. *Toward the Decolonization of African Literature*, vol. 1. 1980. Reprint. Washington D.C.: Howard University Press, 1983.

Clifford, James. "On Ethnographic Authority." *Representations* 1 (1983): 118–46.

———. *The Predicament of Culture: Twentieth-Century Ethnography, Literature, and Art*. Cambridge, Mass.: Harvard University Press, 1988.

Clifford, James, and George E. Marcus, eds. *Writing Culture: The Poetics and Politics of Ethnography*. Berkeley and Los Angeles: University of California Press, 1986.

Crapanzano, Vincent. "Hermes' Dilemma: The Masking of Subversion in Ethnographic Description." In *Writing Culture*, ed. Clifford and Marcus, 51–76.

De Man, Paul. *Allegories of Reading: Figural Language in Rousseau, Nietzsche, Rilke, and Proust*. New Haven: Yale University Press, 1979.

———. *Blindness and Insight: Essays in the Rhetoric of Contemporary Criticism*. New York: Oxford University Press, 1971.

———. *Critical Writings 1953–1978*. Edited by Lindsay Waters. Minneapolis: University of Minnesota Press, 1989.

———. "Hegel on the Sublime." In *Displacement: Derrida and After*, ed. Mark Krupnick, 139–53. Bloomington: Indiana University Press, 1983.

———. Introduction to *Toward an Aesthetic of Reception*, by Hans Robert Jauss, vii–xxv. Minneapolis: University of Minnesota Press, 1982.

———. "Pascal's Allegory of Persuasion." In *Allegory and Representation*, ed. Stephen Greenblatt, 1–25. Baltimore: Johns Hopkins Press, 1969.

———. *The Resistance to Theory*. Minneapolis: University of Minnesota Press, 1986.

———. *The Rhetoric of Romanticism*. New York: Columbia University Press, 1984.

———. "The Rhetoric of Temporality." In *Interpretation: Theory and Practice*, ed. Charles Singleton, 173–209. Baltimore: Johns Hopkins Press, 1969.

———. "Shelley Disfigured." In *Deconstruction and Criticism*, ed. Harold Bloom et al., 39–73. New York: Seabury Press, 1979.

———. "Sign and Symbol in Hegel's Aesthetics." *Critical Inquiry* 8, no. 4 (Summer 1982): 761–75.

Derrida, Jacques. "Des Tours de Babel." Translated by Joseph F. Graham. In *Difference in Translation*, ed. Graham, 165–207. Ithaca, N.Y.: Cornell University Press, 1985.

———. *Dissemination*. Translated by Barbara Johnson. Chicago: University of Chicago Press, 1981.

————. *The Ear of the Other.* Translated by Peggy Kamuf. New York: Schocken Books, 1985.

————. *Glas.* Translated by John P. Leavey, Jr., and Richard Rand. Lincoln: University of Nebraska Press, 1986.

————. "In Memoriam." Translated by Kevin Newmark. *Yale French Studies* 69 (1985): 323–26.

————. "Living On: Border Lines." In *Deconstruction and Criticism,* ed. Harold Bloom et al., 75–176. New York: Seabury Press, 1979.

————. *Margins of Philosophy.* Translated by Alan Bass. Chicago: University of Chicago Press, 1982.

————. *Memoires: For Paul de Man.* Translated by Cecile Lindsay, Jonathan Culler, and Eduardo Cadava. New York: Columbia University Press, 1986.

————. *Of Grammatology.* Translated by Gayatri Chakravorty Spivak. Baltimore: Johns Hopkins Press, 1974.

————. *Positions.* Translated by Alan Bass. Chicago: University of Chicago Press, 1981.

————. *The Post Card: From Socrates to Freud and Beyond.* Translated by Alan Bass. Chicago: University of Chicago Press, 1987.

————. "Sending: On Representation." Translated by Peter Caws and Mary Ann Caws. *Social Research* 49, no. 2 (Summer 1982): 294–326.

————. *Speech and Phenomena, and Other Essays on Husserl's Theory of Signs.* Translated by David B. Allison. Evanston, Ill.: Northwestern University Press, 1973.

————. *The Truth in Painting.* Translated by Geoff Bennington and Ian McLeod. Chicago: University of Chicago Press, 1987.

————. *Writing and Difference.* Translated by Alan Bass. Chicago: University of Chicago Press, 1978.

Descombes, Vincent. *Modern French Philosophy.* Translated by L. Scott-Fox and J. M. Harding. Cambridge: Cambridge University Press, 1980.

Dharàmpal. *The Beautiful Tree: Indigenous Indian Education in the Eighteenth Century.* New Delhi: Biblia Impex, 1983.

Dhareshwar, Vivek. "The Predicament of Theory." In *Theory between the Disciplines: Authority/Vision/Politics,* ed. Martin Kreiswirth and Mark Cheetham, 231–50. Ann Arbor: University of Michigan Press, 1990.

————. "Toward a Narrative Epistemology of the Postcolonial Predicament." In *Traveling Theories, Traveling Theorists,* ed. James Clifford and Vivek Dhareshwar. *Inscriptions* 5 (1989): 135–57.

Doron, Marcia Nita, and Marilyn Gaddis Rose. "The Economics and Politics of Translation." In *Translation Spectrum,* ed. M. G. Rose. Albany: State University of New York Press, 1981.

Dumont, Louis. *Homo Hierarchicus: The Caste System and Its Implications.* Rev. ed. Translated by Mark Sainsbury, Louis Dumont, and Basia Gulati. Chicago: University of Chicago Press, 1980.

Eagleton, Terry. *Walter Benjamin, or, Towards a Revolutionary Criticism.* London: Verso Editions and NLB, 1981.

Fabian, Johannes. *Language and Colonial Power: The Appropriation of Swahili in the Former Belgian Congo, 1880–1938.* New York: Cambridge University Press, 1986.

———. *Time and the Other: How Anthropology Makes Its Object.* New York: Columbia University Press, 1983.

Fahim, Hussein, ed. *Indigenous Anthropology in Non-Western Countries: Proceedings of a Burg Wartenstein Symposium.* Durham, N.C.: Carolina Academic Press, 1982.

Fanon, Frantz. *Black Skin, White Masks.* 1967. Translated by Charles L. Markmann. New York: Grove Press, 1968. London: Pluto Press, 1986.

———. *The Wretched of the Earth.* 1963. Translated by Constance Farrington. New York: Grove Press, 1968. Harmondsworth: Penguin Books, 1967.

Faris, James. "Pax Britannica and the Sudan: S. F. Nadel." In *Anthropology and the Colonial Encounter,* ed. Asad, 153–72.

Feuchtwang, Stephen. "The Discipline and Its Sponsors: The Colonial Formation of British Social Anthropology." In *Anthropology and the Colonial Encounter,* ed. Asad, 71–102.

Foucault, Michel. *Discipline and Punish: The Birth of the Prison.* Translated by Alan Sheridan. New York: Random House, Vintage Books, 1979.

———. "Nietzsche, Genealogy, History." In *Language, Counter-Memory, Practice,* ed. Donald Bouchard, 139–64. Ithaca, N.Y.: Cornell University Press, 1977.

Gadamer, Hans-Georg. *Philosophical Hermeneutics.* Translated by David E. Linge. Berkeley and Los Angeles: University of California Press, 1976.

———. *Truth and Method.* Translated by Garrett Barden and John Cumming. 1975. Reprint. New York: Crossroad, 1985.

Gasche, Rodolphe. "Saturnine Vision and the Question of Difference: Reflections on Walter Benjamin's Theory of Language." *Studies in Twentieth Century Literature* 11, no. 1 (Fall 1986): 69–90.

———. "Setzung and Übersetzung: Notes on Paul de Man." *Diacritics* 11 (Winter 1981): 36–57.

Gearhart, Suzanne. *The Open Boundary of History and Fiction: A Critical Approach to the French Enlightenment.* Princeton: Princeton University Press, 1984.

———. "Philosophy before Literature: Deconstruction, Historicity, and the Work of Paul de Man." *Diacritics* 19 (Winter 1983): 63–81.

Gough, Kathleen. " 'Anthropology and Imperialism' Revisited." *Economic and Political Weekly* 25, no. 31 (1990): 1705–8.

———. "New Proposals for Anthropologists." *Current Anthropology* 9 (1968): 403–7.

Graham, Joseph F., ed. *Difference in Translation*. Ithaca, N.Y.: Cornell University Press, 1985.

Gramsci, Antonio. *Selections from the Prison Notebooks*. Translated by Quintin Hoare and Geoffrey Nowell Smith. New York: International Publishers, 1971.

Guha, Ranajit. "Dominance without Hegemony and Its Historiography." In *Subaltern Studies VI: Writings on South Asian History and Society*, ed. Ranajit Guha, 210–309. Delhi: Oxford University Press, 1989.

———. "The Prose of Counter-Insurgency." In *Subaltern Studies II: Writings on South Asian History and Society*, ed. Ranajit Guha, 1–42. Delhi: Oxford University Press, 1983.

Habermas, Jurgen. "Walter Benjamin: Consciousness-Raising or Rescuing Critique." Translated by Frederick G. Lawrence. In *Philosophical-Political Profiles*, 131–66. Cambridge, Mass.: MIT Press, 1983.

Harris, Marvin. *The Rise of Anthropological Theory: A History of Theories of Culture*. New York: Crowell, 1968.

Headrick, Daniel R. *The Tools of Empire: Technology and European Imperialism in the Nineteenth Century*. New York: Oxford University Press, 1981.

Hegel, G. W. F. *The Philosophy of History*. 1837. Translated by J. Sibree. New York: Colonial Press, [1899]. Reprint. New York: P. F. Collier, n.d.

Hermans, Theo, ed. *The Manipulation of Literature: Studies in Literary Translation*. London: Croom Helm, 1985.

Hulme, Peter. *Colonial Encounters: Europe and the Native Caribbean, 1492–1797*. New York: Methuen, 1986.

Inden, Ronald. "Orientalist Constructions of India." *Modern Asian Studies* 20, no. 3 (July 1986): 401–46.

Jakobson, Roman. "On Linguistic Aspects of Translation." In *On Translation*, ed. Brower, 232–39.

Jameson, Fredric. *Marxism and Form: Twentieth-Century Dialectical Theories of Literature*. Princeton: Princeton University Press, 1971.

———. *The Political Unconscious: Narrative as a Socially Symbolic Act*. Ithaca, N.Y.: Cornell University Press, 1981.

———. "Third-World Literature in the Era of Multinational Capitalism." *Social Text* 15 (Fall 1986): 65–88.

Jauss, Hans-Robert. *Toward an Aesthetic of Reception*. Translated by Timothy Bahti. Minneapolis: University of Minnesota Press, 1982.

Jay, Martin. *The Dialectical Imagination: A History of the Frankfurt School and the Institute of Social Research, 1923–1950*. Boston: Little, Brown, 1973.

Johnson, Barbara. "Taking Fidelity Philosophically." In *Difference in Translation*, ed. Graham, 142–48.

Jones, Sir William. *Discourses and Essays*. Edited by Moni Bagchee. New Delhi: People's Publishing House, 1984.

———. *A Grammar of the Persian Language*. 1771. 8th ed. London: W. Nicol, 1823.

———. *The Letters of Sir William Jones*. Edited by Garland Cannon. 2 vols. Oxford: Oxford University Press, 1970.

———. *Translations from Oriental Languages*. 2 vols. Delhi: Pravesh Publications, n.d.

———. *Works*. 1799. 13 vols. Delhi: Agam Prakashan, 1979.

Kalgudi, Basavaraja. *Madhyakaaleena Bhakti matthu Anubhaava Saahitya haagoo Charitrika Prajne*. Bangalore: Kannada Sahitya Parishat, 1988.

Kālidāsa. *Śacontala; or, The Fatal Ring*. Translated by William Jones. Edinburgh: J. Mundell, 1796.

Kelly, Louis. *The True Interpreter*. New York: St. Martin's Press, 1979.

Kittsteiner, H. D. "Walter Benjamin's Historicism." Translated by Jonathan Monroe and Irving Wohlfarth. *New German Critique* 39 (Fall 1986): 179–215.

Kopf, David. *British Orientalism and the Bengal Renaissance: The Dynamics of Indian Modernization, 1773–1835*. Berkeley and Los Angeles: University of California Press, 1969.

Lackner, Helen. "Colonial Administration and Social Anthropology: Eastern Nigeria 1920–1940." In *Anthropology and the Colonial Encounter*, ed. Asad, 123–52.

Leach, Edmund. *Social Anthropology*. London: Oxford University Press, 1982.

Lefevere, André. *Translating Literature: The German Tradition from Luther to Rosenzweig*. Assen/Amsterdam: Van Gorcum, 1977.

Lentricchia, Frank. *After the New Criticism*. Chicago: University of Chicago Press, 1980.

———. *Criticism and Social Change*. Chicago: University of Chicago Press, 1983.

Lévi-Strauss, Claude. *The Scope of Anthropology*. Translated by Sherry Ortner Paul and Robert A. Paul. London: Jonathan Cape, 1967.

———*Tristes Tropiques*. 1955. Translated by John Weightman and Doreen Weightman. 1973. Reprint. New York: Washington Square Press, 1977.

———. *The View from Afar*. Translated by Joachim Neugroschel and Phoebe Hoss. New York: Basic Books, 1985.

Lienhardt, Godfrey. "Modes of Thought." In *The Institutions of Primitive Society*. Oxford: Basil Blackwell, 1961.

Macaulay, Thomas Babington. "Indian Education" (Minute of the 2nd of February, 1835). In *Prose and Poetry*, ed. G. M. Young, 719–30. Cambridge, Mass.: Harvard University Press, 1967. Originally published London: Rupert Hart-Davis, 1952.

Mani, Lata. "Contentious Traditions: The Debate on SATI in Colonial India." *Cultural Critique* (Fall 1987): 119–56.

———. "The Production of an Official Discourse on SATI in Early Nineteenth-Century Bengal." In *Europe and Its Others*, ed. Barker et al., 107–27.

Marcus, George E., and Michael M. J. Fischer. *Anthropology as Cultural Critique*. Chicago: University of Chicago Press, 1986.

Matthews, Robert J. "What Did Archimedes Mean by 'χευσός'?" In *Difference in Translation*, ed. Graham, 149–64.

Memmi, Albert. *The Colonizer and the Colonized*. Translated by Howard Greenfeld. Boston: Beacon Press, 1967.

Mill, James. *A History of British India*. 1817. New Delhi: Associated Publishing House, 1972.

Mouffe, Chantal. "Hegemony and Ideology in Gramsci." Translated by Suzanne Stewart. Edited by Chantal Mouffe. *Gramsci and Marxist Theory*. London: Routledge & Kegan Paul, 1979.

Mukherjee, Ramakrishna. *The Rise and Fall of the East India Company*. 1955. Reprint. Bombay: Popular Prakashan, 1973.

Mukherjee, S. N. *Sir William Jones*. Cambridge: Cambridge University Press, 1968.

Murthy, Chidananda. *Vacana Saahitya*. Bangalore: Bangalore University Press, 1975.

Narayanan, M. G. S., and Veluthat Kesavan. "Bhakti Movement in South India." In *Indian Movements: Some Aspects of Dissent, Protest and Reform*, ed. S. C. Malik, 33–66. Simla: Indian Institute of Advanced Study, 1978.

Newmark, Kevin. "Paul de Man's History." In *Reading de Man Reading*, ed. Waters and Godzich, 121–35.

Ngũgĩ wa Thiong'o. *Decolonising the Mind: The Politics of Language in African Literature*. Portsmouth, N.H.: Heinemann; London: James Currey, 1986.

———. *Homecoming*. 1972. Westport, Conn.: Lawrence Hill, 1983.

Nida, Eugene A. "Principles of Translation as Exemplified in Bible Translation." In *On Translation*, ed. Brower, 11–31.

Nietzsche, Friedrich. *The Use and Abuse of History*. Translated by Adrian Collins. 2d ed. Indianapolis: Bobbs-Merrill, 1957.

Niranjana, Tejaswini. "Translation, Colonialism and the Rise of English." *Economic and Political Weekly* 25, no. 15 (1990): 773–79.

Norton, Glyn P. *The Ideology and Language of Translation in Renaissance France and Their Humanist Antecedents*. Geneva: Librairie Droz, 1984.

Onoge, Omafume F. "The Counterrevolutionary Tradition in African Studies: The Case of Applied Anthropology." In *The Politics of Anthropology: From Colonialism and Sexism toward a View from Below,* ed. Gerrit Huizer and Bruce Mannheim, 45–66. The Hague: Mouton, 1979.

Paetzold, Heinz. "Walter Benjamin's Theory of the End of Art." *International Journal of Sociology* 8, no. 1 (Spring 1977): 25–75.

Paris, Jean. "Translation and Creation." In *The Craft and Context of Translation,* ed. Arrowsmith and Shattuck, 57–67.

Parry, Benita. "Problems in Current Theories of Colonial Discourse." *Oxford Literary Review* 9, nos. 1–2 (1987): 27–58.

Popovič, Anton. *Dictionary for the Analysis of Literary Translation.* Edmonton: Department of Comparative Literature, University of Alberta, 1976.

Pratt, Mary Louise. "Fieldwork in Common Places." In *Writing Culture,* ed. Clifford and Marcus, 27–50.

———. "Scratches on the Face of the Country; or, What Mr. Barrow Saw in the Land of the Bushmen." *Critical Inquiry* 12 (Autumn 1985): 119–43.

Radnoti, Sandor. "The Early Aesthetics of Walter Benjamin." *International Journal of Sociology* 7, no. 1 (Spring 1977): 76–123.

Rafael, Vicente L. *Contracting Colonialism: Translation and Christian Conversion in Tagalog Society under Early Spanish Rule.* Ithaca, N.Y.: Cornell University Press, 1988.

———. "Gods and Grammar: The Politics of Translation in the Spanish Colonization of the Tagalogs of the Philippines." In *Notebooks in Cultural Analysis,* vol. 3, ed. Norman F. Cantor and Nathalia King, 97–133. Durham, N.C.: Duke University Press, 1986.

Rajan, Tilottama. "Displacing Post-Structuralism: Romantic Studies after Paul de Man." *Studies in Romanticism* 24, no. 4 (Winter 1985): 451–74.

Ramanujan, A. K., ed. and trans. *Speaking of Śiva.* Harmondsworth: Penguin Books, 1973.

Riddel, Joseph N. "Coup de Man, or The Uses and Abuses of Semiotics." *Cultural Critique* 4 (Fall 1986): 81–109.

Roberts, Julian. *Walter Benjamin.* Atlantic Highlands, N.J.: Humanities Press, 1983.

Rosaldo, Renato. "From the Door of His Tent: The Fieldworker and the Inquisitor." In *Writing Culture,* ed. Clifford and Marcus, 77–97.

Rose, Marilyn Gaddis, ed. *Translation Spectrum: Essays in Theory and Practice.* Albany: State University of New York Press, 1981.

Said, Edward. *After the Last Sky: Palestinian Lives.* New York: Pantheon Books, 1986.

———. "Intellectuals in the Post-Colonial World." *Salmagundi,* no. 70–71 (Spring–Summer 1986): 44–64.

———. *Orientalism.* London: Routledge & Kegan Paul, 1978.

————. *The World, the Text, and the Critic.* Cambridge, Mass.: Harvard University Press, 1983.

Sangari, Kumkum. "The Politics of the Possible." *Cultural Critique* no. 7 (Fall 1987): 157–86.

————, and Sudesh Vaid, eds. *Recasting Women: Essays in Colonial History.* New Delhi: Kali for Women, 1989.

Savory, T. H. *The Art of Translation.* 1957. Boston: The Writer, 1968.

Spear, Percival. *A History of India,* vol. 2. Harmondsworth: Penguin Books, 1970.

Spivak, Gayatri Chakravorty. "Can the Subaltern Speak?" In *Marxism and the Interpretation of Culture,* ed. Cary Nelson and Lawrence Grossberg, 271–313. Urbana: University of Illinois Press, 1988.

————. *In Other Worlds: Essays in Cultural Politics.* London: Methuen, 1987.

————. "The Rani of Sirmur." In *Europe and Its Others,* ed. Barker et al., 128–51.

————. "Subaltern Studies: Deconstructing Historiography." In *Subaltern Studies IV: Writings on South Asian History and Society,* ed. Ranajit Guha, 330–63. Delhi: Oxford University Press, 1985.

Steiner, George. *After Babel.* New York: Oxford University Press, 1975.

Steiner, T. R. *English Translation Theory, 1650–1800.* Assen/Amsterdam: Van Gorcum, 1975.

Stokes, Eric. *The English Utilitarians and India.* 1959. Reprint. Delhi: Oxford University Press, 1989.

Śūnyasampādane. Edited by S. C. Nandimath, L. M. A. Menezes, and R. C. Hiremath. 6 vols. Dharwar: Karnatak University, 1965.

Szondi, Peter. "Hope in the Past: On Walter Benjamin." Translated by Harvey Mendelsohn. *Critical Inquiry* 4, no. 3 (Spring 1978): 491–506.

Thapar, Romila. *A History of India,* vol. 1. Harmondsworth: Penguin Books, 1966.

Tharu, Susie. "Tracing Savitri's Pedigree: Victorian Racism and the Image of Women in Indo-Anglian Literature." In *Recasting Women,* ed. Sangari and Vaid.

Thompson, John B. *Studies in the Theory of Ideology.* Berkeley and Los Angeles: University of California Press, 1984.

Tiedemann, Rolf. "Historical Materialism or Political Messianism? An Interpretation of the Theses 'On the Concept of History'." Translated by Barton Byg. *Philosophical Forum* 15, nos. 1–2 (Fall–Winter 1983–84): 71–104.

Toury, Gideon. "A Rationale for Descriptive Translation Studies." In *The Manipulation of Literature,* ed. Theo Hermans, 16–41. London: Croom Helm, 1985.

Trevelyan, Charles. *On the Education of the People of India.* London: Longman, Orme, Brown, Green & Longmans, 1838.

Trevelyan, George Otto. *The Life and Letters of Lord Macaulay*. 3 vols. London: Longmans, Green, 1877.

Tyler, Stephen. "Post-Modern Ethnography: From Document of the Occult to Occult Document." In *Writing History*, ed. Clifford and Marcus, 122–40.

Viswanathan, Gauri. "The Beginnings of English Literary Study in British India." *Oxford Literary Review* 9, nos. 1–2 (1987): 2–26.

———. *Masks of Conquest: Literary Study and British Rule in India*. New York: Columbia University Press, 1989.

Waters, Lindsay, and Wlad Godzich, eds. *Reading de Man Reading*. Minneapolis: University of Minnesota Press, 1989.

Weber, Samuel. "Capitalizing History: *The Political Unconscious*." In *Institution and Interpretation*, 40–58. Minneapolis: University of Minnesota Press, 1987.

Williams, Raymond. *Marxism and Literature*. London: Oxford University Press, 1977.

Winter, Werner. "Translation as Political Action." In *The Craft and Context of Translation*, ed. Arrowsmith and Shattuck, 172–76.

Witte, Bernd. "Benjamin and Lukacs: Historical Notes on Their Political and Aesthetic Theories." *New German Critique* 5 (Spring 1975): 3–26.

Wolfarth, Irving. "Et Cetera? The Historian as Chiffonnier." *New German Critique* 39 (Fall 1986): 143–68.

———. "No-Man's Land: On Walter Benjamin's 'Destructive Character'." *Diacritics* (June 1978): 47–65.

———. "On the Messianic Structure of Walter Benjamin's Last Reflections." *Glyph* 3 (1978): 148–212.

———. "The Politics of Prose and the Art of Awakening: Walter Benjamin's Version of a German Romantic Motif." *Glyph* 7 (1980): 131–48.

Wolin, Richard. "Experience and Materialism in Benjamin's Passagenwerk." *Philosophical Forum* 17, no. 3 (Spring 1986): 201–16.

———. *Walter Benjamin: An Aesthetic of Redemption*. New York: Columbia University Press, 1982.

Index

Abrams, M. H., 36, 94
Achebe, Chinua, 6
Adorno, Theodor: critique of historicism, 149
Ahmad, Aijaz, 46n.95
Allama Prabhu, 175, 177, 178–79, 182, 183
Althusser, Louis: on history, 38; interpellation, 10–11n.16, 11, 14, 33, 33n.71
Anglicists, 17n.32, 29
Arrowsmith, William, 57
Asad, Talal, 70, 78, 82, 83–84
Asiatic despotism, 14, 76
Asiatic Society, 12, 14, 73, 74
Austin, John, 100n.24
Autocolonization, 32; and hegemony, 33

Barthes, Roland, 81
Bassnett-McGuire, Susan, 56, 58n.37, 59
Beattie, John, 72–73
Belloc, Hilaire, 63
Belsey, Catherine, 51
Benjamin, Walter, 4–5, 41, 55–56, 90, 110–62, 168, 171, 172, 174, 179, 185; on accuracy in translation, 117, 120; "afterlife," 133–34, 147, 150; on allegory, 110, 150–51, 154, 158; Arcades Project, 119; on citation, 45, 119, 172; critique of historicism, 110, 111, 113, 115, 118, 120, 137, 150, 154, 159; and fragmentation, 136–37, 156, 157, 173; on historical materialism, 45, 111, 114, 118, 120, 126, 130, 146, 148, 152, 158, 160; history-writ-

ing, 38, 117, 129, 134, 151; legibility, 154; *Nachreife*, 133–34; on reading, 110; on redemption, 115, 126, 139, 145, 157; on remembrance, 157–58; on translatability, 114, 119, 151, 154, 180; *Wehen*, 133–34
Bennington, Geoff, 36
Bentinck, Lord William, 27, 29–30
Bhabha, Homi K., 10, 167–68, 172–73; on hybridity, 45–46
Boman-Behram, B. K., 29n.57
Bourdieu, Pierre: on symbolic domination, 32
Breitinger, Johann Jacob, 55
Buck-Morss, Susan, 149n.18
Burke, Kenneth, 98
Burton, Sir Richard, 82

Carey, William, 35, 180
Chapman, George, 51–53
Charter Act of 1813, 27
Civil society, 32
Clapham Sect, 27
Clifford, James, 46, 80n.104, 81, 82
Colonialism: absentee colonialism, 76; authority of, 45; colonial discourse, 7, 8, 15, 34, 43, 65, 72, 185; colonial enterprise, 1; colonial subject, 1, 2, 11, 32; colonial subjectification, 10; and missionaries, 19–21, 27, 34, 62–63, 72; and proper names, 183; technologies of, 35, 172
Condillac, Etienne Bonnot de, 153
Cornwallis, Lord, 17, 29
Cowley, Abraham, 52, 54

199

Printed in the United States
20099LVS00002B/206